"Slaves of the Depression"

"Slaves of the Depression"

WORKERS' LETTERS ABOUT LIFE ON THE JOB

Gerald Markowitz
and David Rosner

Cornell University Press

ITHACA AND LONDON

First published 1987 by Cornell University Press.

International Standard Book Number (cloth) 0-8014-1956-5
International Standard Book Number (paper) 0-8014-9464-8
Library of Congress Catalog Card Number 87-6671
Printed in the United States of America
Librarians: Library of Congress cataloging information
appears on the last page of the book.

The paper in this book is acid-free and meets the guidelines for
permanence and durability of the Committee on Production Guidelines
for Book Longevity of the Council on Library Resources.

TO ALEX, IRV, AND SOPHIE AND IN
MEMORY OF ESSIE AND SYLVIA—

*they experienced many of the hardships described
in this book and passed on a message of hope
to their children and grandchildren.*

Contents

vii

Preface

The letters assembled here testify eloquently to the struggles of the people who wrote them: Americans who managed to hold jobs during the Great Depression but found themselves little better off than the unemployed and often as desperate. Exhibiting a faith in their government which would be hard to duplicate today, thousands of them wrote directly to the president and the secretary of labor, confident that if only those good people knew about the inhuman conditions under which they labored, such conditions would not be permitted to continue. Their letters bring to life an era often remembered but seldom seen so vividly as in the words of these men and women who suffered through it.

We are grateful to these letter writers for the insights they give us. Other people have contributed much to this book as well. Among our academic colleagues, Roy Rosenzweig of George Mason University was especially helpful, providing us with a detailed commentary that gave the book form and focus. We sincerely thank him for the time and effort he put into this work. Peter Agree, our editor at Cornell University Press, immediately understood the significance of this work and has been supportive and imaginative throughout the months of manuscript preparation. Thomas Frazier, William Preston, Blanche Cook, and our other colleagues in the history departments at John Jay College, Baruch College, and The Graduate Center of the City University of New York encouraged us with their enthusiasm. Elizabeth Blackmar of Columbia University, Michael Meeropol of Western New England College, and Barbara Rosenkrantz of Harvard University also provided enthusiastic support and useful ideas. Of course, we thank our families for their support and love: Kathy Conway and Zachary and Molly Rosner; Billy, Toby, and Elena Markowitz.

Two people who lived through the events that are recorded here were especially important to us. Clara Beyer, assistant director of the Division of Labor Standards of the U.S. Department of Labor during the Depression, gave us many hours of her time, welcoming us into her home and into her thoughts. Well up in her nineties, she provided essential information about events a half century ago with clarity and precision. It is inspiring to have known her, for she represents the best of the New Deal. Dr. Lorin Kerr, the founder of the United Mine Workers' health and safety programs, was also generous with his time and help. The numerous long-distance calls exchanged between us testify to his energy and goodwill. We sincerely appreciate his constant help and support.

Two archivists at the National Archives were also extremely helpful. Gerald Hess, of Record Group 174, and Aloha South, who is in charge of the Public Health Service materials in Record Group 90, were always ready to track down leads, respond to our inquiries, and make suggestions. Thomas Connors and Peter Hoefer, at the AFL-CIO Archives in Washington, and Judson MacLaurey, at the library of the Department of Labor, were also extremely generous with their time. The help of Barbara Salazar of Cornell University Press in checking quotations and improving our prose was invaluable. We also thank Edna Pinckney-Pearlman and Mary Seto, who helped prepare the manuscript. Thanks also to Andrea Ades and Harold Chenven.

Two grants have made this work possible: The Milbank Memorial Fund and the Professional Staff Congress/City University of New York provided needed support for this work. We thank the Milbank Memorial Fund additionally for permission to use portions of our article "More than Economism," *Milbank Quarterly* 64 (Fall 1986): 331–54, copyright © 1986 Milbank Memorial Fund.

Finally, as members of the City University faculty, we want to mention the tremendous loss we both feel at the passing of our colleague Herbert Gutman. He was an inspiration to many of us and gave of himself both to his colleagues and to his students. We miss him greatly.

GERALD MARKOWITZ
DAVID ROSNER

New York City

"Slaves of the Depression"

Introduction

"In the Grime and Dirt of a Nation"

Dear Miss Perkins:

Reading about you as I do I have come to the understanding, that you are a fair and impartial observer of labor conditions in the United States. Well, I'll have to get a load off my chest, and tell you of the labor conditions in a place which is laughingly called a factory. We work in a Woolstock Concern. We handle discarded rags. We work, ten hours a day for six days. In the grime and dirt of a nation. We go home tired and sick—dirty—disgusted—with the world in general, work—work all day, low pay—average wage sixteen dollars. Tired in the train going home, sitting at the dinner table, too tired to even wash ourselves, what for—to keep body and souls together not to depend on charity. What of N.R.A.? What of everything—? We handle diseased rags all day. Tuberculosis roaming loose, unsanitary conditions—, slaves—slaves of the depression! I'm even tired as I write this letter—, a letter of hope—. What am I? I am young—I am twenty, a high school education—no recreation—no fun—. Pardon ma'am—but I want to live—! do you deny me that right—? As an American citizen I ask you—, what—what must we do? Please investigate this matter. I sleep now, yes ma'am with a prayer on my lips, hoping against hope—, that you will better our conditions. I'll sign my name, but if my boss finds out—, well— Give us a new deal, Miss Perkins.

J. G.

This letter, dated March 29, 1935, provides a poignant glimpse into the life of one worker during the worst depression in American history. The man who wrote it was more fortunate than many others in 1935—at least he had a job. Although we know a great deal about the unemployed and the union organizing drives during the 1930s, we know very little about the Depression's effects on working conditions and the lives of the large majority of unorganized and unprotected workers. This book is by and about them, workers who considered themselves "slaves of the Depression."

In order to uncover and understand the ways in which workers reacted to and absorbed the trials of work during the Depression, we turn to a little-used source: the letters they wrote to the federal government as they sought relief from the exploitation and intimidation they experienced on the job. The letters collected here are a sampling of thousands we discovered among the records of the Department of Labor in the National Archives while we were investigating the effects of the Depression on workers' safety and health. Together with the statistical and manuscript sources used by earlier researchers these letters illuminate laborers' suffering and struggles.[1]

The Great Depression devastated the lives of millions of Americans. It is estimated that in this "temporary downturn" that in fact lasted more than twelve years, more than one of every three nonagricultural workers could not find work.[2] Even in 1941, when war-related industries had begun to gear up for production, about 15 percent of the nonagricultural work force were still unemployed. Without employment insurance, social security, health plans, or union benefits, people suffered as few today can even imagine. Starvation was a fact of life for Americans in every city in the country. The malnutrition of rural children, the cardboard shacks

[1]Robert S. McElvaine, in his fascinating book *Down and Out in the Great Depression: Letters from the "Forgotten Man"* (Chapel Hill: University of North Carolina Press, 1983), has presented letters from the unemployed to Franklin Roosevelt to illuminate their experiences. Others have used census materials, oral histories, union records, newspaper accounts, and government records to document the Depression's effects on American lives. See Ann Banks, *First-Person America* (New York: Vintage, 1981), which makes good use of the manuscripts of the Federal Writers' Project's life history narratives; Studs Terkel, *Hard Times: An Oral History of the Great Depression* (New York: Pantheon, 1970); Rosalyn Baxandall, Linda Gordon, and Susan Reverby, eds., *America's Working Women: A Documentary History* (New York: Vintage, 1976).

[2]The figure generally accepted for unemployment at the depths of the Depression, in the winter of 1932–33, is 25 percent, although there are no reliable figures. Stephan Thernstrom uses the figure 37.6 percent for nonagricultural workers. See Stephan Thernstrom, *A History of the American People*, vol. 2 (San Diego: Harcourt Brace Jovanovich, 1984).

of "Hoovervilles," the lack of heat in urban slums, the evictions, the enormous numbers of hobos riding the rails in search of work—all have entered our popular consciousness and have guided our national conscience. The unemployed have come to symbolize the dislocation caused by the Great Depression.

Yet the majority of Americans who did have jobs also suffered severely. If they were not to join the ranks of the unemployed, workers were generally forced to accept long hours, low wages, and inhuman working conditions. In many ways employed workers were only marginally more secure than the unemployed, for they lived with the constant threat of losing their jobs, their homes, and their families. The wages of the vast majority of workers were never enough to guarantee much more than subsistence. From 1929 to 1933 the general cost of living fell almost 30 percent and food prices declined almost 45 percent, but declining wages left most workers no better off than they had been before. Even those few who experienced a gain in real wages were often called upon to support more people as family members turned to them for support. Opportunities for advancement and adequate wages disappeared for the millions of unskilled, part-time, and temporary employees. The tremendous growth in unemployment led to a temporary decline in union membership in the early years of the Depression: between 1929 and 1933 trade union membership fell by over 20 percent, from 3.6 million to 2.8 million workers.[3]

Most important, Depression-era workers experienced speedups. The Depression lowered profits for many hard-pressed small manufacturers and led them to seek ways to increase production while lowering costs. One contemporary government study concluded that "the Depression no doubt stimulated efforts to reduce unit labor requirements by speeding up operations." In fact, despite lowered demand, productivity increases were evident in forty of forty-five industries surveyed between 1929 and 1935.[4] The resultant increase in inventory undoubtedly exacerbated unemployment in the latter part of the decade.

Skilled and unskilled workers alike found their positions eroded by the economic pressures of the Depression. Managers had incentives to auto-

[3]M. Adabeney, *Cost of Living in the United States, 1914–1936,* report no. 228 (New York: National Industrial Conference Board, 1936); U.S. Bureau of the Census, *Historical Statistics of the United States, Colonial Times to 1957* (Washington, D.C., 1960), p. 98.

[4]David Weintraub and Irving Kaplan, "Summary of Findings to Date," U.S. Works Progress Administration, National Research Project on Opportunities and Recent Changes in Industrial Techniques (Philadelphia, March, 1938) (typescript).

mate or reorganize the production process rather than depend on highly skilled and expensive laborers. With demand dwindling, many managers took advantage of government loan programs to retool outdated plants. The codes of the short-lived National Recovery Administration (NRA) brought workers an immediate benefit by limiting the number of hours they could be required to work, but the codes' long-term effects were often detrimental to all workers' positions. When the NRA code worked out by the textile manufacturers set maximum hours for any factory at two shifts of forty hours each a week, manufacturers soon saw the wisdom of modernizing their plants in order to get maximum production in this restricted time period. Under the pressure of automation in a depressed economy, workers had to accept low wages and deteriorating work conditions or seek jobs elsewhere.[5]

Other manufacturers used automation to eliminate their dependence on skilled laborers whose specialized knowledge could interfere with their control over production. Paper, steel, and auto manufacturers introduced such combustion-control instruments as the pyrometer to "reduce costs and the labor associated with production," according to a contemporary government study. The cooking of paper pulp, for example, had been considered a skilled occupation, as the quality of paper depended on the judgment and attention of the worker. But with the "introduction of temperature, pressure, and flow devices . . . the process was so simplified that an inexperienced worker could cook pulp merely by observing the instruments and following instructions." In automaking, as well, the development of automatic combustion control of heat-treating furnaces virtually eliminated the skilled heat treaters who had previously judged the temperature of the metal by observing its color. The introduction of pyrometers in the mid-1920s had begun a process that destroyed the control that skilled workers exerted over production. When, in the early 1930s, "automatic temperature control of heat treating was developed, the process became highly standardized and the last elements of skill were eliminated." The overall effect of automation was devastating to skilled workers, for in undermining their control over the work process it eroded their bargaining position with management. A government study of the late 1930s noted the significance of this long-term change in the production process by citing the words of an industry spokesman who claimed that the labor difficulties in the auto industry

[5]Alice Kessler-Harris, *Out To Work: A History of Wage-Earning Women in the United States* (New York: Oxford University Press, 1982), pp. 266–68.

were "reduced" by this deskilling process. "The men seem more satisfied, principally, he felt, because they realized they had a good job, but a job which can be taken by some other man at a moment's notice."[6] The process of automation was clearly uneven, affecting various industries and laborers according to the differing rates of technological innovation and patterns of adaptation. But it is clear that the distinction between skilled and unskilled workers had seriously eroded by the middle of the 1930s. In their follow-up on their classic study of "Middletown," Indiana, Robert and Helen Lynd pointed out that by June 1935 "the general hourly wage rate for skilled men in industry was only 45 cents as against 43 cents for the unskilled."[7] For laborers, all of these changes in employment, wages, and production added up to an intense sense of insecurity and lack of control over their everyday work. While the Depression brought these issues to the fore, the problems of displacement, deskilling, and poverty were the typical lot of the American worker in the twentieth century.

The Depression exacerbated the exploitation of the employee by giving management a free hand to change the methods of production, often abusing the worker in the process. In factory after factory, the physical environment in which workers labored rapidly deteriorated. As unemployment grew and workers' dependence on their employers became more extreme, filth and the dangers of unguarded and undermaintained work sites and machinery increased. Working conditions in the 1920s had hardly been impressive, for the period was marked by repressive antilabor activities by management and government alike. But during those relatively prosperous years, workers' real wages had increased and their lack of control at work was balanced by some modest financial reward. During the Depression the illusion of job security and the promise of future abundance were stripped away to expose the cruelest aspects of industrial capitalism.

There is no better way to appreciate the suffering of workers and their families than to read their own descriptions of it. During the New Deal, thousands of workers wrote to government officials about their strug-

---

[6]George Perazich, Herbert Shimmel, and Benjamin Rosenberg, *Industrial Instruments and Changing Technology*, Works Progress Administration, National Research Project, report no. M-1 (Philadelphia, October 1938), pp. 86, 88, 94. David Montgomery, *Workers' Control in America: Studies in the History of Work, Technology, and Labor Struggle* (London: Cambridge University Press, 1979), discusses factory automation in the late nineteenth and early twentieth centuries.

[7]Robert S. Lynd and Helen Merrill Lynd, *Middletown in Transition* (New York: Harcourt, Brace, 1937), p. 67.

gles, their hopes, and their endurance during this most trying time in American history. The small selection of letters presented here is poignant testimony not only to their pain but also to their ability to articulate their vision of a more just society built on economic and political democracy. The letters came from people of every sort—women and men, immigrants and native-born, black and white, rural and urban, industrial and agricultural. They all called on their government for social justice. Yet their pleas reflected the diversity of opinion and of approach that we must expect from as varied a people as we are. Their letters at times seem almost revolutionary, but the very fact that workers wrote to their government seeking redress indicates a profound faith in the willingness and ability of the nation's leaders to act on their behalf. Despite their hardships, workers exhibited a profound belief in the ideals of political democracy and economic security, which they saw being perverted by the avarice of a few. Most called on the federal government and on Franklin D. Roosevelt in particular to take a strong role in protecting democracy by restoring economic stability and social justice. Many workers, however, also voiced a militant class consciousness that was extremely radical. These people recognized no community of interest with the owners and managers of the plants in which they toiled. The writers described working conditions and power relationships that they often compared with slavery—a slavery that destroyed family life and introduced constant fear and insecurity. But their suffering also engendered pride in their ability to withstand the nightmare through which they were living.

Ordinary people's descriptions of their actual working conditions are the most troubling parts of the letters. A group of workers in a plastics plant in Pennsylvania pleaded with President Roosevelt to investigate their exposure to an acid that was causing their fingers to "look like a piece of raw meat." "Oh! nobody knows how we suffer," one lamented. A laborer in a South Carolina textile mill protested against long hours and speedups. "We are stretched out so even the young people are complaining that it is too hard for them," she wrote. A Pennsylvania man, describing the "terrible" conditions in a steel foundry, wrote that "the men that start to work there are healthy and strong and in a short time they become sick, short of breath cough and spit up substances." A worker who was employed by a private company on a federal road construction job was concerned that men who arose at 4 A.M. and worked until dusk "usually went without breakfast" and got only a cold sandwich on the job, "when their hands would be so cold they could hardly hold it." Even after one worker cut off most of his foot with an ax and another badly

burned both hands, "no first aid kit or attendant was at this camp." It
was the desperate need for a job at any cost that kept workers working.
The need to support their families made laborers stay in these jobs despite the dangers to their health and well-being. The wife of a bakery
worker in Nebraska worried that when her "husband gets home he is absolutely too weary to eat"; in one horrendous period he worked "thirty
hours without stopping only to 'gulp' a few bites and watch the motor
while he did that. . . . If one has a family they must do something but this
is slavery."

The imagery of workers shackled to their jobs and whipped into submission appears and reappears throughout these letters. To be sure, such
imagery pervades the rhetoric of labor organizers and leaders throughout
American history, but it had a special import during the hard years of the
Depression. "We have slavery in many of the mills mines and factories in
the United States of America," wrote a worker in Pittsburgh. J. G. lamented the fate of millions of workers as "slaves of the depression," for
they often felt helpless and vulnerable in the face of the economic need
that kept them from improving their condition. A Cleveland steelworker
echoed J. G.'s sentiments when he wrote that "American workers are not
'free.'" Describing in graphic detail how millworkers were burned by
molten metal, he bitterly denounced their treatment as "just as bad as
black-snake-whip slavery." Slavery was more than an abstract idea found
in schoolbooks for this generation of Americans, both black and white.

Industrialists and foremen had taken the place of southern planters in
the slave economy, and the whip they used to control workers' lives was
the Depression. Workers understood that human bondage could take
many forms. "Truly," wrote a copper and brass worker in Detroit, "there
is such a thing as economic slavery." Some saw their own poor economic
condition as a conscious tactic employed by management to exert control
over them: "Why must the worker suffer every time they want to put on
depression?" asked a sixty-year-old worker in Youngstown. The new
slavery was as demoralizing as the old. "What can there be left in life for a
man who has to keep going all night . . . 365 days a year for a mere existence," wrote the wife of a night watchman in Washington State. Faced
by declining profits, managers pressed their workers to the limits of human endurance. Some owners sought to avoid costly technological renovations and increased labor costs by increasing production speed and
lengthening the workweek without raising compensation. American
workers feared for their jobs. Some also understood that people could
not be forced to endure these work conditions without experiencing an

erosion of the spiritual base on which they assumed America had been built: "We workers are losing our moral, our integrity is on the decline."

Many workers described the destruction of their family life. Grandparents, spouses, and children were being victimized by the severity of working life. A chain store clerk in Paterson, New Jersey, wrote that the long hours he was forced to work had undermined his relationship with his wife and children. He begged the government to protect him and his fellow workers for "WE WANT TO SEE OUR MOTHERS AND WIVES SOMETIME, TOO!!" Suffering sapped the bodies as well as the spirits of workers. An Iowa housewife explained to the president that her family could not long survive on her husband's wage of $1 a day. "We don't have anything to eat but my husband [goes] to work any way and I am pretty weak. . . . I know Mr. Roosevelt you will understand one must have something to eat. . . ." The wife of an injured worker who had been laid off by his company with minimal compensation pleaded with Frances Perkins, the secretary of labor, for advice on how to get enough money to survive: "I will forever be grateful to you to know that I can raise my two daughters and not have to worry how I am going to do it." Another wife, describing her husband's state of "utter exhaustion," plaintively wrote that she was "about at the point of breaking up my home and heading for nowhere." Much has been written on the plight of the unemployed; here we see that the inadequacy of wages and the conditions of work itself could lead to the same results for the employed.

Workers and their families lived in continual hardship and constant fear. Even after the passage of the National Labor Relations Act, most workers were unorganized and were subject to arbitrary reprisals for real and imagined protests. An Alabama knitting mill worker, complaining about her lack of rights on the job, noted that her co-workers were "treated so bad they are afraid to do anything for they will be fired if they do." Conditions were apparently little better at an aircraft company in New England: a foreman sympathetic to the plight of his workers wrote of the "feeling of fear" that permeated the plant. "Today through a spying system all men go around with sealed lips. Afraid to even talk about anything relating to their regular work." Many who wrote to the government refused to sign their names for fear of retribution. A writer in Bloomington, Indiana, identified herself simply as "a tired office worker." Others begged the president and Secretary Perkins to keep their letters confidential. Many workers were so afraid of losing their jobs that they could not bring themselves to discuss working conditions with government inspectors. A writer in Massachusetts explained his co-workers' fears: "They are so afraid of their jobs that if questioned by inspectors they would doubtless say they were satisfied." A miner in the Mesabi iron range of Minnesota graphically explained why he refused to sign his letter: "I'm in U.S.A. but can't sign as the Missabe range isn't Americanized yet. I do not know who will get this letter first and I have no right to sign, as these companies have spies, even underground." The much-heralded pro-labor legislation of the New Deal could not protect the vast number of unorganized and vulnerable workers.

These letters reflect not only the intimidation and fear of workers struggling to hold on to their jobs but also their enormous pride, anger, and outrage. A machinist in California denounced the regimentation that employers imposed upon their workers, "as though the employer were buying a mule." A black worker in North Carolina objected to the fact that nobody "ever investigates our working conditions and the greatest portion of us are colored people and I think every body hates a colored man." The Pennsylvania steelworker quoted earlier charged that his company was "committing wholesale murder." Others wanted retribution: "They do not seem to need to care for the country or the people. Only profit. Sometimes I wish it would come to a shooting match."

Most workers did not despair of a peaceful and equitable solution. Demoralized and intimidated by the prospect of unemployment, they still expressed outrage and a fundamental faith in the ideals of a democratic America. As one distraught worker put it, "I'm only asking for justice and fair play." Even if he and his fellow workers could not improve their own condition, he still entertained hope for future generations: "If we do not benefit by it now maybe someone else will in years to come." Four chain store employees, sending "a plaintive cry from a lone outpost among the corn rows of Indiana," described their struggle to "make a decent living." They did "not demand a Shangri-La on earth but . . . would like to have a small bit of the good works created here." A Pennsylvania laborer pointed out that "God did not make this world just for rich to enjoy he made it for every living soul."

Many writers believed that the democratic principles on which the nation was built had been perverted by the greed and excesses of a few. A steelworker in Pittsburgh said that "our Fathers and Fore Fathers left there homes years ago and shed there blood on battle fields and many gave up there lives to banish Slavery and to make this a happy Christian country to live in." A Detroit wife and mother wrote, "I and my husband are and have been Americans for three generations and we are proud of what our parents did . . . to help America progress. They were builders of our country not destructors as is now going on to make the rich man richer and the poor man poorer. . . ." Hotel workers in Brooklyn asked "in the name of GOD is this a free country or is it dominated by the few millionaires and money changers. . . ." Describing the hotel as a "veritable Salt Mine of Siberia," they charged that renovations then in progress were being paid for "with Human Blood." A Louisiana sugar cane worker, describing conditions that hadn't "made any progress or improvement since slavery days," assured Secretary Perkins that such conditions were un-American. "I am sure that the lowest places in China or Mexico or Africa has better places to live in." Some saw the exploitation practiced at their workplaces as an anomaly; others, politically more radical, saw horrible conditions as endemic to capitalism and feared that such exploitation would undermine America's moral fiber.

It is impossible to read these letters without feeling the suffering and struggle that working people had to experience every day. The letters eloquently testify to the depth and immediacy of their writers' need. In the end, what workers were asking for was deceptively simple: they wanted shorter hours so that they could spend time with their families; they asked for higher wages so that they could feed their children; they demanded safer, cleaner, more humane working conditions and relief from fear. In short, they wanted control over their lives so that they could feel a sense of purpose and integrity at work and at home.

All of these writers clearly believed that the government of Franklin D. Roosevelt shared their concerns and would work to help them. It is remarkable how many workers felt that the president and Eleanor Roosevelt, Secretary Perkins and other government officials would pay attention to their pleas. Some letters are strong and forceful, demanding action to redress particular grievances. Most often, though, they are humble and personal appeals for help. One writer begs forgiveness for presuming to write to the president. "Please excuse me if I am abusing to write you these few lines, because you are in head of the United States of America," wrote an Italian worker who was dying of asbestosis. A black worker who had been fired from a defense plant wrote that Roosevelt had "done much to help out our people, and if you will, please look into this matter." Some began by admitting their own insecurity: "I have never gone as far as writing to a person of your rank in office." All of the writers believed that their concerns were small in comparison with the issues that the president had to face. One wrote: "I regret that I had to bring this matter to you, but I don't know any one else to whom I can appeal."

People appealed directly to Roosevelt because, in the words of a Detroit factory worker, they saw him as "the savior of the labor class of people." "You are the one & only President that ever helped a Working Class
of People," wrote a Texas furniture worker. The wife of a worker at a
brewer's warehouse in Detroit saw the president as a modern-day Moses
and reported that her "minister said Sunday, that Roosevelt would lead
us out of bondage, so we are hoping." These people sincerely believed
that Roosevelt would listen to their problems. Other historians have
pointed out the extraordinary power of Roosevelt's radio personality. As
he broadcast his "fireside chats," listeners felt that he was communicat-
ing personally with them. Why, then, should they not write personally
to him? The wife of an Illinois craneman wrote, "We listened to your talk
yesterday over the radio and feel certain that you are in favor of the working men of this country therefore would appreciate a little advice." A laborer from a small town in Connecticut asked the president to enlist the
aid of the first lady in addressing his problem: "Please have Mrs. Roosevelt say something concerning this when she speaks over the radio."

The belief that the president would deal with the problems one faced if
only he were informed about them was exhilarating. A domestic worker
in Pittsburgh, wondering "how can we make it [on] such little money,"
asked Roosevelt, "Please see what you can do . . . and many thanks all
good wishes to you and family." Other writers sought legislative relief.
One worker wanted the government to "pass laws to stop this curse [of
speedup and overproduction] for prosperity and welfare for our beloved
country." A coal miner in Pennsylvania despaired of doing "anything
myself" but asked the government to "step right in here at once without
any delay."

The faith that workers placed in Roosevelt was due in large part to the
labor legislation pushed by his administration. Although Roosevelt himself was a reluctant advocate of union rights, the National Industrial Recovery Act (NIRA) of 1933, the National Labor Relations and Social
Security acts of 1935, and the Fair Labor Standards Act of 1938 altered relations between industry and labor in ways that are still being felt.

The NIRA created the National Recovery Administration, which provided that each industry was to establish a code to govern its own management. Section 7(a) provided for the establishment of minimum wages
and maximum hours, improvements in working conditions, the elimination of child labor, and the right of unions to bargain collectively with
management. While this provision was widely evaded—many businesses
used it as a justification for forming company unions—it gave workers

confidence that the federal government supported their organizing efforts. Some union organizers told workers in plants they were attempting to organize that "FDR wants you to join the union."[8]

When the Supreme Court declared the NIRA unconstitutional in 1935, Congress passed the National Labor Relations Act (the Wagner Act), which guaranteed workers the right to organize and bargain collectively and set up a permanent board to supervise elections for union representation. The National Labor Relations Board (NLRB), in conjunction with active organizing drives by the Congress of Industrial Organizations (CIO), led to the rapid growth of trade union membership, from 3.7 million workers in 1935 to 7.2 million in 1940 and 12.5 million in 1945.

The Social Security Act of 1935 was also taken as a sign of the federal government's concern for the poor, employed or not. Although it did not cover about a quarter of the labor force—public employees, farmworkers, and domestic servants—it established for the first time a national system of unemployment insurance and old age pensions. Three years later, Congress passed the Fair Labor Standards Act, which expanded the protection offered employed members of the work force. This act initially set a minimum wage of 25 cents an hour and a maximum workweek of 44 hours; these standards were later raised to 40 cents and 40 hours.

Most of these pieces of labor legislation were carried out through a newly energized Department of Labor. The Labor Department of the 1930s, like other New Deal departments and agencies, attracted to it persons whose political and social commitments were far to the left of Roosevelt's. These administrators and staff members often sought to develop programs that aided labor and thereby represented an important break with past government policy. Before the New Deal, the national government had rarely assumed any but a research and information-gathering role in regard to labor. There were no national standards for hours, wages, or working conditions; each state and every industry had its own formal and informal methods for controlling its labor relations. Some states—New York, for example—had developed relatively extensive regulatory devices for controlling excesses on the shop floor; in the vast majority of states, however, regulatory activities were ineffective or nonexistent. In light of the dismal status of most state programs and in

[8]Alex Rosner, interview, June 12, 1978; see Irving Bernstein, *The Turbulent Years: A History of the American Worker* (Boston: Houghton Mifflin, 1970) and *A Caring Society: The New Deal, the Worker, and the Great Depression* (Boston: Houghton Mifflin, 1985).

the context of the Great Depression, when most workers were subject to even greater exploitation than in earlier years, it is significant that the Department of Labor had as one of its major goals "improvement in the working and living conditions of wage-earners and their families."[9]

The secretary of labor was deluged with requests for help. Perhaps because Frances Perkins was the first woman cabinet member, or perhaps because she shared Roosevelt's activist image, she too received highly personal appeals. A Florida worker wrote that he and his co-workers were all "looking to you [for] we believe that your heart and life are wrapped up in this work."

Perkins' commitment to workers' interests was reflected in the attention she paid to their letters and queries. She not only attended to many letters herself but organized within her office a special division to address workers' complaints about deteriorating working conditions. It was to this Division of Labor Standards that she referred all correspondence about problems at the workplace. The division's files are filled with appeals for help from both organized and unorganized workers, and its administrators' responses, some of which we reproduce in conjunction with the letters that prompted them, show a respect and concern we rarely associate with government bureaucrats today. When a foundry worker in Pennsylvania complained of "terrible" working conditions that should be investigated, he added, "Please do not notify the bosses you are coming make it a surprise they are very tricky." Verne Zimmer, the division's head, not only responded directly to the worker but sent a copy of the complaint to the Pennsylvania Bureau of Inspection and Enforcement. "You will doubtless wish to make a complete investigation of this plant," he wrote, "keeping in mind the last sentence of this letter which suggests that the Company management not be advised of your contemplated inspection." When a union lodged a more formal complaint, Zimmer went beyond the specific issue raised and suggested a broader program to address a wide range of health and safety issues. When a Connecticut local of the International Brotherhood of Paper Makers asked for information that would "help us to safeguard our health in industry," Zimmer offered to send a safety engineer to consult

---

[9]Memorandum, "The Division of Labor Standards—Its Functions and Organization" (Clara Beyer, November 1934), National Archives, RG 100, ser. 1, 1934–1937, 1-1, Box 24. See also Gerald Markowitz and David Rosner, "More than Economism: The Politics of Workers' Safety and Health, 1932–1947," *Milbank Quarterly* 64 (Fall 1986): 331–54; David Rosner and Gerald Markowitz, "Research or Advocacy: Federal Occupational Safety and Health Policies during the New Deal," *Journal of Social History* 18 (Spring 1985): 365–82.

with the union's safety council. A meeting was arranged, and the union secretary reported that the "visit helped us more than we expected."

World War II brought important changes in the lives of laborers and in the work of the Department of Labor. The enlistment of millions of agrarian, black, female, and untrained workers for war production made accident prevention and "human conservation" a national concern. It came to be generally understood that protecting workers on the home front was as important as protecting soldiers overseas. Consciousness of the cost of industrial accidents was heightened by the fact that during the first three years of the war more Americans were killed and injured in work-related accidents than on the battlefield.

The department's personnel saw the war as an opportunity for direct involvement of the federal government in protecting American workers. Just a month before Pearl Harbor, the department developed an extensive program to protect workers against the threats of speedup, involuntary overtime, and poor working conditions. The first and most important project was to begin federal inspection of plants engaged in war work. The Walsh-Healey Act authorized the federal government to inspect plants doing work under federal contracts, but such inspections were carried out at only a small number of plants and were confined almost entirely to checking compliance with the wage and hour regulations of the Fair Labor Standards Act. During World War II the Division of Labor Standards, working with the National Committee for the Conservation of Manpower in Defense Industries, directed a volunteer force of several hundred safety engineers who personally visited each contract plant, "checking conspicuously high accident rates," working with state and regional labor officials, "recommending corrective measures, analyzing and appraising trends and recording progress and improvements." Under this program, more than 21,000 plants were inspected in the first eighteen months of the war, and after the first inspection, the division claimed, approximately 75 percent of them showed a "decided downward trend in accident frequency."[10]

The letters presented on the following pages—all from Record Group 100 in the National Archives—vividly describe life during the terrible years when the American dream became a nightmare. They span a 13-year period, from 1932 through 1945, when the death of Roosevelt and Perkins' retirement formally closed a critical period in political history.

[10]Safety and Health Section, Division of Labor Standards, National Archives, RG 100, 3d ser., 1941–1945, 1-1.

These letters tell us more about the period than that working conditions were terrible. They also give us insight into the lives of workers and their families and an understanding of the complexity of workers' own analysis of the American political and economic system. Politically, the sentiments expressed in these letters are traditional and sometimes conservative. When these workers needed help, they turned to the federal government, not to radical political parties. The very act of writing to the government was an expression of faith in the political system and specifically in the New Deal. As most of these workers were unorganized, it is possible that they had few places to turn other than to FDR and the government. But the values repeated over and over again reflect a faith in democracy, republican government, and the centrality of "the people" to the survival of the political system.

Their faith in the viability of the political system did not blind them to the oppression of the economic system under which they toiled. They understood exactly what was happening to them during these trying years. They knew that business owners were using the Depression to exploit their labor, to undermine their self-reliance, to control their actions, their words, and even their thoughts; that they did so to increase their own profits; and that these profits were gained at the expense of the health and well-being of workers and their families. In short, these letters exhibit a class consciousness that has all too often been ignored.

The letters also tell us something important about the culture of the American working class. The rhetoric of many of the letters sounds strange today. Often the letter writers use the language of the socialist and communist left, though the vast majority could have echoed Will Rogers' joke: "I'm not a member of any organized party. I'm a Democrat." The frequent use of leftist rhetoric by people who trusted their government suggests two important points: first, that class consciousness was deeply embedded in the working class; second, that the impact of the organized parties on the left, both Socialist and Communist, may have reached unorganized workers in ways that are now little understood. We do not know how consciously such rhetoric was used or if people understood its origins in working-class culture or in the relatively new political movements. But we do know that workers of the Depression and even during World War II recognized no identity of interests with their employers and defined their differences in class terms.

Locations, dates, salutations, and signatures have been regularized. The names of government and organization officials and of companies and other organizations are reproduced as they appear in the letters; all other persons are identified by initials only. Otherwise the letters are reproduced as they were written, their inaccuracies and idiosyncrasies faithfully preserved.

1. *"The Working Class of People"*

Academics have often asked why socialism has failed to take root in American soil. What is it about the American experience that has militated against the creation of a strong socialist movement in this country? The answers that have been offered reflect differing political and social commitments and types of academic training. Some scholars have simply seen the United States as an exception to the political trends that prevailed in the stratified European societies, where class antagonisms flourished; the unique American political, economic, and social environment, they say, militated against the development of a strong working-class consciousness and socialist tradition. Others have offered social and economic mobility as partial answers to the question, while still others have seen the organized repression of the 1920s as responsible for the dissolution of a socialist tradition.[1] The internal organizational, tactical, and ideological problems of the Socialist and Communist parties have also been held responsible for socialism's failure in the United States.

A major assumption of the exceptionalist arguments is that American workers, lacking a tradition of class stratification, never developed a consciousness of themselves as a class. The uniquely American ideology and experience of social mobility stifled class consciousness. Some historians, such as Herbert Gutman, have looked at the culture of working-class life, both at home and in the workplace, for clues as to why a lasting workers' movement has not developed in this country. Others, such as Stanley

[1]See David M. Gordon, Richard Edwards, and Michael Reich, *Segmented Work, Divided Workers: The Historical Transformation of Labor in the United States* (New York: Cambridge University Press, 1982), pp. 4–8, for a brief discussion.

Aronowitz, have argued that workers' identification with particular ethnic or racial groups has worked against class identification.[2]

It is beyond the scope of this book to address the question of socialism's failure to flourish in the United States. The letters reproduced here,
however, should cause us to question the widely held assumption that
American workers have not historically identified themselves as part of a
particular class. We shall see that the people who wrote to the government in the 1930s and 1940s clearly identified themselves as workers and
just as clearly identified the people responsible for their misery as owners,
managers, and capitalists. These workers assumed that the interests of labor and of capital clashed. This was a reasonable view, given the pitched
battles between workers and owners during the 1930s over such issues as
wages, hours, and the right to form a union. The extraordinary power of
capital to control the lives of workers and their families was laid bare by
the Depression. In more prosperous times, workers' hostility was muted
by their ability to find other work if wages were cut, hours lengthened,
or jobs eliminated. Now those options had evaporated. The theme of
class exploitation and class antagonism surfaces too often throughout
these letters to be ignored. Whatever the workers' specific complaints —
conditions on the shop floor, speedups, pay cuts, forced overtime, kick-
backs, requirements that families buy their food at the company store at
exorbitant prices — the realization that workers as a class were being ha-
rassed and exploited was explicit. Some writers used traditional Marxist
and socialist terms, identifying managers and owners as "capitalists" and
themselves as "the working class." Most of them, though, wrote only of
the way "we poor workers" were being treated by foremen, managers,
and owners. The writers often used terms that historians now associate
with Roosevelt's "fireside chats." They spoke of "the common man,"
"little people," or simply "the people."

Given the rhetoric and attitudes expressed in these letters, it is remarkable that so many Americans wrote to their government in the expecta-
tion of a sympathetic response. The writers were not revolutionaries, and
the volume of such correspondence in government files demonstrates a
widely held faith in the basic goodness and integrity of the federal government, a belief that the government and especially the president were
the workers' allies and would take concrete administrative and legislative

[2]See Herbert Gutman, *Work, Culture, and Society in Industrializing America* (New York:
Knopf, 1976); Stanley Aronowitz, *False Promises: The Shaping of American Working-Class
Consciousness* (New York: McGraw-Hill, 1973).

action to remedy conditions on the shop floor. It is also remarkable that most of these letters are from individual workers, not from organized political groups.

Class-conscious language is to be found throughout the correspondence in this book. In this chapter we present a few letters that demonstrate the expression of class consciousness in the writings of working Americans during the Depression. Workers today may find such language alien or alienating, and we may wonder what happened to workers' class consciousness in the postwar years. The vibrancy of the 1930s correspondence gives us reason to look closely at the cultural and political importance of the organized repression of the Cold War years. While many of these writers may have supported socialist alternatives, class-conscious rhetoric was also used by such demogogues as Huey Long and Charles Coughlin to foster their own personal agendas.[3]

The writer of the following letter fears reprisals because he was unwilling to inform on his co-workers. Though he had a white-collar job, his alliance with the workers on the shop floor was more important to him than the rewards promised by his employer.

Detroit, Michigan, September 21, 1936

Dear [President Roosevelt]:

Having served five years in the Regular Navy I feel it is the Federal Governments intent to do what is right. I will attempt in a[s] brief a manner as I am capable to outline what has occurred. Truly it may be said that there is such a thing as economic slavery.

To commence: I was employed by the Michigan Division of the Revere Copper and Brass Co. in the Cost Dept. My job was to establish the cost of production and to do whatever Time Study work the was necessary. I am thirty-two years old, married, and support my wife and two children. One a boy of six and a half years and a girl of five months. On September 4th. at 3.00 p.m. I was informed by my superior, F. S., that starting the following Tuesday I was to commence a Time Study of the

[3]Gary Gerstle is currently working on a book that discusses the phenomenon we outline here. He seeks to ground the destruction of class consciousness among American workers in the demographic and cultural events that took place during and after World War II as workers' ethnic communities were dispersed. See Gary Gerstle, "The Politics of Patriotism, Americanization, and the Formation of the CIO," *Dissent* 33 (Winter 1986): 84–92.

three mills. I was further instructed to pay particular attention to the promptness with which the operator started his machine at the start of his shift. If the machine was at any time left idle. If any one of the crew left the machine. If the foreman or subforeman pushed his men. In other words it was the company's intent that I should be nothing other than a stool pigeon. Further on each Saturday morning I was to make my appearance at the office and in so many words tell my Department Head and the Mill Supt. everything I had seen or heard. Further, if I did a real good job I was receive a raise the first of the year.

As any man who holds himself to be decent I could not accept such an assignment and within the hour I quit. However in quitting I appreciated the fact that this country today is no longer one of free speech, therefore, I stated the reason for resigning was that I would not work for fifty five cents per hour. Further I carefully refrained from making any further statement. You understand such things as referring to your previous employer for a recommendation. Now here comes the rub. I know for a fact that it is the intent of the Company Officials to do everything possible to prevent my obtaining employment. I am further informed that they wait the day when failing to obtain employment elsewhere I return to them. At that time (They believe it will occur) it is their intent to turn me down. To boil the matter down then it is their intent to persecute me because I dared to refuse to do their bidding and actually had nerve enough to risk the welfare of myself and the ones at home by quitting. I know it all sounds cockeyed. Nevertheless I am prepared to prove what I say before competent authority.

You must appreciate the fact that no country however great can long continue if these conditions exist.

During the depression I lived with my wife and boy on the pension we receive account of a Medical Discharge which amounted to twelve dollars per month. True we moved to the country and our hardships were many but we did not go on the Welfare. I am prepared to do the same thing again. I believe it is useless for me to look for a job in view of the Company's apparent intent.

F. D. J.

The writer of the following letter, a foreman in a furniture factory, clearly identified with the workers he supervised rather than with management.

Please the reader of this letter let the meaning reach the one intended.

Paris, Texas, November 23, 1936

Dear President now that we have had a land Slide[4] and done just what was best for our country & I will Say more done the only thing that could of bin done to Save this Country I do believe you Will Strain a point to help the ones who helped you mostly & that is the Working Class of People I am not smart or I would be in a different line of work & better up in ever way yet I will Know you are the one & only President that ever helped a Working Class of People I have Writen you several letters & have always received a answer from Some of you officials clerks or Some one & I will know you have to much to think about to answer a little man letter like my Self yet I will Say I and thousands of men just like me were in the fight for you & I for one will go down for you any day I am a White Man American age 47 married wife 2 children in high School am a Finishing room foreman I mean a Working foreman & am in a furniture Factory here in Paris Texas where thaire is 175 to 200 Working & when the NRA came in I was Proud to See my fellow workmen Rec 30 Per hour in Place of 8 cents to 20 cents Per hour yet the NRA did not make any allowance for Skilled labor or foreman unless they rec as much as 35.00 Per Week & very few Furniture Makers rec Such a Price I have bin with this firm for 25 years & they have Surly reaped the harvest. . . . I can't see for my life President why a man must toil & work his life out in Such factories 10 long hours ever day except Sunday for a small sum of 15 cents to 35 cents per hour & pay the high cost of honest & deason living expences is thaire any way in the world to help this one class of Laboring People just a little I admit this class of Working People should form a union but ever time it talked the big boy owners say we will close down then it is more releaf workers to take care of more expence to our Government and more trouble to you what we need is a law passed to shorten our hours at a living & let live scal & take more men off the Government expense & put them in the factories & get things to running normal but if a co cuts hours & then tells Foreman shove & push them & keeps putting out as much with short hours & driving the men like convicts it will never help a bit you have had your load & I well know it but please see if something can be done to help this one Class of Working People the factories are a man killer not venelated or kept up just a bunch

---

[4]In 1936 Roosevelt won over 60 percent of the popular vote against his Republican opponent, Alfred M. Landon. Roosevelt won every state except Maine and Vermont.

of Republickins Grafters 90/100 of them Please help us some way I Pray
to God for relief. I am a christian . . . and a truthful man & have not told
you wrong & am for you to the end.

H. M. L.

Marshalltown, Iowa, February 3, 1937

Dear President:

I am writing you about work and what they pay. My husband work for
1.00 a day and we must pay 8.00 month rent but we are back, have of the
time. We don't have anything to eat but my husband go to work any way
and I am pretty weak and we have not been in Marshalltown long to get
aid but in April we will be I know Mr. Roosevelt you will understand
one must have something to eat and sleep and there ist no other work my
husband also belong to Co. H he get 1.00 every Monday night. they pay
every 3 months I vote for you the 1st time also for the 2nd time. for you
are the man for the office. My husband work from 7:30 till 5:30 for only
1.00 day. I will give you this man address he work for C. K. 205 So. 7th
Ave Marshalltown. Please help us this town has no union to keep wages
up. it should have. There is where us working man is to day. Maybe if
you write him a letter I think that would help a Married Man just can't
live on it yes he is making money he run a gramberg [?] truck so please
see if you can do something.

Mrs. F. M.

Washington, D.C., February 15, 1937

Dear Mrs. M.:

The President has referred your letter of February 3 to the Department
of Labor.

I am afraid the President cannot help you directly as you ask, since he
does not have the authority to require an employer to increase wages.

As Iowa does not have any law by which the hours of men may be limited, I am afraid it would not be possible for the State Labor Commissioner to help you either.

If you and your husband are entirely dependent upon his earnings of a
dollar a day, I can easily see that your situation is a very serious one and
while I know that you are probably very reluctant to ask for assistance, I

think that under the circumstances you may have to, temporarily at least, ask for some help. If you find that it is necessary to do so, I suggest that you write to Mr. J. Carl Pryor, Chairman, Emergency Relief Committee, Oransky Building, 8th Street, Des Moines, Iowa.

V. A. ZIMMER, Director
Division of Labor Standards

Ronceverte, West Virginia, April 20, 1937

Dear Mr. President:

By newspaper reports I see that you will in the near future put before Congress a plan for the regulation of wages and working hours and perhaps a weeding out of the many persons employed by the various industries that have incomes or other means of livelihood. As an illustration of what I mean, I will tell you of my own condition of the practices of the company for which I work.

I am employed by the Ronceverte Ice and Produce Company of Ronceverte, W. Va., a comparatively small concern, working a yearly average of perhaps twenty men. Besides making ice, they are engaged in a varied line of business, manufacturing ice cream, and other dairy products, carry a full line of produce, fruit, vegetables, etc., wholesale and retailing oil and gas, auto and truck sales agency, refrigerator agency, wholesale and retail coal, wholesale beer distributors, dealer in automobile tires and other accessories. This plant operates on-a twenty four hour basis. I am employed as a third shift man; my duties are as follows: taking care of the refrigerating machine or machines, as the case may be (in winter one or two, in summer three or four), looking after storage rooms and storage conditions as required, pulling ice to load out early morning trucks, looking after filling station trade, also ice cream and dairy products trade, cleaning fire box and cinder pit and having steam up for early morning crew. This winter I worked on an eight hour shift. During March I notified them that I would be leaving April first, as I could not continue to exist on the small salary of $50.00 per month. I am a widower and have two daughters, one in High and the other in Junior High School, have an old lady who helps with the house work. I do not own property. Out of this wage I pay house rent, lights, water, fuel, buy groceries, school supplies, which leaves nothing for clothing nor recreation. When they learned that I was leaving, they offered me $75.00 per month, but they tacked on two hours more per day, making it a ten hour day. All this

I gladly accepted because I needed more money. I am not writing this as a complaint against the company but am trying to show the conditions existing in smaller plants as well as the larger ones. The service required of me is even less than is required of many others.

The company has two men employed that own farms and paid for. Now it seems to me in justice to the fellow that doesn't have a job that these men should be on their farms. I know of a number of cases of husband and wife, without children both working. At least five more persons could be employed here if hours were properly regulated, for example the engineers pull ice; there is no regular ice man. Truck drivers working from ten to sixteen hours, big three to five ton beer and produce trucks, making trips to Baltimore, Florida, and various other points with only one driver. Men in various departments are frequently worked over time without extra pay. Chiseling in various other ways, almost too numerous to mention. The place is notorious for its petty thieving, caused very much by low wages, and unfair treatment.

I believe that conditions are worse in the smaller industries because of a lack of organization or leverage for bargaining. It leaves small groups at the mercy of unscrupulous employers. Again, I want to say I have no quarrel with this company for which I am working but seeing the injustices practiced and intolerable conditions existing, I believe that similar conditions exist in various plants throughout the country. I feel there is an urgent need for some drastic relief.

I was born a Methodist Episcopal, and a Republican, I have stood by my church but have strayed far politically. I left the old line Republicans with the Bull Moosers and I have continued to stray farther away, until today I find myself heartily supporting the New Deal. I believe in the law and an orderly course of procedure, but if time prohibits and the occasion demands it, and it is the only way to alleviate suffering and distress of the masses of people, I would be in favor of taking the nine old men [on the Supreme Court] by the scruff of the neck and the seat of the pants and lift them wholly and bodily out of their sanctuary of usurped authority. As to sit-down strikers I don't approve of the method but it seems to be an only means to an end. From them I turn my mind's eye to the ever right and infallible corporations that flout the law which says the working man has a right to organize for collective bargaining.

Pardon me for writing all this well-meant stuff and if it never reaches you, at least it will relieve a mind that feels this an urgent duty.

J. H. Y.

P.S. Please keep this letter confidential.

Detroit, Michigan, November 29, 1937

Mr. President:

It has taken me a long time, to have enough courage to write to you.

You Mr. President are the savior of the labor class of people. Things this fall looked bright, but they changed a lot. I am a member of the U.A.W. affiliated with the C.I.O. Just the other day the factories have laid off thousands of men. Some of these men have four to six children, some are single planing to marry. What are they going to do? Please help them.

I myself am begging you for help. At present time I am employed at the Briggs Mfg. Co. in Detroit. How long will I work? I don't know. But Mr. President do everything in your power to help these people, they have faith in you. I am not educated enough to have an easy life, but all I want, and everybody else is to make an honest living. I would like to have a talk with you hand in hand so you could really understand what I mean.

I would like to have an answer on this letter. Please forgive me for my mistakes because I was to nervous.

Mr. President the people of United States are behind you, The labor class backs you one hundred percent in everything you say or do.

We the people of these United States, the labor class all we ask for is "An honest way to make a decent living." We are the backbone of the nation.

I would like you to see me but I have no way of getting to see you. 1. my education 2) my financial standing. If I could see you, I am sure I could explain it in a different form.

R. K. (a real Dem.)

Washington, D.C., December 8, 1937

My dear Mr. K:

The President has asked me to reply to your letter of November 29.

I can assure you that the President is doing everything in his power to stabilize employment and we hope that the wage and hour bill which is being considered by Congress may be one of the means of spreading employment, and also of assuring workers of living wages.

Thank you for your interest in writing to the President.

V. A. ZIMMER

Kokomo, Indiana, December 27, 1937

Dear President:

Wish to forward to you what I believe a general opinion that's prevalent in the rank and file of labor.

The New Deal and its fundamental principles had some progressive and economic value, but obviously the two vital issues have been dodged at every instance (underpaid labor and excessive profits) and until you and Congress prescribe a remedy for those two ailments there is no New Deal and the advancement of civilization as you so often speak of cannot and will not *move*.

I or may I say we laborers of America don't believe in confiscation and we don't want radical socialism in fact we are more or less like monkeys. let us earn an adequate living and we will be well satisfied.

I'm not much on prognostication neither do I profess to be a prophet, but surely you great intelligent leaders can see the hand-writing on the wall. Unfortunately I'm a man without an education entering my late forties overflowing with tranquility and energy yet unable to make a decent living.

I assure Hon. President we workers are losing our moral, our integrity is on the decline but within us intrepidity is gaining.

The man who is fortunate enough to deposit money in a bank is safe and agriculture has been well taken care of which I congratulate the present administration, but labor is still in the rut.

There is only one solution make a cut in those excessive profits and add it on to labor its feasible without doubt.

Lets get off of relief permanently.

Trust you will consider this little missive and find no espionage infringement I day say however it carries some Patrick Henry inspiration.

O. B.

Pittsburgh, Pennsylvania, February 28, 1938
(Part 1)
(note) Read very carefully

Dear [Mr. President]:

The United States Representative form of Government through an elected Congress and Senate by the votes of the people are not doing there duty as law makers for the people of these United States of America. Our Fathers and Fore Fathers left there homes years ago and shed there blood on battle fields and many gave up there lives to banish Slavery and to make this a happy Christian country to live in. That every young or old person may be contented and live in peace and happyness throughout there entire life. But what have we on our hands at the present time which every human person knows who can reason. We have Slavery in many of the mills mines and factories in the United States of America where many people young and old are employed trying to make an honest living for themselves and family by the sweat of there brow that there children may be raised with decency and respect and when they grow up may be of some use to there parents in there old days. It has been told to me by many of these people who are employed in some of these factories that since they have improved machinery in these places many of the employers are now compelled to do two and three peoples work with one persons pay. What kind of a profit system is this when these Corporations are making such big profits dividends and giving the Slave drivers under them a bonus to drive the working class of people to death at there work at small wages and long hours. These Capitalists and the Board of Directors and the slave drivers who do the dirty work for these Corporations should be tried by Court marshal or by new laws made by Congress and Senate that they should be put in prison and kept there the remaining days of there miserable lives if they cannot be true to man they cannot be true to God. Our Lord in his times drove the money changers out of the Temple for using the Temple for a place to trade and carry on there business. They killed no one in the Temple at that time through there business transactions. But in the mills mines and factories of the United States thousands are killed and crippled yearly by what is known as the speed up Profit system. Human life in America under the Capitalist system is very cheap to these mongrels.

(Part 2)

When many of these people working in these mills mines and factories reach the age of 40 or 50 years of age they are broken down in health and body with hard work. the remaining days of there life is a life of misery. They must finish there old days in a refuge or prison. Until our good Lord and Savior Jesus Christ calls them to his home in heaven where Slavery and the greed for profits does not exist. When the Constitution of the United States was confirmed and ratified by the 13 States it did not say that Slavery should exist in the United States. So why have Slavery in this country at the present time. Congress and Senate should make laws for the people to abolish wage Slavery from these United States nothing can ever be accomplished where Slavery and misery exists. Many of these rich mongrels go to church on Sunday sit in the front pew praying to our good Lord that he may give them more power to blindfold the people. Gods chosen people the very poor. What is needed more than anything else in this country is a Safety Council now the Labor board by a law passed by Congress and Senate in giving employees the authority to vote whether they wish to join a union of there own or not is a very good plan concerning human nature now the Safety Council should be appointed the same way by an act of Congress and Senate in looking after the interests of the employees in mills mines factories to see that they are not made Slaves of by being over burdensome with hard work at there labor. There work would be to see that every thing is safe in mills mines factories laying water lines gas lines erection of buildings and Sanitary conditions. This is what makes a happy and prosperous country to live in. Thousands of employees in mills mines and factories are killed and crippled every year. How long are we in this country going to live in these stone ages. Congress and Senate of the United States must decide that question themselves by making laws to overcome these barbarian laws which we are now going through.

J. M. G.

Youngstown, Ohio, March 1, 1940

Dear [Mr. President]:

Why must the worker suffer every time they want to put on depression they lay thousant of men off can't you send anyone to check why they shut down when and w[h]ere they want to. They have lots of orders and month's ahead the way they say. If they try to put something over we need someone to protect the worker and there family from starving. Many loosing their homes, their life's earning. The way I see [it is to] stop there overproduction. [But there are] men on top of you with book and pencil to put in all delays. Worse than slavery. Ain't there a way Loveable President. They call workers Reds when they say one word. Why? The corporation do every thing in the world to hurt the worker and from making our country one of the best in the world. Taxes they need for their surplus for they make plenty and more taxes when they shut down to no cause at all. Men have freedom for colectave Bargaining. But do they. They load up with thousands of cots amonition and tear Gas. When the work goes down they pay thousands of dollars of Bonus to Foreman and Superintendent, money that belongs to the worker.

Everytime they lay a man off means more compensation. Why must this go on. Every wage earner wife and child love you Honorable President. I beg you to check this unamerican tactic. Know you will. Thank you. Been a steel worker all my life. Today it's slavery. Got injured t[h]rough their fault. Hurry and over production. Please pass laws to stop this curse for prosperity and welfare for our beloved country. If they ever change Presidents Pity the workman for they sure need someone Honorable beloved president.

I close and I thank you from the bottom of my heart. Please consider heart aches about condition in the Steel mills. Employee Republic Steel Corp Past 60 years old and a Democrat all my life.

H. W. D.

York, Pennsylvania, March 8, 1940

Dear Miss Perkins:

I am writing to you in regards to Wagner labor law, I see in our Daily Papers here that some Republicans Congressmen wants it modified. I ask you to fight against that don't let them do it, they want a working man in these shops to work 60 hours per week they want to go back to Horse & Buggy days & make a man work for 12½ cents an hour. A night watchman before Wagner labor law was working 7 nights per week 12 hours a night 72 hours per week, what pleasure has a night man all he knows is work eat & sleep he cannot even go to Church now our night men works 42 hours per week, I am a night man myself & know what I am talking about & look at new jobs it made instead of two night men now they have four in these shops. Who is running our country today why it is the States Factory Insurance Co., they are the ones that are throwing our men out of our shops at age of 40 & 45 years of age & yet our State Governors stand idle by & let them do it & they wonder why there are so many men on W.P.A. jobs. Why don't our State Governors put that in Supreme Court & see if it is constitutional right to bar an able bodied man out of job at that age, or what authority the Insurance Co. had to do such a *rash act* they are throwing our best experienced men out of shops & putting in young boys who are turning out bumb work that is why our Mfgr., dont have much work today when people buys something they want it made right not half. So I say the working class will fight to uphold Wagner Labor Laws, that is the finest Law ever gotten up for labor, it gives a man a chance to rest up a little & enjoy life. God did not make this world just for rich to enjoy he made it for every living soul. So I urge you to fight to uphold *Wagner Labor Law*.

Will look for reply.

J. C. S.

P.S. Look what Congress done cut W.P.A. men down $12.00 per week ask them if they can live on that, why don't they work for that?

The language of class was also used to justify nativist, antidemocratic beliefs.

Chicago, Illinois, August 4, 1940

Mr. President:

I am writing to thank you for certain laws which have been passed by Congress, of which you are responsible, one is that all civil service employees must pay income taxes, Federal, State, County, & municipal, because they are paid larger salaries than most employee's in private industry. That was a very good law. Another was the minimum wage and hour law. Although it has not been ratified by many of the states, right here in Chicago the five and ten cent stores are employing girls for ten dollars and eleven dollars per week, eight hours per day so I am told. In Kansas City, Mo., the State Free Employment Bureau is sending girls and women out on private industry jobs at seven dollars per week, . . . the clerk who sits there and draws a big salary will tell them they are asking too much, that Kansas City does not pay that much, that they are not like Chicago and San Francisco and other places, *think of that.* I think, Kirk, Sear's and a lot of those employees should be discharged. The State Free Employment Bureau's in any state is N.G. they place very few people, when they do, it is at starvation wages. I never got a position through one in my life, I do not know of very many who did. It does not pay our Government to keep them open, for the expense and overhead is terrific. It only favors a few political men and women with good jobs at big salaries and the rent of these large offices, light, heat, cleaning, printing materials etc., costs the taxpayers more money than it is worth to the public, I think it would be a good idea to close all of them. . . . Another thing I asked you to do was to have a government labor man go into all shops and factories of private industry and unionize all the workers so that they would receive better wages *which you did.* . . . I think there should be *one government union labor man* and he should continue going into all shops and factories, stores and offices organizing all of the employees in every state in the U.S. I do think communists and German bunds should be *outlawed*. I think *there should be a federal law prohibiting immigrants or their offspring from organizing any organization* whether it be labor unions or subversive organizations and that only the Son's and daughter's of the American revolution be allowed to organize any organization, and this law should specify that all Americans whose ancestors fought in the American revolution to preserve this nation, and whose descendants have paid taxes in this country many generations, must be looked up to with respect and must be given employment first of all *in any state* wherever they may go, or if they need relief or work on W.P.A. they must be taken care of *first* and without a lot of red tape and given protection first of all. This is their country and there is *no other way* to figure. Without their ancestors we would still [be] under the British rule, there would be no America today. . . . I think there should be a federal law, that no one could hold public office in the U.S. unless their ancestors fought in the early wars to preserve this nation, or be entitled to civil service jobs, welfare offices, military, navy or marine officers except the old stock Americans who has lived here three hundred years or more. . . .

F. S.

Calimesa, California, May 20, 1941

Dear Miss Perkins:

I applied for a position as machinist (first class) to the Lockheed Aircraft Corp. at Burbank Cal. and received the enclosed questionnaire by return mail.

You will note there are some 150 questions and not more than a half doz. have any bearing whatever on my mechanical ability.

Most of these questions are irrelevent, and impertinent, I understand they also require a physical examination, and resort to fingerprinting, and photographing the employee, as though he were a criminal, before proving their case; their excuse being that the Gov. requires it.

Just what kind of Democracy is this, where a man has to undergo such indignities in order to get a job to make an honest living?

Is this our way of life?

Are we to be taxed to pay for this sort of thing?

The working class are regimented today as never before in the history of this country, as though the employer were buying a mule.

The workers today are driven at breakneck speed, until at thirty-five or forty, when worn out, they are kicked out in the street, to starve to death, or get on relief and exist on a reduced diet.

These Corp. have millions in Gov. contracts and are paying the lowest wages on the pacific coast, hiring mostly high school boys, while competent men with twenty years experience still hunt a job.

Needless to say I have not complied with their requirements and have no intentions of doing so, as they must not need competent ability.

The above is for your information as I thought your office might be interested in these UnAmerican conditions.

C. E. K.

McKees Rocks, Pennsylvania, July 29, 1942

Dear Mr. President:

Freedom from want! What a great inspiring phrase. How easily it can be said. But much, oh so very much more blood will be shed before those words will be in actual practice.

Groups, before the war and now, are everlastingly seeking to deny human beings the opportunity to earn their bread and in the words of Vice-President Wallace, "a quart of milk every day."

How can there be freedom from want when every day machines are being invented to replace people? The machine can produce in an hour what a man can't produce in eight.

How can we enjoy freedom from want when labor is considered as a cost and overhead?

We must first change our attitude and behavior before we can even think of such a noble idea.

I am wishing and praying that your great strength will gain in bounds and may you be our guiding light for more and more years to come.

C. P.

2. "Won't You Please Investigate Our Poor Sore Fingers"

Working Conditions in Selected Industries

Between 1921 and 1929 manufacturing production nearly doubled; during the next four years it dropped more than 62 percent. Some industries experienced even greater declines. Rolled iron and steel production, for example, fell nearly 75 percent, from 41 million tons in 1929 to 10.5 million tons in 1932. In 1929, 11,000 locomotives were produced; in 1933, only 63 left the assembly line. The value of automobiles produced in 1929 was $2.5 billion; in 1932 it had fallen to $600 million, a drop of more than 75 percent. Similarly, the value of industrial machinery and equipment fell from $2 billion in 1929 to $525 million in 1932. Even the superrich were affected: production of pleasure craft fell by over 80 percent.

The letters in this chapter give us a glimpse into the effects of this economic devastation on the lives of ordinary people. We generally associate the Depression with unemployment, homelessness, starvation, and dislocation. But when we read the correspondence of bakers, autoworkers, foundrymen, night watchmen, window cleaners, hotel workers, salesmen, clerks, farm hands, hospital workers, carnival employees, and a host of others, we get a broader sense of the myriad ways in which millions of marginally employed workers were affected. Most of the occupations of these workers have received little scholarly study. The nature of their jobs, the culture of the workplace, the special problems that each experienced have escaped most historians' attention. Yet together these workers accounted for a significant part of the teetering economy. Dayworkers in a carnival, tied to their jobs by the lack of a permanent home and

33

by the ever-changing locale, develop their own community through their shared experiences. A night watchman, isolated for days at a time, forced to work long hours that preclude a family life, struggles to control his workplace through the only means at his disposal. A baker's wife complains that her husband's job has left him too weak to eat. A hotel worker begs Roosevelt to establish some minimum standards of hours, wages, and days of work so that he can have some time to "do some little things." The humble way in which people explained their enormous suffering speaks to the devastation that the economic disorder created for most working Americans.

Most Americans were working. And most were working in these unorganized and often barely recognized occupations. Contrary to our general perception of labor during the Depression, most workers were not employed in such heavy industries as steel, rubber, autos, or mining. Of 48 million employed workers in 1930, fewer than 5 million were so employed. Another 13 million were in the professions, management, or farming. The remaining 30 million were employed in a wide variety of jobs: there were 1,654,000 domestic workers; 292,000 cooks; 310,000 janitors; 148,000 watchmen and doormen; 259,000 service workers; 21,000 employees making synthetic fibers; 28,000 bakers; 17,000 carpet makers; 1,097,000 stenographers, typists, and secretaries; 249,000 telephone operators. Some of our letters come from workers whose occupations all but defy classification: potato seed pickers; carnival workers; window cleaners; ragstuffers and sorters. All saw themselves as honest, hardworking, and deserving of respect and some minimal protection.

"So Tired We Can't Eat":
Conditions in Miscellaneous Industries

The unorganized workers in small businesses throughout the nation used a wide variety of means to protect their integrity and sense of self-respect. Even the carnival workers, isolated by the very transitory nature of their work, learned the lessons necessary for unionization from each other and from other workers throughout the country. A Polish immigrant window washer in Pennsylvania asks the government to investigate working conditions and company practices. None of these letter writers held highly skilled jobs; the very marginality of their jobs, and hence their susceptibility to harrassment by management, led them to seek redress from the government.

Men and women were forced by the circumstances of the Depression to work under conditions that few today would tolerate. The writer of the following letter sorted dirty rags for recycling.

Brooklyn, New York, March 29, 1935

Dear Miss Perkins:

Reading about you as I do I have come to the understanding, that you are a fair and impartial observer of labor conditions in the United States. Well, I'll have to get a load off my chest, and tell you of the labor conditions in a place which is laughingly called a factory. We work in a Woolstock Concern. We handle discarded rags. We work, ten hours a day for six days. In the grime and dirt of a nation. We go home tired and sick —dirty—disgusted—with the world in general, work—work all day, low pay—average wage sixteen dollars. Tired in the train going home, sitting at the dinner table, too tired to even wash outselves, what for—to keep body and souls together not to depend on charity. What of N.R.A.? What of everything—? We handle diseased rags all day. Tuberculosis roaming loose, unsanitary conditions—, slaves—slaves of the depression! I'm even tired as I write this letter—, a letter of hope—. What am I? I am young—I am twenty, a high school education—no recreation—no fun—. Pardon ma'am—but I want to live—! Do you deny me that right—? As an American citizen I ask you—, what—what must we do? Please investigate this matter. I sleep now, yes ma'am with a prayer on my lips, hoping against hope—, that you will better our conditions. I'll sign my name, but if my boss finds out—, well— Give us a new deal, Miss Perkins. The address of the concern is Simons Wool Stock, 20 Broadway, Brooklyn, N.Y.

Yours hoping,
J. G.

Washington, D.C., April 5, 1935

Dear Mr. G.:

The Secretary has asked me to acknowledge your letter of March 29 and to thank you for your expression of confidence in her desire to bring about better working conditions. We must remember, however, that the present situation is the result of many years' growth and its problems will require time for adjustment.

I am afraid your letter does not give quite enough information for us to say whether or not you are receiving as much protection as the code can give you. There are two codes applying to the handling of rags—one for the wiping cloth industry and the other for waste materials. I think you might write directly to the N.R.A. Compliance Officer, 45 Broadway, New York, New York, giving the name and address of the firm which employs you, and stating particularly whether or not the rags are sterilized in the plant. On the basis of this information the N.R.A. office can send you a copy of the code which applies to the work, and can assist you if you think its provisions are not being carried out.

I think you, yourself, have found the answer to your question when you say that you are young and have a high school education. This means that while you have at present the only job which is available to you, and which is thoroughly distasteful to you, you are equipped for something better and will, I sincerely hope, find a better opportunity when general employment conditions improve. You may be interested in getting in touch with the Brooklyn office of the Bureau of Junior Placements, 214 Duffield Place, where you may be given advice as to more desirable future employment.

> MARIAN L. MEL
> for Clara M. Beyer, Assistant Director
> Division of Labor Standards

Manatee, Florida, May 12, 1935

Dear Secretary Perkins,

We the employees of the Manatee Crate Company and the crate industry are wondering if you as Secretary of Labor know the conditions as they actually exist here in this industry. Some of the mills are paying from 12c to 15c per hour for white labor. We are wondering why the N.R.A. should not be extended or why it is not being enforced.

To us it was the only assurance against destitute poverty. The New Deal had helped us. We were getting a minimum wage of 8 or 9c per hr. with ten hrs. per day or more if we were needed— The N.R.A. put our code at a minimum of 23c per hr. and 40 hrs. pr. wk. Little enough it's true, less than $10 per week on full time— We only get full time about half the year. But it was much better than we were getting and we were encouraged because we had found a President and an administration that were really reaching down and pulling the fellow up from the bottom a little. The crate and carrier industry employs thousands of people here in the South east corner of the country— in Fla. Ga. and Ala. . . . An N.R.A. man told us that all the mills in this territory had abandoned the Code but one.

Now Secretary Perkins: We are looking to you as the head of this great labor department of this country and we believe that your heart and life are wrapped up in this work. Can't this condition be adjusted? They have adjusted prices in agriculture, they have adjusted the banking business. Why not labor and prices through the N.R.A. with penalties for violation.

This company will be glad to go back under the workings of the N.R.A. if it is re established among the crate industry. . . .

J. J. B. AND OTHERS

can send petition with hundreds of names.

Even the Rockettes, the famed precision dancers at New York's Radio City Music Hall, complained about their working conditions and about the tactics used by management to thwart their attempts to organize.

New York City, April 14, 1936

Dear Miss Perkins:

We are appealing to you to give us help in our task of trying to improve working conditions of the Radio City Music Hall of New York City. We have written repeatedly to Mr. V. S. managing director of the theatre but have been cast aside and conditions continue.

At the present time, the performers are working on a basis of 82 hours a week and are receiving salaries ranging from $35 to $42.

The irony of it is that they have organized groups in the theatre who are being justly paid but when the Equity Organization tried to enter its folds, they had these unfortunate employees refuse to recognize them under threats of losing their jobs. This is not the first time that they have used these methods. Once again, perhaps you would recall, during the period of the N.R.A, two girls were picked, rehearsed what to say and sent down to Washington to tell how much they loved their organization etc. before a group of investigators of conditions at this Theatre.

Miss Perkins, please help us for while these people are the ones who bring joy into the hearts of thousands, they themselves are being shoved into a hot bed of communistic feeling.

Thank you.

The following two letters are from a young woman who had been out of work for five years before she landed her current job. She was soon unemployed again.

Hamilton, Ohio, August 13, 1936

Dear Madam [Perkins]:

I am writing to you concerning the conditions of the Leshner Corporation on Central Ave, near South Ave. in Hamilton, Ohio.

I've been working on the cutters, and it's a shame how the girls have to work and what they have to do to earn $12.80 per week, also a little bonus, that's if you make any bonus.

There's three shifts, 7 A.M. to 3 P.M., 3 P.M. to 11 P.M. and 11 P.M. to 7 A.M. On this 11 P.M. to 7 A.M. shift, the girls are mostly ill as the hours and work make the girls ill. We work 6 days a week, and worst of all, have only 15 minutes to eat our lunch, also have to ring our time cards in this 15 minutes. It's really impossible for a person to feel good when you have to eat your lunch so fast in such a little time. Sometimes we are so tired we can't eat.

On the third floor the women cut cement sacks by hand . . . standing up-right. The cement dust is so terrible, the women have to tie rags over their faces so they can work in the dust.

On the second floor the girls sort out dirty old rags for the washers. Such rags as rayon pants etc. aren't washed but make girls cut the filthy garments. Of this they make cotton etc. I think such filthy garments should be washed as they're not fit to be handled. I wouldn't handle them. On the first floor are cutters, washers and dryers. . . . The heat is terrible as they have very little ventilation. An electric fan was installed, but the air from the fan makes us feel bad. The rags brought to our tables direct from the dryers are so hot you can hardly touch them, but we have to cut them or else get fired. A man used to fill our tables and clean up the roofing, but they got women doing this sort of work. It's not a woman's job as its too hard.

Also have girls bailing rags. A man should be had, but mostly its a girl doing such work as bailing, sewing these bails of rags up, and trying to push them around while bosses look on.

Also they mix some sort of a bleach which is used for washing the rags. They mix the bleach and it gags the girls terribly, some turn sick, we almost choke, as its terrible to smell and inhale. I think this should be mixed someplace else so the girls don't inhale it. All the bosses yell, is that we don't work fast enough. The girls are afraid to move as afraid of being fired. A girl really needs a job to work in such a place. They are worked as they are men. When a girl does slow up from being tired etc. the bosses yell that, "they'll fire the hell out of us." They don't seem to care what sort of language they use.

The toilets are so dirty, a person doesn't feel as though they care to go to the dressing room.

The drinking fountain is dirty on the first floor but you should see X what the girls drink out of on the third floor. Cement dust all over this they drink out of.

To keep from drinking this water, the girls on the first floor got a barrel and bought ice every day out of their own wages. The barrel was filled with water into which the ice was put; so that they could have cold ice water to cool them off as the place is so hot to work in cutting hot rags. I never drank any ice water as it tastes terrible. The barrel would get full of lint on top and I was afraid cockroaches would crawl into the barrel.

The elevator isn't safe. The cable, I was told, is broken in several places. I know myself as I had to pick up roofing and had to use this elevator. When I pulled on the cable, tiny wires stuck into my hands and hurt. Sometimes the elevator stops and sometimes it don't. Its not regulated right. I don't think girls have any business on such elevators which are not safe to be on. I took the time to write this to you, other girls wanted to, but was afraid the bosses would find out who did it and would get fired; so I myself am reporting these conditions.

I only hope you'll look into these conditions as girls are getting tired of being like slaves.

Other factories have conditions suitable for their girls and live up [to] the law. Why don't the Leshner Corporation do the same?

P.S. I was told that Leshner's are usually tipped off several days ahead of time when the inspectors come through. If you look into this matter don't let them be notified ahead of time so they can straighten things up in the shop. I could tell more than I can write.

Attica, Indiana, August 17, 1936

Dear Madam [Perkins]:

Last Friday August 13, 1936, I wrote you a letter concerning the conditions of the Leshner Corporation on Central Ave. in Hamilton, Ohio.

I'm writing once again to tell you that Mr. D. *fired* me and my partner

Sat. Aug. 15. at 3:00 P.M. Mr. D. couldn't tell us, but wrote it on paper, and gave it to the other boss on the 3:00 A.M. [*sic*] to 11:00 P.M. shift. This boss was hurt about it, and couldn't hardly tell us we were fired . . . "on account of not coming up to the standard in the shop.

Of course I refused to do certain kinds of work like other girls do, but was told I was a good worker on the cutters.

On the 3rd floor they have Hog Machines into which heavy pieces of cotton from mattresses is thrown and made into fine cotton. On the day shifts men run these machines, but on the night shifts they have women to run these dirty machines. It's really ashame to see how they work these people. The women work like men, and do men's work for $12.80 per wk. The wash bowls in the dressing room is so dirty they're not fit to wash in. These washbowls were put up by men working at Leshners. Old iron pipes were used for water connections. When the water is turned on, green and rusty water pours from the faucets.

I cut my finger badly one morning about 7:10 A.M. on the electric knife. The floor lady wanted to use an old dirty rag to wrap my finger up. I refused and used my handkerchief instead, as my handkerchief was clean, towards those rags they cut in the cutters. I waited like this till 8:00 A.M.—One hour till the office opened up. Then I made the Floor Lady dress my cut finger, which was hurting me badly by then. They really haven't any system of any kind in this plant.

But all they do is yell "Step on it," drive the girls all day long. After 5 hrs. of work on the cutters a girl is ready to lay down, for you can't hardly go any faster, but they insist for you keep up speed.

Of course I needed a job, but I'm happy to think I'm out of this dirty old shop. My back doesn't ache no more, my clothes aren't wet from sweat, and my hands and arms aren't being burnt from hot burning rags. I've seen rags so hot, put on tables for the girls that they were burning. The buttons on those rags were so hot they burnt blisters on our hands when we handled them. It was a torture to work as such as this.

I wish you will kindly look into this matter in the near future.

I was out of work for nearly 5 years. I got this job at Leshners May 1st 1936 and work just 3 months.

I'm 27 years old, and am single, I really need work badly, I want to work but I don't think it is right to work girls such as Leshners Corporation does.

I only hope I can obtain employment in some other factory in the near future.

The Division of Labor Standards prepared the following summary of a letter written in Polish by the wife of an immigrant window washer.

Interpretation of the attached Polish letter:

The writer of the letter, addressed to the Secretary and dated March 19, 1935, states that her husband is doing work for the Globe Window Cleaning Company, 8 Walnut Street, Philadelphia, under the rules of N.R.A. He is supposed to work only 8 hours a day and 5 days a week, altogether 40 hours a week. But he is required to work 9 hours a day and on some days even much longer. He earns $16.35 a week, that is, about 25 cents per hour of work. This means that no overtime is paid, as the required hourly wage is higher. He applied for a transfer to another foreman in a different section, but he was refused.

The writer's family consists of 10 persons. She has to pay $38.00 in taxes and $45.00 in mortgage interest. At the present earnings are not enough to keep her family going and pay the above taxes and interest, she is afraid of soon losing her house and home.

The other workers with the same concern work long hours also—from 4 a.m. until late evening. They are paid from $27.00 to $30.00 a week. This means again that their overtime is not paid. But everybody is afraid either to ask the company to pay overtime or to make a complaint against the company.

Now, the writer asks the Secretary to investigate the labor conditions, especially the wages paid by the above-named company, and to compel the latter either to pay the overtime or, still better, not to work overtime at all and employ more workers.

The writer also asks the Secretary to consider this letter to be strictly confidential, for if the company learns that she has made a complaint, her husband will be fired at once.

She signs: (Mrs.) M. P.

New Hope, Pennsylvania

The writer of the following letter, a native-born worker, complains about both the treatment of immigrant workers and the threat they pose to the native-born.

Philadelphia, Pennsylvania, May 26, 1935

Miss Frances Perkins

Dear Friend:

I am writing you to inform you about a carpet mill in Frankfort—Phila. There are hundreds of carpet weavers out of work and will never get a job the way this mill is operated. There are 13 looms and 2 seldom runs. They are all foreigners and none citizens learning the trade by being a (scab). There seem to be no management of the firm, they have them work as long as they want. They start 7 o'clock in the morning, go home for supper go back again and work sometime until 11 o'clock at night. The looms run by motor and they are told they can work as long as they want. (Sunday also) They have a man that rings the time clock for all the men at ¼ of 4 o'clock letting on they work 8 hours, but the men only ring the clock going in—in the morning. Instead of them working 8 hours some of them work 13 to 15 hours a day. This mill has been running like this all through the code. . . . Some time they get a scare and make the men stop at ¼ of 4 o'clock but it only last a week then they are all working there long hours again. I think if this would be investigated they could put another shift of men on and not let all of those foreign scabs get all the work and Americans walk the street. Hoping you investigate and will find if you catch them it is true.

YOURS RESPECT IN LABOR

Sandusky, Ohio, November [25?], 1936

Office of the Secretary of Labor

Dear Sir:

I do not know if I am addressing the proper office or not, but probably will receive advice from your office if I am wrong.

The question concerns a small amount of people in a very insignificant firm in the city of Sandusky, O. and the conditions under which they work. But nevertheless it is in the U.S.A. and the existing conditions are those of the old world under foreign employers.

Women work 50 hours a week at hard labor for $10 under unhealthful conditions their hands in cold water and lifting heavy weights. Men work 56 to 60 hours per week at a comparative low wage scale in cellars heated with gas stoves without fume flues throwing the fumes into the room and without proper protecting devices from the explosive champagne bottles as masks and gloves. No hourly wage scale is set and the workman receives what the employer decides to pay him at the end of the week many times receiving nothing for overtime. When one is hurt by flying glass and can't work he is promptly laid off. The concern is the *Mon Ami Champagne Co* of Sandusky O. . . . Please keep this confidential address correspondence to me at Doylestown, Ohio. thanking you for advice or the designation of proper executive for this matter.

F. L.

The following letter reveals the dangerous conditions endured by workers in the developing plastics industry. Central to this worker's concerns were the intensification of work in the plant and its effect on health. In the two subsequent letters, the director of the Labor Department's Division of Labor Standards puts pressure on his colleagues at the state level to investigate and rectify conditions in the plant.

Lewistown, Pennsylvania, November 20, 1936

Dear President Roosevelt:

We work in the Reeling department of the Viscose Co. in Lewiston, Pa. Won't you please investigate our poor sore fingers. The acid or whatever is on the cakes eat our fingers so terrible sometimes they look like a piece of raw meat, then we get acid sores—they are terrible—they eat almost to the bone—they take a core out of them, and oh! nobody knows how we suffer, if we don't have these acid sores—and our fingers are just sore—they send us home and often times won't give us compensation. They had been paying us ⅔ of what we made; and for Saturday and Sunday but last week a note was passed down No. 5 Reeling room—no more Sat. and Sunday compensation and 20 cents an hour—signed by the Supt. of the plant.

Please President Roosevelt won't you see the proper ones will look into this and see if something can't be done that our poor fingers won't get so sore—we can't tell you the agony we work in.

They put big pieces in the paper about the raises they give us—it does help the hour workers but us poor reelers, it don't do much good—for they use that stretch out system and when the raise comes, they add so much more yardage to our cakes and in the end we make very little if any more—and we have to buy wire brushes to clean our machines, cream for our hands and rubber aprons to wear, every couple weeks and a girl who has board and Bus fare to pay—don't have much left. Ten years ago we run ten machines made good money and did a good days work, but now we have from 40 to 50 machines and make a little over half what we did then, and didn't know what sore fingers were.

Please President Roosevelt—don't show this letter or get us in wrong in any way for writing it—but we wanted you to know the agony in which we have to work, and thought you could help us—and we thank you for what you have already done for us.

We are your friends and may god Bless you in your good work for the next four years.

SOME GIRLS FROM THE REELING ROOM OF THE VISCOSE CO.

P.S. If we are on compensation, say Friday and Saturday of one week, Monday, Tuesday and Wednesday of another week and they do give us compensation, they will make a Break on our time card for Monday and even cheat us out of that days compensation if we are not working. Is it right?

Washington, D.C., December 14, 1936

Mr. Ralph M. Bashore, Secretary
Department of Labor and Industry
Harrisburg, Pennsylvania

My Dear Mr. Bashore:

I am enclosing a copy of an anonymous letter addressed to President Roosevelt and referred by his Office to the Department of Labor.

You will notice that the writer makes a point of asking the President to exercise care in making use of this information. I thought, however, that it might be possible for you to include this plant among those in which you are making regular investigations, without jeopardizing the complainants, and I have, therefore, called it to your attention.

V. A. ZIMMER

Harrisburg, Pennsylvania, December 17, 1936

Dear Mr. Zimmer:

Your letter of December 14 addressed to Secretary Bashore has been referred to this Bureau for attention.

For quite some time this Department has been investigating conditions in the Viscose plants in Lewistown, Marcus Hook and Meadville, and benefits have been derived as the results of these investigations. However, we shall again go into the plant in Lewistown which is the source of the complaint sent to President Roosevelt and try to remedy conditions without jeopardizing the complainants.

RAYMOND J. NICAISE

The following two letters, from the wife of an assembly-line worker in Detroit, illustrate the variety of ways in which workers, especially older workers, were tied to their jobs. This man's pay was cut 25 percent and he was forced to work on Sundays even when he was injured.

Detroit, Michigan, January 30, 1937

Dear Miss Perkins:

I am coming to you as the only available recourse.

May I ask your good offices to have your representatives investigate the Timken Detroit Axle Company of this city, with regard to employees' hours and wages—while they are in the act of investigating other labor conditions here. The fact of the matter is that ever since the NRA went out of being this firm has been working its men practically morning, noon and night to the point of utter exhaustion, without adding to the force to take up the surplus strain: and I am just about at the point of breaking up my home and heading for nowhere, since the nervous atmosphere created by reason of this pressure is just about intolerable. My husband's nerves appear to be taxed to about the limit.

I gleaned from him that men down there are working 12 hours a day, as you will note is borne out by the attached copy of schedule (which please hold in strictest confidence) and a suggestion was even made to re-make the week a 10-day proposition instead of seven. My husband has been with the firm here in mentioned for the past 20 years, and despite the fact that his services rendered are apparently classed as entirely satisfactory, nevertheless his wages total but $30.00 per week, (he had received $40 and better before the depression, but they have never restored the factory men's wages to their normal rate since that period) with a heap of nervous strain thrown in for good measure. His work is that of "stock chaser" which necessitates keeping the assembly line moving. On various occasions when he has approached his superiors for a higher wage consideration, he is promptly apprised that "his job doesn't pay any more, regardless of length of service; that his pay is the limit for his particular line of work, etc."

Due to my husband's age (he is 50 and well preserved for that age) he, of course, as you will readily understand, cannot very well say "quit" and hope to run into a position very promptly elsewhere. So, I am, therefore, bringing this letter to your good attention to see if something cannot be done to alleviate the terrific strain under which, not only he, but the other Timken employees as well, are compelled to work.

In conclusion, may I further ask that you treat my communication as *strictly confidential*, for very obvious reasons, particularly insofar as the firm mentioned and even my husband are concerned.

And, thanking you in advance for your very kind and just consideration, and assuring you that the working element of this town are certainly more sinned against than sinning, believe me

Most respectfully yours,
Mrs. G. F

Detroit, Michigan, February 3, 1937

Dear Miss Perkins:

Since writing the enclosed letter (which I have been waiting to take to the Post Office a little further in town) I would like to add just an inkling to a condition that has popped up in the meantime:

On Sunday last my husband slipped on the ice and hurt his knee. Inasmuch as his work consists of constant walking and climbing of stairs throughout the entire day, naturally he was unable to report for duty Monday and Tuesday by reason of a stiffening that developed. He, however, went in Wednesday and was met with the reception "You fellows who try to duck out of work Sundays and then take time off for little or nothing; if you can't take it then why don't you check out." The fact of the matter is that as in my husband's case the men do not get paid for a minute they lose, and they are compelled to line up with two different company benefit associations for sickness and the like out of which they never receive a cent unless at the very threshold of death's door. The men are in constant complaint against this Sunday work, but it doesn't do any good. A glance at exposed machinery (wheels, etc.) without any protection or safeguard for the workers, tells the tale of the consideration here about of the average employer for his employees.

The foregoing is just for your good information.

Mrs. G. F.

Even the clergy was not exempt from the indignities suffered by workers who were forced to take any job they could get, as the following letter from a restaurant worker reveals.

Cleveland, Ohio, February 12, 1937

Dear Miss Perkins:

These few lines on the behalf of a neglected group of good American Citizens, are, I am convinced, absolutely necessary!

This is my experience, and I feel the same experience has come to many who are in no position to better themselves for the present. On Wednesday, January 27, 1937, I started to work as a "dishwasher" in the Old Log Cabin Inn, 14,108 Euclid Avenue, Cleveland, Ohio. My hours were from 11 A.M until 9 P.M. When I started to work I was allowed two and sometimes, three dough-nuts and a cup of coffee! This was just a few minutes before 11 A.M. Between 3 and 4 P.M. I was allowed a piece of pie and a cup of coffee. After 9 P.M. I was allowed what would be called a meal. In other words, there was only one *real* meal, according to "the *good* American standard of living."

In addition to both washing and drying dishes—by hand—I was *expected* to help mop up the floor and peel potatoes and perform other various and sundry tasks!

I went to the position from the Ohio State Employment Bureau, with headquarters in the basement of the City Hall, in Cleveland, Ohio. I went to work one day, *on trial*. My employer was pleased enough with my diligence to "call me for steady work" as he termed it, the next day. I worked five days, when my hand became infected. My employer, seeing the condition of my hand, laid me off." I had to go to the City Hospital, Cleveland, Ohio—location—Scranton Road & Valentine Avenue. I had to have my hand lanced, had to have a drain inserted, and of course suffered considerable pain. For my labor I received $1.25 per day. The position, if one may call it that, was on a "seven day a week" basis.

I was "growled," at by my employer, for eating a piece of pie and drinking a cup of coffee between 3 and 4 P.M.

I have been told by others who have secured dish-washing jobs, thru the same employment agency, that they only have been allowed *two meals* a day for hard, laborious work!

I am told that the average wage of the waitresses, working in Cleveland restaurants is $6.00 per week! In my opinion, for a young lady to dress properly, keep up her self-respect, and have *healthful recreation*, considering the hours that the average waitress is obliged to work, I believe $12.00 per week *would not be too much*!

I only accepted my position because I have utterly no use for loafing!

I am an Ordained Minister—if that counts for anything—I have supported our beloved President twice, morally and with ardor!

I feel that someone "with a heart" and with courage should champion the cause of the poorly paid and poorly privileged restaurant employees of Cleveland, *and so I state a case in fact!*

Hoping this letter shall be of some benefit, not only to myself, but to some others who have been no doubt less fortunate.

(REV.) P. P. H.

N.B. When my employer noticed my hand was injured he did not even have the courtesy to direct me to go to a physician.

Washington, D.C., February 24, 1937

Dear Rev. H.:

The Secretary has asked me to acknowledge your letter of February 12 and to express her appreciation of your interest in calling her attention to the reported conditions existing in restaurant work. As you probably know, the Secretary has made every effort to impress upon states the importance of passing laws which will limit hours of work, require the payment of minimum wages for workers and to provide safe and healthy working conditions. All she can lend to this cause is her influence, which she is always glad to do, but the action depends upon the people of the state itself.

Letters are always helpful, however, in pointing to the need for such action and recording the fact of the existence of such conditions.

V. A. ZIMMER

The next three letters testify to the strains and pressures of the long hours and low wages endured by nonunionized workers during the Depression years.

Bellingham, Washington, February 26, 1937

Dear Madame Perkins:

I am taking the liberty of writing to you in regards to the new N.R.A. which I see by the newspapers you are making out for the President.[1]

---

[1] The writer is probably referring to the legislation that resulted in the Fair Labor Standards Act of 1938.

And I humbly ask. Please remember the night watchman. My husband has night watched 13 years on the same job. from 7 to 6 making 12 rounds 7 nights a week. only when the N.R.A. was in effect before he had 8 hours 7 nights a week. As soon as it was outlawed he was put right back to the 12 hour round again. In addition to the hourly rounds he has janitor work in five offices rooms and during working seasons he has to keep up steam in the boiler also attend the freight boat as they come and go. And keep pressure in the retorts [?]. He is kept busy these 12 hours for which he gets $75 a month and a shack to live in. What can there be left in life for a man who has to keep going all night and lay in a close darkened room all day 365 days a year for a mere existence. I am not writing merely for one but for all night watchman. It seems there should be some way out. I do not wish this letter published. I am only asking for justice and fair play. and if we do not benefit by it now maybe someone else will in years to come.

E. J.

P.S. This is the Salmon cannery industry.

Detroit, Michigan, February 27, 1937

Dear Miss Perkins:

Here's one more vote for President Roosevelt's shorter hours and larger wages bill.

My husband's job is one more example of such a measure being necessary.

He work's in the warehouse for Anheuser Busch's distributing plant here. Works from 7:30 A.M. till all hours of the nite. The earliest he has ever got home is 8 P.M. and in warm weather it usually is near midnight. We wouldn't mind the long hour's if he were paid accordingly but $90.00 a mo. isn't much for his long hours and the amount of work he does. The co. wont unionize so they feel they can get by on this, but for a wealthy co. like the Busch's they can pay more money.

When N.R.A. was in effect he received 35.00 a week for the same work, but as soon as it dropped, so did the wages. We have to pay 30.00 a mo. rent. Impossible to rent a house for less. Everything is for sale and with the cost of living rising so rapidly we need 35.00 a mo for food and household supplies. then when gas, elect. and coal are taken out and husband's transportation, we haven't anything left to even buy clothing. $90.00 a mo. is merely an existence.

We aren't the only one's living under this strain. Its impossible to buy dental or medical care or to even revive lapsed insurance.

I'm not writing this for an answer but telling you facts to help people like ourselves who can't do any thing about the condition.

We are hoping and praying this measure of our beloved President will become a law soon, and force some of these wealthy manufacturers to pay living wages. Our minister said Sunday, that Roosevelt would lead us out of bondage, so we are hoping.

Mrs. C. E. A.

Lincoln, Nebraska, May 20, 1937

Department of Labor
Dear Sirs:

Is there anything done or being done, or ever to be done about big, wealthy concerns working a poor man way too many hours and giving him scarcely an existing wage? and then scold & drive all the time.

Goochs Baking Co of Lincoln pay such very small wages and nearly work their men to death. When my husband gets home he is absolutely too weary to eat till he rests a while and sometimes he doesn't get home to eat, we carry his meals to him and they never pay him a cent for overtime.

Two weeks ago he worked 30 hours without stopping only to "gulp" a few bites and watched the motor while he did that, then he came home at 2 o'clock, bathed & went to bed and at 7 that evening they wanted him to go back and work again and they never paid him an extra dime.

From Monday to Friday one man only had 4 hrs. off duty so he said and never got any extra pay. They are so mean to their help those who don't have to have work won't stay, but if one has a family they must do something but this is slavery. What is the matter with our Democratic government I was sure those kind of things would be cleaned up long ago.

For the kind of work some of the men do there, they should be paid about twice their salary.

I'm doing this for us first and then for all the men there.

Mrs. W. A. B.

I appealed to the State Labor here but they don't do anything like that. Is there nothing to protect the poor man and make the Co. and corporations be fair?

That is all I ask is fair play. We want to work, when we were without work we did without before we took charity and I feel we deserve fair play as well as the others who are being mistreated. Please look into this and then *do* something about it and also about other places like this one. Thank you so much.

MRS. B.

Washington, D.C., May 26, 1937

Dear Mrs. B.:

Your letter of May 20 has been referred to me.

As you probably know, since the NRA was declared invalid by the Supreme Court, the Federal Government has had practically no control over the wages and hours in private industry. However, new legislation on this subject has just been introduced in Congress and if enacted into law, may provide the protection you desire.

We are very glad to have your comments since they serve to bring these matters to the attention of the proper authorities.

CLARA M. BEYER
Acting Director

☎The writer of the following letter, a college-educated chemist in the dairy industry, looks to the passage of a new NRA or the formation of a strong national union as the only means of improving working conditions.

Weymouth, Massachusetts, October 2, 1937

Madame Secretary:

I am not writing this letter with any ideas of directly helping myself, but to give you an idea on sectional conditions in one of the largest industries in the country, the milk business.

Working conditions, and hours as well as wages are very poor. The few exceptions are a very few large companies or cooperatives if unionized. Since the N.R.A. code came to a stop, conditions have gone back to the old poor conditions. The N.R.A. codes worked wonders for the working man. I am and always have been a loyal supporter of President Roosevelt and the New deal.

I am twelve years out of Mass. State College, have followed the milk business as milk plant foreman, milk chemist, milk buying and producer supervision.

I have for the past two years been plant foreman where conditions were so bad that I have become sickened on my line of work.

What I say about myself is only an example of many others. Working a minimum of twelve hours per day up to sixteen and seventeen, due to lack of equipment and cooperation, at bare existence wages, so a man if he has a family keeps sinking more hopelessly in debt, and cannot even then afford the necessities of life.

The owners are making money in most cases, but expect a man to be chemist, engineer, sanitation engineer, and laborer at less than W.P.A. wages per day.

I have made quite a name for myself in bacteria control work and have lately inherited some money, so I gave up my job to get back my physical health as well as nerves which were pretty well ruined after the years of slave driving work, I never was on W.P.A. or relief, would have been better off if I had I guess.

Since I have been away from my job several have tried to hire me including my last employer.

This is the point I wish to bring out, of all the jobs offered me only one employer gives a day a week off. Others seven days per wk. until one can't stand to work anymore. Pay small for what is expected. The conditions for route salesman are about as bad, especially in the small companies.

Unless the N.R.A. code can be installed again to cover this business, the only hope is a union strong enough, and countrywide which will *make* the employers give the help enough money to support a family, and time enough to get acquainted with their families.

This line of work requires more specialized training, and accurate work than many other industries, yet a man is better off with a pick and shovel job.

The N.R.A. code was a wonderful thing, and I deeply regret its passing. I also dread to think of conditions when this administration comes to end of term.

If this letter can do any good toward better conditions in this business for the workers, I shall certainly take great pleasure.

P. S.

Not all federal construction was performed under government supervision. Here the conditions of life for laborers on a road construction crew are described by the wife of one of them. Away from family and friends, workers were forced to live in unsanitary conditions, laboring from before sunrise till sunset. Under these conditions, workers' resentment built until they found themselves sabotaging the job.

Ogden, Utah, December [11?], 1937

To the Honorable Frances Perkins:

My husband went to work at a road camp, a federal job. The contract in the hands of the contractor read—The contractor agrees to maintain a camp with high moral and sanitary standards, with suitable living conditions for workers. And the following conditions are a few of the things he found prevailing. I, his wife send them to you, hoping that you will receive them in the spirit in which they are given. I wish to place this information in the hands of the most interested in the cause. I am sure you would never know this specific case, at least, unless I told you. Regarding equipment, the tents were leaky, and kept out neither the heat by day or the cold by night. Gasoline lanterns were supposed to supply light. The greater part of the time they were not lightable on account of the mantles being broken and new ones not available. They washed their faces in a spring of water near by, breaking the ice each morning to do so. The water bags froze solid each night by the side of the cots. The cots were bare, each man was supposed to furnish his own bedding. Many men arrived there without bedding and lay on the bare dirt floor by the fire as long as it lasted, then got up and walked around to keep warm. One fellow was seen to crawl in another mans bed when he went to work. The man without a bed changed beds this way three times during the night trying to get himself a little rest. My husband reports he slept cold every night, although he had his own bedding. Men arose at 4 A.M. dressed in the dark, fumbling in the dark trying to find their clothes; cussing and raving, and who wouldn't? Their shoes so stiff and cold they made their feet ache. Men who went to work on this shift, usually went without their breakfast, expecting to return later to eat. Sometimes they would be handed a cold sandwich out on the job for their breakfast, when their hands would be so cold they could hardly hold it. All this in the face of a contract which read "Suitable living conditions for men." No first aid kit or attendant was at this camp. I believe the law requires one. A man who cut his foot partly off with an ax, was thrown in the back of a truck and taken a distance of about 25 miles, where he was treated inadequately, the truck driver who brought him in assisting in the job of dressing the foot. The same thing happened when a man got both hands badly burned. He was taken away in the truck for mere first aid. No doubt there were many more such instances but these two came under his observation, and the details were supplied by the man who took the men to the nearest assistance, many miles away. My husband's leg was badly cut and bruised with a rock, he dressed the wound with water. There is an ugly scar to remember. To quote my husband "I can't think of one convenience the workers enjoyed."

The workers—Hated their bosses, blaming them for their plight. They seem to aim to destroy and waste material in every manner possible. Superiors were repeatedly invited by their workers to go to hell, or its equivalent. One sunday they had, thru mismanagement, potatoes and meat only for their dinner. The boss disappeared all day. When he showed up for breakfast the next morning he was greeted with you couldn't eat your own food, eh? Better stick around next time, we nearly blowed your outfit to pieces with dynamite. Boss asked My husband what he thinks is the matter. He replies "The fellows resent the living conditions around here. When will you guys learn how to get the best and most out of men. Instead of provoking them to wrath, you, with your experience should know that we men after all are still human, and respond to kindness and consideration the same as anybody else."

Eight or ten new cooks in one month. One cook took a look at the kitchen and walked off, without preparing one meal, although he had come a long way to take the job. Another prepared two meals and left, declaring that the food, kitchen and everything connected with it were beyond him. And yet, with this poor food, and the preparation of it the board was very faithfully deducted from their wages. At least they were efficient in this one thing. Much gasoline was used. In depositing the gasoline where it was needed, a bucket was used to pour same. The gas drizzled and spilled during the process of pouring. If there happened to be a gallon or two left in the bucket after the tank was filled, it would be thrown away on the ground, for convenience to the man doing the pouring. My husband deplored this waste of gas, as he does all waste, and asked for a 10 cent funnel with which to use in pouring the gasoline. The funnel was not supplied. And what could the poor man do? Men in all manner of work seemed to aim to see how much they could destroy. Valuable tools were broken and destroyed recklessly. Dynamite and drills were handled without thot of cost. It looked like a case organized sabotage.

The men laughed when fired, as tho that was what they were aiming at. They said it was an honor to be fired from such a place.

Here is the opinion of an educated Indian. Bitterly he complained to my husband "You white people taught me to be clean to cultivate high standards of living. Look at me. I haven't had my clothes off only once in five weeks, and then only long enough to wash the dirt and grime off, in an icy pool. Why, my ancestors lived like princes compared with this. Bah, it makes me sick, the thought of it all. They at least had some standards to go by. They knew where they were at. But not me. I follow in the white man's ways. Part of my work is so dangerous that I leave word for them to come and dig me out from under the truck in case I do not get back at a certain time. Happy thought, isn't it? One of my duties is ambulance man. It is I who haul the poor suffering men to the country Dr. twenty five miles. Their groans and suffering is something I hope some day to be able to forget, but know I never shall. I've had enough. I'm thru." And who could blame him?

In submitting this report to you I hope to show that the working man is very often in a position to explain why things go wrong and why the results that our leaders aim to accomplish are thwarted. My husband says that it is not the fault of the administration, but the small bosses, who are not efficient, who are too eager to keep their jobs, who get away with all manner of irregularities, unchallenged. No one, probably knows of his doings but the working man, who is associated with him, and he, when he gets too disgusted, or can stand it no longer, quits. And that is all there is to it. When I was told of conditions as related here I thought that the proper person to report them to was our Secretary of Labor. And in conclusion may I suggest that we, the working people, could without doubt be of great service to you, if you care to contact us further. My husband is a keen observer, and has a valuable supply of knowledge pertaining to the workers problems, which he has gained thru observation thru the years, and in many cases he has a remedy. He certainly has a good solution of the problems that prevailed in the camp of which I have written.

Mrs. L. P. D.

Milwaukee, Wisconsin, October 12, 1937

Dear President, Friend & Leader of our beloved U.S.A.:

Just heard your address this evening and would like to tell you we certainly enjoyed it very much. Somehow it gave me the assurance that perhaps after all you do occasionally take time to read letters sent you by your humble citizens since part of your talk seemed to contain some of the very words I asked you about some time ago. Also was glad to hear

you discuss some of those farm problems. Tho we are not farmers ourselves, we visited relatives who are and who discussed that topic yesterday. They of course are very much opposed to regulating crop control
the way you said. However, we were and always will be on your side.
However, what do people mean when they say in a couple of years we
shall have inflation. Is there any truth to that? I don't understand it yet it
seems to be quite a topic these days also socialized medicine. I don't
think I would favor that. In spite of the fact that for the past three years
we have had a big share of sickness in our life, and right after my husband
was again able to find employment after being out of work for the three
years it made it doubly hard for us. It means we just can't seem to get
caught-up financially. We try to skimp and deny ourselves as much as
possible, yet it just seems we get nowhere. We have three children, who
we love dearly, and it certainly hurts us deeply that despite our efforts we
cannot provide for them the way we should like. None of us were able to
buy much of anything in clothing, the last three years we don't spend
money for foolishness we do not own a car nor do we spend money for
taverns, etc. Not that we would not occasionally enjoy some sort of
amusement once in a while but we can't afford it. However, in spite of
this, I think I would rather have it this way and be able to have my own
Doctor, who is to us one of the best, kindest and most understanding
friend. Yet every laborer is worthy of his hire. My husband would not
work without pay and neither would we expect our doctor to donate his
services without his due reward. However, as you said tonite if only employers would realize how much it means to pay reasonable wages it
would certainly mean much to the laborer. My husband works for a place
called the Cream City Trimming. They do work on cars, repairing bodies, fenders, and everything else that might be wrong with a car. Well
they pay the men union wages by the hour. They must be at the shop all
day in order to be there when work comes in but get paid only for the
number of hours they *work* not for the time they spend at the shop.
Would you consider this fair. My husband is considered an A1 worker is
rated very highly and is well liked by employer & fellow employees. he
works hard and does not stall on the job. yet will we ever get anywhere at
this rate. He has done this line of work for almost 20 years. He is 36 and
was 16 when he started. One of the bosses died suddenly and now the
head boss would like to have my husband take this other employee's
place. however in order to do so he must buy a share in the Company.
One share I believe he said at $45.00. We don't quite see our way clear to
accepting this offer, in view of the fact that we haven't the money on
hand we would have to borrow or have it taken off the pay check what

little there is and with all the expense we have, we don't like to do this unless we are certain it is for our & our children's benefit. Besides, due to a fall, and also from giving birth to the children I was injured to such an extent that my health is not anywhere near what it should be. I am unable to take the active part in life, as I should like and also as a wife and mother I cannot perform my duties as I should like so for the past nine years this should have been taken care of and an operation is the answer. after consulting several specialists besides my own doctor all who emphatically advised me not to wait, but have it taken care of immediately, my husband wants me to go this month. I dread it, to think of making still more expense which means still more denial for a couple more years. But whichever way I chose, I feel health is worth more than gold. But don't you see how much proper wages would keep us. How much more we could do for our children. They are getting older. Billy will be eleven this month. Alita is nine and Baby Karla, just six months old Friday. But what greater joy can parents have than to provide adequate comforts and yes some other things too for their little ones. I would love to have some sort of musical instrument for them. Alita is very good in school in Music, and to have a Piano in the home to have the children play and the family gather together and sing old fashioned Hymns. Well, we won't ever have those things at this rate. With rents so high and nobody wants to rent their homes to children. Maybe America doesn't need children like an old man said some time ago. Only wives who work everyday for their personal pleasure, and who don't want children, are wanted they get the breaks in this country, while we fathers and mothers get kicked around with our children. The future citizens of America those who will someday take our place are they loved and wanted? I wonder too sometimes.

Sent you a little book with my compliments under separate cover and I do hope it will reach you and that you may be able to use it. that it may be of help to you in many ways.

Am enclosing a snap shot of Billy & Alita. the picture was taken at one of your W.P.A. Projects which we visited this summer. It is indeed a place of beauty compared to what it was before.

Hope the next time you pass through Milwaukee you won't be sleeping tho, and perhaps we will have a chance to see you.

If possible would you please return those snap shots after you have seen them.

With best wishes and Gods blessing to you and yours.

JUST A CITIZEN OF DEAR OLD U.S.A.

P.S. The clothes Alita is wearing were made over from old ones.

P.S. Just read an article in the Milwaukee Journal of a typical American Family. The husband has an average income of $1,300. Rent is $20 to $22.00—This from Beaver Dam Wis also is pictured their home a very neat and cozy little bungalow. They have two children. Well I wonder how many typical homes like that can be truly found. Our income is by no means $1,300. We pay $32.00 a month for a cottage which is just about devoid of sunshine. Its so dark that we must burn light in the kitchen almost all day. Then the gas & electric & the water bills amount to almost $10.00. After buying food & paying off old bills can you budget this better so there is money left for much of anything else. That's where I guess I'm getting grey hair from trying to figure a way out. And we sure do worry regardless of how much we try not too. Why are not more families given such advantages in this Land of plenty where, as you say there is a superfluous supply of materials when the greatest number of us can not even buy half the things we need not even a decent pair of shoes nor a warm coat for the kiddies for winter and this is the honest truth. God knows I'm speaking the truth. Surely this is not right. We don't know what its like to actually go out & enjoy ourselves for a change to go and forget there is a worry and care in the world and it sure is no pleasure looking forward to an operation with all this to think about. How would you like that. We are living at our present home 4½ yrs—at $32.00 per month makes enough to almost pay for a little home of our own. I'm afraid after everyone was supplied [with all their necessities] there would not be much overproduction, but would furnish employment to a host of husbands & fathers to manufacture more products. I know God would smile on our country and bless it richly if someone made this possible for those who actually need this help. What a joy to actually look forward to Christmas if one could forget worry and cares to know that Uncle Sam really cared enough for his citizens to show them a way to be happy. I'm sure there would be less strikes less suicides and a happier atmosphere would again prevail in this good old U.S.A. If there is over production in meat, why are the prices so high that we can't afford to buy it? Lower prices would increase the demand, or are poor people not supposed to have meat?

Conditions in the fast-food establishments of the 1930s goaded the writer of the following letter to express her support for legislation establishing minimum wages and maximum hours in this service industry.

Denver, Colorado, April 14, 1938

Dear Mr. Roosevelt:

I listened to your address over the radio tonight and want to tell you how much I appreciate what you are trying to do for the people and can see what a fight and struggle you have. Wish it was so you could see and know how things are here in Denver. You can't even buy a job and if you do get one they expect you to work 9 to 10 hrs a day and the most you can get for cooking and such is $10.00 a week. Something should be done with these chain eating houses as they work their boys 12 and 14 hrs and just give them a 14% of earnings charge them for shortages dishes broken, their eats and etc, and when they get their weekly salary sometimes they have from $7.00 to $9.00 coming to them for their long hrs of service and they keep taking in boys to learn and lay off the regular help as the boys they break in has to work a week or so without pay. Its no wonder so many are without work and can't eat half the time. Its no wonder so much crime exists. These chain sandwich shops are the AVB and the owners are out of Wichita Kans. They have seven of these shops here in Denver at this time and are figuring on putting in more. They should be made [to] pay a certain salary as well as every other place of business. Do hope you can get a wage and hour law here that will put more people to work and at least give the head of the family wages that they can at least pay the rent and have enough left to eat a week on. My husband has been out of work since Jan 1st and all we have had is what I can earn at Restaurant work and have a family of five to try to care for. Sure wish could have some good hours and then some one to see that they were enforced. I was sick in the winter and was off of work and the W.P.A. wouldn't give my husband a days work because he had worked out of Denver and out of town 3 months out of year. He works for the Great Western Sugar Co each year during their campaign. I am truly thankful for all you have accomplished so far and hope you may be able to see much more realized.

Mrs. A. F. T.

A carnival worker provides insight into the importance of other workers' unionization efforts as models for the unorganized.

Chippewa Falls, Wisconsin, August 3, 1939

Dear Madam Secretary:

After some deliberation I write you of these conditions because I feel you do not know of them or you would not allow them to exist.

An undercurrent of discontent has been increasing on the Beckmann & Gerety Midway since the opening date April 17th, 1939.

I look for an outbreak within the next 2 or 4 weeks, as that time covers the Picnic and State Fair dates of Springfield, Ill. and Detroit, Mich. All trades unions are 100% organized in those cities.

To show you why I foresee a tidal wave of strike and sabotage I will enumerate a few facts.

Many old employees expected a raise in general pay rate because of betterment of economical conditions in the territory the show covers each year. Also there has been addition of work with strict supervised maintenance for all equipment. Work, that could have been rightly done in winter quarters, was done "on the road." Addition of neon lighting on some riding devices not only increased working hrs. while neon containers holders and equipment was under construction but also the handling time and labor during dismantling and loading and unloading and erecting at each location.

Still no pay increase.

Seven ($7.00) dollars per wk. per man is deducted from the pay of those employed out of the B&G office and contracted similar to the one attached to this letter. This seven dollars is credited to Cook House (C.H.) for berth and board. The berth car is #43 of the B&G train.

The berths are 3 high. A child might sit up in a berth but not a man. The berth car leaks when it rains and it has been a wet spring tour. How much rest can anyone get in a wet bed.

The windows are either too tight they will not raise or are so loose the cold and rain blows in. The aisle is narrow and the berths on either side are very narrow too, many berths must sleep 2 men. The blanket (no plural) is not thick enough. The only really good thing about the car is the porter who keeps things shipshape and does his best to keep a poor toilet sanitary. The light at night is a few scattered low watt globes burning D.C. mfg. by a popping gas machine. The light is not bright enough to read by without injuring the eyes.

The food is served (on location) in a large airy tent, which has long since lost its fly netting. There has been several times that a pure food inspector would have had apoplexy just by looking—There are many of us who have to eat there regularly who have suffered digestive pains and those pains which improper food will cause. No! Not all the food is bad all the time. "On Location" there is always plenty even if some things are portioned. But on the move when the meals are served on the diner on the train almost everything is portioned although one has to eat on the train the first meal after working most of the night to dismantle and load his particular ride etc. and the last meal before the big job of erecting his particular ride or act.

Caesar said "an army travels on its stomach". Well one might (?) work hard on a small meal but he sure as wants a full meal afterwards.

There has been some agitation for organization but some feel that the present set-up of organized labor in U.S.A. is doing good only for a selected few and they fear to be misused. The employees are divided as yet in the means but are 90% in the cause for more pay and better living conditions.

Unless adjustments are made I fear for the worst since requests and complaints are frowned upon and some of the men feel as if they were being treated as minors.

Bad living conditions and low pay breed discontent and a discontented person can be persuaded.

An expression often heard is a mimic of "Well if you don't like it you can quit"—The weaker ones have quit but those who remain are either vassals or are standing by for a fight to the finish when the opportune time arrives.

Personally I dislike strike and strife but I have yet to run from a fight. (I learned a lesson in 1922)

All trades are concerned in the operation and upkeep of a carnival— painters, blacksmiths, carpenters, metal workers, erectoral steel workers, mechanics of many classes, actors, musicians, electricians, neon lighting workers and sound technicians, cooks, waiters, lecturers, cashiers, rail car loaders & repairmen, tractor drivers, machinist.

So you see that any intervention by one trades council would bring in others and you can imagine the results.

The attached contract shows the petty bluff the management puts up in its "compliance" with laws and conditions in the Seat of Freedom Washington, D.C.

I sincerely hope you can do something about this as the 40 hr. wk. law and some of the others seem to leave traveling companies a free hand to subdue the working man.

> A. E. T.
> Precinct #64, Harris Co., Texas
> Poll tax receipt #79537

Despite the organizing efforts of the CIO, auto workers, especially older ones, were still subject to unfair labor practices.

Detroit, Michigan, February 15, 1941

[Dear Mr. President]:

I would like to place before you the truth about one of our motor car company's in this city.

The policy of this company is to place men at work rush out production then lay the men off.

I have been working for this company since 1934 and only have credit for 730 days. At present I have been out of work since October 29, 1941. I am 50 years old and find it impossible to find employment at this age.

I can't understand why some kind of a law couldn't be passed to stop this kind of practice. Say a law requiring these company's to pay a certain percentage of the amount of wages earned each week during the lay off.

I think this would put quite a big hole in the unemployment of today.

Today I am behind in my rent the landlord is after his money I have 4 to feed besides myself.

It is quite a hardship on me as it is hard to get welfare aid and also on W.P.A. my unemployment insurance is run out and I am up against it.

The only encouragement you get from this company is to stay at home till we send for you.

How am I to feed, house cloth my family this way.

I would be very glad to have you give this letter your deep consideration and hoping to hear from you about same.

Thanking you for your time in reading this note and hope you can do something about the aforementioned law.

Thanking you very much.

J. E. D.

P.S. The above mentioned Motor Co is the Hudson Motor Car Co. E. Jefferson Ave, Detroit Mich.

Even in a unionized shop at the end of World War II, this foundry worker was exposed to dangerous chemical fumes that imperiled her health.

Portsmouth, Virginia, May 31, 1945

Dear [Mr. President]:

I no you have a hold lot on your mind without me bothering you, but I hope that if you can you will. I been treated awful bad down here in Virginia. I am working down here in the America Brake Shoe and Foundry Company an got poison gas. The gas man come after I told the boss, but I had suck so much poison that I am not well. An the boss which is Mr. G., won't give me a break—let me stay off an pay me. Or let me come in early enough in the morning so I can have time enough to do my work and get of before they start pouring in the afternoon so I won't inhale the gas of the iron witch mix with that other gas that escape from the stove and it make me sick. Instead he ask me had I better quit my job and go somewhere else an get a job after I become sick from escaping gas there. No one else would want me on a job sick after I gotten sick on this one. They say they pay me for time of an doctor bill but I am still sick an taking doctor medicine. He should given me time of so I could get real well, but he haven't.

I come in early one morning to escape iron pouring an he say come in 8 o'clock. And he no I inhaled poison gas from the stove and he no I can do the same work early, as I can late. I don't no why he doing. He always say my work is good. I would not like to loose my job an not still like to get well. An would get well if it wasn't for inhaling in gas of the iron.

But still want me to give up my job witch I been working for one year are nearly to. I been working to the foundry for 5 years witch I got gas no body will hire me now while I am gasted. You can call up the gas co. portsmouth, Va., and they will tell you about coming an fitting the stove I don't wont to loose my job. I work as janitor and wire maker and core maker which got gas.

I am a poor widow with one child to support. My boss name is Mr. J. E. G., phone Port 2639W. Will you please help me if can not will you please send this letter to the president of the CIO union which I am a member. I don't no his name are where he lives. My doctor is Dr. J. W. J., telephone Port. 5716. I work at American Break shoe an casting division.

J. C.

"But What about the Poor Domestics?": Workers in Homes, Hotels, and Restaurants

When employment opportunities for working-class women were limited, many sought work in domestic service. Throughout the late nineteenth century and the first decade of the twentieth, the number of domestics grew steadily. In the cities, most domestic workers were immigrants; in small towns and rural areas they tended to be native-born whites, except in the South, where they were overwhelmingly black. Of 1.43 million domestic workers in the United States in 1890, 40 percent were native-born whites, 29 percent were foreign-born whites, and 31 percent were black. By 1920 the total had fallen below 1.4 million and there had been a dramatic shift in the proportions of these groups of women in domestic service: now 33 percent were native-born whites, 18 percent were foreign-born whites, and 49 percent were black.[2] Three factors account for the shift toward the employment of black women outside of the South: white women found new opportunities available to them in offices and department stores, immigration declined during and after World War I, and black women began to migrate to the growing industrial centers of the North.

Along with these shifts came changes in conditions of work and life. During the decades before World War I, most domestic workers lived in the houses of their employers, and no group of workers worked longer hours. Isolated and exploited, often with no other home to go to, many domestics worked seven days a week. During the 1920s, however, domestics increasingly "lived out." As growing numbers of middle- and upper-class families lived in apartments where space was limited, many domestics found themselves living a long trolley ride away from their place of employment. Increasing numbers of women who went into domestic service had families of their own to support. Though these women were no longer tied to their employers as they had been when they "lived in," their circumstances still compelled them to submit to harsh working conditions.

Men and women who did similar work in hotels, restaurants, and institutions apparently fared no better. Whether they worked in private homes or in larger establishments, domestic workers expressed their anger and appealed to the government for help as the conditions of their work disintegrated further during the Depression.

☎The following three letters describe the plight of women domestic workers.

[2]David Katzman, *Seven Days a Week: Women and Domestic Service in Industrializing America* (New York: Oxford University Press, 1978), p. 73.

Quincy, Illinois, February 23, 1937

Dear Miss Perkins:

There is so much discussion at present on social security acts, and labor legislation in general. But it appears to me that those who need protection most are completely overlooked and disregarded. I have in mind the domestics and farm help. You, in Washington, are making provisions for old age annuities for minimum wages and maximum hours in industry, why not extend this scope and include a larger group of individuals. The trade unions are well organized and act in unison (sometimes to the disadvantage of the public). Many industries are organized or could easily organize because they work in concentrated areas. But what about the poor domestics, both in private homes and private institutions? What have you done for them? NOTHING. There are usually only a few at one given place which would not be conducive to any organized effort on their part. Why should the government disregard this element when they are already the under-dogs, and at the same time represent such a large element of our population, especially the female population.

I my self, have no complaint to make for I have struggled for and received a good education, and hold at present a respected remunerative position. But I am imploring aid for my fellow men. It was brought home clearly to me when my own sister became a domestic after her husband passed away. They had owned a ranch in Oregon, purchased a short time before the depression started. They succeeded in holding it and making their heavy interest payments thru their miserly thrift until he passed away, and then all was lost. My sister, not wishing to depend upon me, found work at a religious institution where she works from 7:00 A.M. until 8:00 P.M. with two hours free in the afternoon, but which scarcely gives her an opportunity to leave the building and get back in time, working seven days per week with only one-half day off per week, all this, for the paltry miserable sum of FIFTEEN DOLLARS PER MONTH, with maintenance such as it is. This to me cries to Heaven for vengeance. Institutions dispense so called "charity," but charity should begin first with their own employees. As long as a major portion of those employing domestics and farm hands refuse this, why does not the government come to the rescue of these unfortunates? You would not work for five or six hours of one day for the amount that these women are receiving for eleven hours per day and thirty days per month of labor.

I appeal to you, Miss Perkins, in the name of common decency, please, think it over, and make future labor legislation to serve a larger and less fortunate element of our population.

(Miss) T. A. H.

Washington, D.C., March 4, 1937

Dear Miss H.:

On behalf of the Secretary I am acknowledging for her your letter of February 23. It is certainly a fact that domestic service has been disregarded in the setting of many labor standards as for instance in the regulation of hours and fixing of minimum wages, and in the application of the Social Security Act.

I think this type of exclusion is due not to those who are in the first instance responsible for the passage of labor laws, but are the result of compromises which are forced when the legislation is being passed. I think you will be interested in knowing that there is a growing interest in the welfare of domestic workers under the State hour laws and in some instances have attempted to apply minimum wage rates to them, also.

We are very glad to have your letter as additional evidence of the needs of this group and we sincerely hope that the protection which is given to other workers will, before long, be offered to them also.

V. A. ZIMMER

Pittsburgh, Pennsylvania, October 1, 1941

Dear Mr. Roosevelt:

I am Writting you to ask you to help the domestic workers. All public workers have had raises and hours are shorter except we domestic workers. We have long hours and little pay if we ask for a raise an others will work for less. I thank we should have a union among the domestic workers. Some of us works for two dollars and two fifty a day an the don't want to raise us. Some works for three dollars and we hafter feed ourselves and everything is so very high how can we make it of such little money and we hafter pay the same for what we buy as the rich does I wish you would help us because we can't make it at all on such little Please see what you can do something to help us and many thanks all good wishes to you and family.

MRS. E. O.

Grangeville, Idaho, January 30, 1943

Dear [Mr. President]:

I am enclosing 20 cents in coin for crippled children.

Mr. President I am asking if you and those working with you, can do something about the wages for me and other women working in country homes we are expected to work for $1.00 per day or less. It don't seem fair that we should work 16 to 18 hours per day for such a small wage, we can not help support a war and live on $1.00 per day. I wish the wages could be $50.00 or $60.00 per month, I don't think it to much pay for such hard work.

I trust you can do something to help change this problem.

May the lord bless & guide you in the future.

A. A.

Washington, D.C., February 16, 1943

My dear Miss A.:

This will acknowledge receipt of your letter of January 30 addressed to the President, and your contribution of 20 cents to the fund for crippled children, for which we thank you. We frequently receive descriptions of long hours from workers in domestic service. The Federal wage and hour law does not cover these workers, and there is nothing we can do to get a higher wage for you under existing regulations. Public interest in domestic workers is increasing and at least one State now fixes maximum hours for this group.

V. A. ZIMMER

Some domestic workers looked to unionization rather than legislation as a means to improve the conditions of their work. Attempts to form a domestic workers' union had been made earlier, but none had been successful. The Knights of Labor sought to organize domestic employees as early as the 1880s, and other attempts were made during World War I. In 1920, ten local organizations of domestic workers were affiliated with the American Federation of Labor; by 1923, all had disappeared.[3]

Philadelphia, Pennsylvania, January [1], 1935

Miss Perkins:

We are deeply concerned about conditions facing the laboring class of people in the United States. We notice that one particular class, namely,

[3]See Katzman, *Seven Days a Week*, pp. 234–35, and Daniel Sutherland, *Americans and Their Servants: Domestic Service in the United States from 1880 to 1920* (Baton Rouge: Louisiana State University Press, 1981), pp. 134–36.

the *domestic workers* have been over-looked or neglected by the law-makers in practically all laws pertaining to labor. This, in our opinion, is exploitation of a class which occupies a very important position in the nation. The adjustment of wage and working hours for this class would be a step forward in solving the problem of unemployment.

As a government official, you are urged to cooperate with all measures looking towards the introduction and the passage of such laws as would guarantee the domestic worker the following:

1. A living wage
2. Shorter and more standard working hours
3. Better working conditions
4. Unemployment insurance
5. Compensation insurance for domestic workers
6. Compensation for occupational diseases
7. Authority for the departments of labor to collect unpaid wage claims of workers, and such other legislation as would guarantee the rights of the *domestic workers* and protect the interest of *all labor*.

Hoping you much success, we pledge our loyal support.

THOMAS J. HUNT
President, Domestic Workers of America

Washington, D.C., January 21, 1935

My dear Mr. Hunt:

Your letter addressed to the Secretary, asking for her cooperation in securing legislation which will insure adequate standards for domestic workers, has been referred to me for reply.

The Department of Labor is very much interested in this question. I am sending you, under separate cover, Bulletin No. 12 of the Women's Bureau, which I believe will be of great value to you and the members of your organization if you have not already seen it. The States have hesitated in the past to enact legislation for the protection of domestic workers because of the difficulty which is inevitable in enforcement, especially of hours regulations. Public opinion in support of such legislation is, as you know, essential and exact information as to the existing conditions of employment must be ascertained in order to gain support of public opinion. I believe that if you will get in touch with Miss Emma Gunther who is on the National Committee on Household Employment, 525 West 120th Street, New York City, and also, Miss Dorothy Wells, Secretary of

Employment on the National Board of the Y.W.C.A., 600 Lexington Avenue, New York City, you will find that they will be glad to have whatever definite information you have secured through the members of your organization, as they are both very much concerned with this problem.

I can assure you that the Secretary is thoroughly sympathetic with the idea of fair standards for workers in this group, as in any other industrial group.

CLARA M. BEYER

Here a group of workers complain of the tyranny of hotel work. As their references to Father Coughlin make clear, exploitation did not always lead to leftist political sentiments.[4]

Brooklyn, New York, April 2, 1936

Dear Madam [Perkins]:

Will please be so kind as to encourage an investigation of some sort at the Hotel St George in Boro of Brooklyn City and State of New York to remedy the Slave tactics employed at this Hotel. In the past two months one third of the Maids and Housemen were laid off, and the remaining personnel are forced to do double the work as formerly. When the N.R.A. was in force we were told we would better conditions, we were to be given an increase in salary but as it is we have received nothing but abuse from a crew of Tyrant Housekeepers we are forced to work 48 hours and more per week for a mere pittance of twelve (12) dollars per week, we have no time for lunch and have to eat our sandwich if we are able to do so while we are making up the rooms if we are sick we are not allowed to take time off under threat of instant dismissal, we are given either 20 or 22 single rooms to clean and make up or if the rooms are double rooms you are given 17 or 19 of that lot to do if any of the Maids

---

[4]Charles E. Coughlin was the pastor of a small Roman Catholic parish in Royal Oaks, Michigan, a suburb of Detroit. A rousing speaker, he gained a national following as "the radio priest" when sixteen CBS stations began to air his broadcasts in 1930. After CBS dropped his controversial program, he developed his own network of twenty-six stations and at his height was reaching an audience estimated to number 30 to 40 million people. His message was a populist amalgam of class analysis, racism, and anti-Semitism. See Alan Brinkley, *Voices of Protest: Huey Long, Father Coughlin, and the Great Depression* (New York: Vintage, 1983).

should collapse from the terrific strain under which we are forced along the other Maids or Housemen are given six to ten extra rooms to do, I ask you in the name of GOD is this a free country or is it dominated by the few millionaires and money changers as The Honorable Rev. C. E. Coughlin calls them. This very Hotel St George at the present time is expanding its redecoration of rooms and they are paying for these improvements with Human Blood, cannot something be done about this veritable Salt Mine of Siberia. Trusting in both Almighty GOD and your sane judgement.

THE CO-WORKERS OF HOTEL ST GEORGE

The writer of the following letter, head chef in a hotel, complains about competition from "cheap foreign labor" and offers his observations on the effect of mechanization on the demand for labor.

Concord, California, September 16, 1937

U.S. Department of Labor
Gentlemen:

I am writing with the sincere wish to be of some help in the present unsettled labor conditions, by presenting to you the views of a laboring man who is not, and has never been a member of any union, while in sympathy with all labor. I do not honestly believe that the union as now existing, is the remedy of our evils, though it may serve as a means to an end. I firmly believe that a stringently enforced restriction of hours, to divide the work to be done among those who depend on their labor for a livelihood, together with enforced payment of living wages, to be the only ultimate solution. Human nature has not yet reached the stage where an employer—or employee—can resist taking advantage of an advantage. I do not expect you to take up my individual case, but I wish to state some facts.

I am head chef at the Los Medanos Hotel, at Pittsburg Calif purported to be the best hotel in this section. I work from ten to thirteen hours a day, six days a week, averaging about 65 hours a week, for which I receive at the end of each half-month, a check for $43.73, net after deductions for room and board, tax, etc. I am the only married man on the staff of 12 persons, and I find it difficult to support a family, pay rent, etc. on this wage. Efforts to secure an increase have failed; the fact is kept before me that Chinese cooks without families are available at even lower wages. In other words, a white man with a family to support is expected to lower his standard of living to compete with an unmarried chinaman! Is this the principle of free America, to displace honest American citizens with cheap foreign labor? If so, there is no longer a Free America. This policy does more to foster Communism, revolution, etc. than the strongest propaganda the Communists themselves put out. And many men like myself, forced to work ungodly hours for less than a decent living wage, are ready to turn to anything that offers any relief.

Much has been said about the persecution of the large interests, steel, oil, etc. May I call attention to the Federal road building as an example of how labor is faring. Crossing Nevada you may see many miles of new construction. Formerly a man with four horses and a fresno scraper moved one-third of a yard of material at a trip. Now the new Le Torneau scraper, with a capacity of twelve yards, is operated with a caterpillar tractor—by one man. And as if that were not enough, they are hooked in tandem, and one man moves twenty-four yards of material, which would formerly have employed 72 men and 288 horses! What the contractor makes is nothing compared to what Steel makes in the manufacture of machinery, and Oil makes on the motive power. Labor's share is very small. I do not advocate a return to the horse and buggy, but I only cite this instance to prove the crying need of some *COMPULSORY* shortening of hours to provide work for those who have to work. There is no justice in forcing one man to work unreasonable hours, while another man as willing and as capable is refused a chance to work at all.

E. N. J.

Flushing, Long Island, New York, October 18, 1937

Dear Madam [Perkins]:

I would feel very unappreciative of yours and our President's efforts to bring about our country a basic and firm prosperity were I to fail to express to you my humble but most sincere congratulations for a well done job, and I am more than sure that the U S joins with me in this sentiment. I would seem indeed foolish if I were to expect the country which has been left to drift hopelessly during the administration of our former republican presidents to be perfect in such short time, you all have done more than any other administration has ever done, and the country is more than sure of.

It is for this reason that I have taken the pains to investigate the condition in my line of employment. I must say that things in the hotel line are still at a stand still. The hotel employees are about the only forgotten industry in the United States. We never seem to get anything or anywhere, nothing is ever done to help us. We never see day light, yet it takes just as long, if not longer to be a baker or a cook as it does to learn any other trade.

In season jobs especially in the south we are called the imported slaves, it is the truth. We are employed without knowing the hours. They say our pay is small because we are going to get a bonus of from one to three hundred dollars; we are to have a little check on a side if business is good, and the season is to last at least from 3 to 4 months, to our surprise, we find that our managers keep none of the said promises, and we haven't even the fare back.

The hours are from 12 to 18 hours per day, and on a holiday longer if we are needed. If we dare complain we are told—if you don't like it you know what to do. They know that we are some two thousand miles away, and that we cannot afford to leave.

In times as these I cannot understand for the world why they are permitted to do such merciless things. Why aren't these conditions investigated—not by some polished political mocker, who has no knowledge of what's going on, but by some competent and well experienced hotel man—and a complete report made to you directly. I am sure that if this is done honestly, the long line of unemployment would be cut to less than half. The same could be done with any other line of industry for the betterment of our country.

While our Government is worrying about the Far East or the European situation, because of such conditions as these in the hotel industry, we can find the brewing of the truest propaganda of communism, and as a man whom has served two years during the world war with the 29th Inf. I feel it is my duty to the country to make report of such things. As I speak six languages I can find out things that the average American can not.

The mission of this letter is not to impress you as a work of art, but it is to serve the purpose of helping the condition of our country and to relieve many suffering modern slaves from the clutches of our modern Simon LeGrees.

Please forgive this bother if it is such, and PLEASE DO SOMETHING TO HELP US AS YOU DO ANY OTHER HUMAN BEING. May God Bless you united the Democratic administration whom has and is doing a lot for all other industries, and in the truest sense of my sincerity I send this letter not as a criticism, but as a suggestion of a loyal American citizen.

J. R.

Washington, D.C., October 25, 1937

Dear Mr. R.:

The Secretary has had your letter of October 18 which she has requested this department to acknowledge for her.

The NRA hearings in the hotel and restaurant industries made very clear the need for State laws, limiting hours, setting minimum wages and standards of general working conditions which would protect the health of men and women engaged in such work.

As hotel and restaurant work is entirely interstate [*sic*] in character, Congress cannot set standards for this work by Federal law. The power does lie, however, in State Legislatures. Pennsylvania, during its last legislative session, passed a 44 hour law for both men and women which will become effective in a short time and which applies to hotels and restaurants as well as to other kinds of work. We have every reason to believe that the successful administration of the Pennsylvania law will encourage other States to take similar action, as well as to extend the protection of living wages and proper working conditions to the men and women in this industry.

While the Industrial Commissioner of New York does not at present have the authority to regulate the wages and hours of men in these industries, I am forwarding a copy of your letter to Elmer Andrews, Industrial Commissioner, Department of Labor, 80 Centre St., New York, N.Y. as I know that your report will add weight to the evidence in favor of securing the necessary State laws to correct the abuses you report.

I know that the Secretary is deeply appreciative of the help of those who, like yourself, make the effort to write her, giving a clear statement of conditions which they know to be harmful and which they believe she can help to correct. I want to thank you on her behalf for your expression of good wishes, and for the assistance you have given her.

V. A. ZIMMER

"It's Hard for This Mill to Keep Hands Here for the Way They Treat Them": Textile Workers

Cotton has occupied a central place in American history. In the antebellum years, much of the nation's economy depended on the growing and transportation of cotton in the South and the manufacture of cotton textiles in the North. After Reconstruction, the production of household fabrics and clothing began to shift southward, to North and South Carolina. One informative article has concluded that "by the end of the Great Depression, the Southeast replaced New England as the world's leading producer of cotton cloth, and the industrializing Piedmont replaced the rural Coastal Plain as pacesetter for the region."[5]

Workers in these new industries experienced severe hardship even before the onset of the Depression in 1929. During World War I, the industry grew dramatically as wartime demand spurred factories to expand in number and in size. Profits and wages increased. In 1920, however, as demand slackened, the industry went into a prolonged tailspin. The economic downturn that surprised the rest of the country in 1929 had begun for the textile industry shortly after the end of World War I. Faced by stiff competition, companies responded with a variety of cost-cutting measures, the most important of which introduced labor-saving machinery, reorganized work, and introduced new supervisory practices aimed at increasing labor discipline. Increasing numbers of workers balked at such tactics. In 1927, individual resistance turned into large-scale labor conflict. In the next few years, Gastonia, Dan River, and High Point became scenes of major strikes.[6]

The onset of the Depression worsened already harsh working conditions. The establishment of the National Recovery Administration led to a short-lived revitalization of the industry and stimulated organizing drives by the United Textile Workers Union. Within a year, however, mill owners had begun to undermine the codes that gave minimum protection to workers, and in 1934 a national strike was soundly defeated. Industry reclassified jobs and cut piecework rates. With speedups and stretchouts, workers were doing as much work in eight hours as they had formerly done in ten or twelve. The quickened pace and intensity of work led managers to replace women workers with young men. Even

[5]Jacquelyn Dowd Hall, Robert Korstad, and James Leloudis, "Cotton Mill People: Work, Community, and Protest in the Textile South, 1880–1940," *American Historical Review* 91 (April 1986): 245.
[6]Ibid., pp. 265, 271.

women who were their families' sole providers found themselves laid off.[7]

El Paso, Texas, June 15, 1936

Labor Department
Messrs:

Perhaps I'm wasting my time writing this, but I feel there should be something done to change a few conditions existing in a cotton mill here at El Paso.

There is no use to go to any one here, so I thought maybe one could get results by writing there.

I have a mill worker staying with me. A faithful and willing worker. She goes to work at 6 o'clock a.m. and works till 4 and sometimes 6. She runs 28 looms. Ofttimes works 8 and 10 hrs. overtime for which she gets no pay whatever. Her pay checks amount to $10.00 and $11.00 per week. There are no conveniences for the workers whatever. Some of the workers fare worse than she does as she is an adept at her work naturally gets more. It might be a good plan to send an investigator. One of the foremen is a prince of a man and wants to better conditions for the workers but is powerless as the one over him has no mercy. Of course there are many Mexicans working there, not all aliens and they chisel on them more than the whites and they are beginning to resent it with just cause. Living conditions are going up and its impossible for them to carry on with such meager pay, specially when you have a few mouths to feed and bodies to clothe. The lady with me has made no complaint just has told me of these conditions and I think it wrong. Hoping there can be some way of changing things. This lady said while the NRA was in effect conditions were much better. Now they get orders for large amounts of material and crowd the work thru, at top speed to prevent them from paying more. It is a regular sweatshop. No fans and no ventilation. Now please don't direct me to Chamber of Commerce here as they are not interested in such things. I've had experience before. I am signing my name but would like to be withheld when investigating. I have no interest in the affair whatever—only a humanitarian one.

Mrs. G. M.

[7]Ibid., p. 256.

Knoxville, Tennessee, January 20, 1937

Dear President:

I am addressing this letter to you, because I believe you will send it to the proper department for right consideration.

The labor conditions at the Appalachian Cotton Mills here are worse than miserable—they are no less than slavery. The mill has only two shifts, day and night shifts, and each of them 10 hours long. The scale of wages is very low, and the mill is a veritable sweatshop. None of the women workers know what they are making, until they draw their pay check at each weekend, and their wages is not sufficient for them to live on.

The mill should have 3 eight hour shifts, or two 8 hour shifts with a considerable increase in their wages. The women and men too, draw from $4.00 to $12.00 per week. Mr. Roosevelt, men can not live on such wages as this, and feed even a small family. Such conditions as these are worse than coersion, it will force men and women to steal, and it surely is not good Americanism. Am I to think that this great big civilization is going to stand for such intolerable conditions as these I have mentioned above. I believe sir, that they are worse than criminal. Such conditions bring sufferings to the unfortunate poor, that have to reak out a miserable existance without even a slaves opportunity to attend worship on the Lord's day. It will take sharp detection to get the facts from this mill, but someone should see to it, that the long hours and short wages be put to an end. If the workers were to rebel against these unfair, and unamerican conditions, then the authorities would pronounce them Reds, or communists. The women have asked me to write this letter to you, because they believe you would remedy the conditions, and lighten their burdens. Now that I have wrote it I have used the fifth chapter of St. James in the N.T. as a base for the letter, which is literally fulfilling every minute.

Let us hope for the best.

R. H. O.

Burlington, North Carolina, March 4, 1937

Dear Mr & Mrs Roosevelt:

I just had a great desire to write and tell you something that I hardly know what to say for I am a poor widow woman with 4 children and uneducated and don't know how to word a letter but in my simple way am going to try and explain what I am about to write we poor working people love you and Mr Roosevelt our President and we done everything we could do to make him our President again now what I am about to say is this the firm we all work for *works us all just as long as they want to and pay us just as little as they please* to which we poor people can not live on never do we have a dime for Doctor are medicine are any thing else and it sure looks hard and it is hard please Mr. Roosevelt in the name of our Lord isn't there something that can be done about it if we get sick we have to die are get well the best we can for the Doctors have got so they won't treat people without money and that is something the working class of people don't have since the NRA was killed down at Raleigh the senate have passed a law to work men 55 hours a week and more and women 48 hours are more even if we worked that many hours we couldn't make a living with the wages we all get it really isn't fair for the poor working class of people to be treated like slaves never have a showing in this world just toil and worry day in and day out with half enough to eat and half enough to keep warm.

God Bless you Both.

Please give this to our President Mr. Roosevelt am sending you a clipping out of the paper of what they are doing down at Raleigh for us we don't think it is fair please do something about it if you can for our sake do.

Mrs. L. B.

Washington, D.C., March 11, 1937

Dear Mrs. B.:

Mrs. Roosevelt has referred your letter to the Department of Labor with the request that we reply for her. I know that both the President and Mrs. Roosevelt appreciate the interest of the many thousands of persons who are writing reports of conditions of work and have asked the President for assistance in improving these conditions. Until Congress makes it possible for the Federal Government to set standards, I am afraid there is nothing which will insure shorter hours and better wages, unless the states themselves pass the necessary laws. We realize that families with low earnings are unable to meet their responsibilities and we are looking forward eagerly to some action which will enable the Government to help you.

V. A. Zimmer

South Carolina, May 3, 1937

Dear Miss Perkins:

Wonder if you could get the men in Washington to do something for the laboring people. Here where I work we have 40 hours a week but in the weave room they start from 15 to 20 minutes before 7 o'clock in the morning and same at noon they do not force us to be there then but we have the batteries to catch up so you see we do about 2½ hours a week without any pay.

When the NRA came on spinners were running around 8 sides two weeks after NRA they had to run 10 sides to get $12.00 they speed up so much it makes it so hard, and now they are adding more to the frames and not adding much to wages of course they have raised our wages a little twice in the last few months.

I am sure they use as much cotton and make as much cloth in the 8 hours as they did in the 10 before they speeded up so much. The S.C. law makers never do any thing to benefit the laborers. We are stretched out. So even the young people are complaining that it is too hard for them. Where will it end? If some one does not do something I notice where wages and hours are to be taken up next week if we get shorter hours and more money please see that there is no more speed up or stretch out for it is bad now. Thank you.

I will have to be nameless or lose my job.

JUST A WORKER

Greensboro, North Carolina, April 19, 1938

[Dear Miss Perkins]:

My purpose in writing you is that you ought to know some things are going on in Rayon industries especially at Carter Fabrics corporations. We think a larger percentage of workers are from near by towns and cities and the people in and around Greensboro stand little or no chance. As proof of this the public service co. made a survey with end in view to put a trolley car to said plant. But found as stated above a larger portion of workers at said plant were from Riedsville, Highpoint, Burlington, Randlman and other places. Of course you know why they do this and it's this. Should there be labor trouble it would not be centralized. Help are brought in by car loads from places mentioned above. We have known help to be laid off here that lives in Greensboro without any cause and people from elsewhere to be put in their place in fact the basis of the whole job is run on friendship. Overseers came from elsewhere. We want to mention too the stretch out system. We do not see how they can hardly stand it anymore. It seems something could be done about this. This is a new plant started up last year. We have heard the plant cost completed 70,50000 [*sic*]. Women on standing jobs have no rest stools. N.C. Law says they must have. H. C. is Supt. He is a young man recently married. I don't guess he would want his wife to work eight hours without resting some. Remembering Mr. Roosevelt's opening speech to Congress in Jan. they stretched out the same day. Their wage scale is less than other smaller plants. We want to speak of the union briefly. This writer does not belong to any union. We know of one man laid off on account of union activity. But he was told that his work was not satisfactory.

I'm withholding my name. Drop this letter in waste basket *after having it typed off for Greensboro News* if you will. Would be glad of any thing you can do to help in this matter. This Co. says they are not making any money. But surely they must be because the help is not getting very much pay for their labor. Wish you would see that it is put in sunday's news. Do not send this letter back to any one as I am an employee and have only stated some facts you being head of our Labor department. Maybe you can bring about some adjustments.

BY A WORKER

Greenville, South Carolina, January 22, 1942

U.S. Department of Labor
Dear Sirs:

I am writing you for my benefits of work I am working at Judson Mill Spinning Room I am laying up roping for the spinning room the job has stretched me out untill I cant hardly make it to save my life it is awful the way we have to work in this spinning room and I work on saturday and I am sent out one day through the week to keep me from getting six days or 48 hours and time and half time for eight hours I have been working like this for over a year and I don't think it is right and I would like to know what to do about it I need the job for I have to work to make a living I only had 104 frames to lay up roping on and they put in 30 more frames up in the old spinning room and have got 24 of them running now and I have to take roping up there for the 24 frames and the 104 frames downstairs is more than a job. More than a year or two when C.

M. was Boss Spinner some of us boys was sent out for two or 4 hours each day and had to go back in and finish working until stopping time to keep down the expense we was running our job in 4 and 6 hours which we should have had 8 hours for the job and this was not right so I hope you can till me what to do. If you will send some one to my house I can tell you more than I can write but I don't want my name mentioned to any of the mill officials for I would not have any job at all if they even knew I wrote to you but I guess others have wrote you many letters nor does Judson Mill pay the wages that the other mills pay for the same job but I know it is my privilege to go to another mill but I don't want to change jobs because I might have to take another shift I go to work at 4 o'clock and quit at twelve at night. It is hard for this mill to keep hands here for the way they treat them. I think it is awful and I have to work for I am poor. Of course some people would not tell you anything about this now way if you send a man to my house I will give him all the information he wants about the spinning room at Judson Mill some of the other hands would tell you if they was not afraid to talk see the hands and talk to them for they are afraid to say much but I am not afraid to tell you if you came to me about my work but I don't want my name mentioned to them.

So I will close for this time

T. W. B.

Washington, D.C., January 29, 1942

Dear Mr. B.:

This will acknowledge your recent letter describing working conditions which exist in the plant in which you are employed. There is no department of government which has authority to require a firm to operate a certain number of hours . . . which an individual can be required to do.

I am enclosing for your information a pamphlet describing the Fair Labor Standards Act. This law does apply to the kind of work you are doing and if you believe that your employer is not carrying out the terms of the act, I suggest that you report that fact to the Wage and Hour Division as suggested by the pamphlet. I can assure you that your present letter will be regarded as confidential.

V. A. ZIMMER

"Our Voice Is after All Very Weak": White-Collar and Sales Workers

Throughout the twentieth century, white-collar workers have been the fastest-growing segment of the American work force. Between 1900 and 1930, the number of white-collar workers as a whole increased by 300 percent while the total work force expanded 59 percent. Even during the Depression, when the number of manual workers grew at a paltry 1 percent, white-collar employment rose by 12 percent.

C. Wright Mills, whose study of white-collar workers focused the nation's consciousness on this segment of the work force in 1951, paid close attention to the expansion of the professional and managerial class;[8] but during most of this century, the major increase in white-collar work occurred in secretarial, clerical, and sales positions. Between 1900 and 1930, the ranks of secretaries and clerical workers increased by almost 500 percent and those of sales workers by over 200 percent. Between 1930 and 1940, when total employment increased by only 6 percent, clerical positions increased by 15 percent, and the number of sales workers more than doubled.

The following two letters speak to the problems of traveling salesmen who worked on commission.

Atlanta, Georgia, December 30, 1936

Dear Madam Secretary:

Because the nature of their business makes it practically impossible for them to organize or protect themselves the travelling salesmen of America are being exploited as no other group in the industrial and commercial field. For that reason, I am writing you requesting that you give some of these ills consideration. Please bear in mind that there are notable exceptions to this but these practices are becoming more prevalent every day.

The nature of their work requires that they spend a large percentage of their time away from home. This varies from a few days to weeks and months. Until a few years ago it was customary to give these men the weekends off where they were gone four or five nights and in instances

---

[8] C. Wright Mills, *White Collar* (New York: Oxford University Press, 1951).

where they were gone several weeks to give them a few days with their families to recuperate from these trips. Now he is expected to work six days in the week and spend Sunday traveling to the next point. Since the beginning of the depression employers have cut their sales forces constantly and doubled up on territory until it is now necessary for the average salesman to work from ten to fourteen hours a day and then spend from thirty minutes to two hours making out reports. Instead of increasing salaries in proportion to this increase in work they have decreased both salaries and expense allowances to the point where it is necessary for them to stay in places hardly decent and eat food out of cans uncooked or in places less than sanitary. To be separated from one's family is bad enough but not to have even the necessities of life either at home or on the road without recreation is the next thing to being slaves. Bear in mind that a large percentage of traveling men are either high school or college graduates. It is true that to anyone not knowing the cost of traveling their earnings sound high but investigation would show that net earnings are very low in proportion to the education, ability, type of work and dress required.

In addition some employers, even some of the largest tire manufacturers in the nation, have men especially hired to place advertisements in the papers promising lucrative employment. When men apply they are promised a wonderful future if they will go out get the license numbers off automobiles, find the owners from the registration department and sell them tires. This is at the expense of the man applying and with little or no training. Not one man in a thousand stands a chance of making a living yet each man who attempts it spends a part of his meager savings and the tire company has sold a few more tires with little or no selling cost.

Several book publishers have men out whose business it is to rent a room in a high type hotel, place an advertisement in the paper offering employment. The applicant is told that if he will buy so many books he can secure a job. This is not only true of publishers but a large group of other manufacturers as well. In most instances all anyone ever gets out of it is merchandise for which they have no need. Some so-called employers require a cash bond which is never returned.

In most instances there is no way for the prospective employee to investigate the prospective employer because he has neither money, time nor facilities to do so.

In my own case there are two instances I would like to call to your attention. For fourteen years I have traveled in the South and naturally during that time I have developed a large clientele. About three years ago Mr. A. C. Jr. came to me after I had made application to his firm and informed me that if I would secure the business of Talmadge Bros. & Co. of Athens, Ga. he would give me a job. In less than twenty four hours I had secured an order amounting to nearly ten thousand dollars. In addition after entering their employ I switched a large number of my other customers to them. I was never given the privilege of handling this business and shortly afterward was transferred to a territory in which eight men had failed in succession, promised cooperation which I was never given. This was an effort to make me quit. After this failed I was let out with the excuse that the territory would not stand the expense.

In July this year Mr. G. C. M. of the G. C. M. Co. of Boston Mass. contacted me in Atlanta, hired me and told me I would be fixed if I got the business of the Eli Witt organization with headquarters in Tampa Fla. In addition he told me that I would be doing well if I got the territory on a paying basis within twelve months. I secured the business of the firm mentioned and in October had already built the business to the point where I earned for the company $130.00 more than my drawing account. After a territory is organized and outlets secured the work is much easier and does not require the intensive effort nor ability to handle and less contact is needed. As a result I received a letter from Mr. M. saying that the directors had decided to combine the two southern territories and as the other man had been with the company longer and had sold more merchandise than I they were giving him the combined territory.

Incidentally, in several instances I had to write letters and send telegrams to secure the drawing account promised me. This was in spite of the fact that they had definite instructions where to send the checks.

The heads of both these firms are very bitter toward the present administration and in all my life I have never heard any man as maliciously maligned as was the President last January by Mr. A. C. Sr. in a sales meeting attended by the salesmen and executives of that company.

One of the biggest groups of employees in this country is the salesmen. I, as one member of this group, request that something be done to help them. We do not desire things unreasonable but we do desire a living wage in proportion to our contributions to industry and commerce; security; the privilege of a few hours at regular hours with our families; that we do not have to spend hours over needless reports; that employers be forced to pay us a living wage and all expenses which we would not incur if at home and that unscrupulous employers and manufacturers who prey on the desire of man to earn an honest living be forced out of business.

J. G. C.

Hollywood, California, January 30, 1937

Dear Mr. Zimmer:

I deeply appreciate your very kind response of the 25th inst. to my letter addressed to our worthy President regarding the unfair conditions existing in the Vacuum cleaner and Kindred fields in compensating their salesmen.

However, I would like to correct a wrong impression concerning the activities of these much exploited unfortunates.

These men all work under the closest form of supervision, and territory cards are furnished in addition. It is also a regular routine for these firms to furnish as often as possible "leads" to these men. These "leads" scattered from one end of the city to the other, entail considerable expense to salesmen for gasoline money, and in the great majority of cases, these leads are mere idle inquiries about the product, for purchase at some future date. The industry as a whole enjoy an incalculable amount of word of mouth advertising on which they later on capitalize while these salesmen actually are starved for want of food. Without close supervision, sales volume would be impossible to get.

As an executive and organizer in this business for years, and in my present capacity as California Sales Manager for one of America's largest Appliance Manufacturers, I know whereof I speak.

During the N.R.A., when it was suggested that these men be placed on a substantial basis, these chiseling specialty firms attempted to fog the vision of the government with a false cry that these men worked "when" and "if" they pleased, were uncontrolled and unsupervised, etc.,—so as to avoid paying salaries. Those who listened, fell for that story, much to the misery and suffering of those exploited men.

The truth of the matter is that these men report for work at 8:00 a.m. or 8.30 a.m. each morning—attend the morning meeting and leave for the field with the supervisor who is with them from morning until night. Lazy men who don't work are soon fired—with the entire situation comparable to any man working in a factory punching a clock—the exception being that the salesman doesn't get paid unless he high pressure's an order.

I have seen dozens of honest men forced to lie, misrepresent and turn crooked in this business—a condition brought about thru this rotten system of exploitation.

Personally, I have no kick, I get a salary, expense allowance and override on all sales; I know what the score is. These firms know definitely that a man cannot make a living selling their products on a commission basis, because of the method of marketing. They have a wholesale branch, resale branch and retail branch, with the result that they compete with their own wholesale customers on their own product. They are not satisfied with wholesale business alone, they go out and sell it retail too—and that added value from retail sales is the sweat off the backs of these misled and exploited unfortunates.

With 100 large dealers handling a certain advertised electrical unit (Department stores included) what chance has a solicitor to do a necessary volume of business by soliciting its sale from house-to-house? Very often when he lands a prospect—she has a charge account in some large store and prefers buying thru that particular store. Many a sale of a particular product has been enjoyed by a Department store handling the line, due to the selling effort on the part of a solicitor representing the factory—and in such cases, the solicitor who stimulated the desire for that particular product, does not receive one cent for his work, while the dealer made a profit and the factory likewise a profit.

I am sure that the Department of Labor never has been fully and definitely familiar with the true situation. The fact that you mention in your letter that it would be difficult to set standards since employees do not work directly under supervision, proves this.

While standards as to working hours could not be set advantageously—a standard of minimum wage is simple to demand—say $16.00 per week plus actual car expense.

In this way—exploitation of men will be done away with. Only men of experience will be considered for such employment—and men won't be dragged into their wrong vocational pew.

Salesmen in every line today are being exploited in shameful fashion—and the inconsistency lies in the fact that during N.R.A., automobile salesmen, who function no differently from other salesmen, were given a minimum wage guarantee.

I shall be glad to render my service to your department at any time should you choose to take advantage of my knowledge and seasoned experience in this field. My reasons are purely humanitarian.

When an end and death sentence is dealt this "Straight Commission Racket", the greatest Racket of all will have been wiped out.

Al Capone was an angel in fairness, compared to many of these firms in their treatment and inconsiderations and ridiculous demands to salesmen, many of whom are not qualified for the work, but hired regardless for exploitation purposes.

I hope something will be done to help deserving salesmen in the very near future.

Kindly pardon the detail of this letter, it is written in the hope of giving you a better and truer picture of the situation.

J. M. D.

Pittsburgh, Pennsylvania, February 22, 1937

Madam Secretary:

As a stenographer, I would like to speak for the five-day week and short working day. Why should we not have some time for mental and physical development; aren't we as much entitled to it as those of the so-called leisure class? At the end of a seven and one-half hour day, our eyes are too tired for further use.

If we are to understand and take an intelligent interest in the affairs of the World, we should have time for study and reading.

Then, too, more people could be employed, if the shorter day and shorter week were generally in effect. I was unemployed for nearly two years and can sympathize with those who are now unemployed.

The Corporation by whom I have been employed for the past fifteen years, tried the five-day week for five months during the Depression. The great majority of the employees were delighted with it; they felt better physically and mentally and life took on a new meaning.

(needless to say, I cannot sign my name)

Steubenville, Ohio, April 15, 1937

Dear Mr. President:

I am writing this in an unconventional mood so was not particular as to the kind of stationary I used. However, knowing you from N.Y. yet when you were governor that such things do not matter to you I am writing these few lines.

Mr. President, as you are the only true fighter for the cause of the forgotten man and woman and because of the fact that you have already accomplished so much for the oppressed of all races and groups, may I too address myself to you as a duly registered Pharmacist to do something for us too. After all we the drug clerks of this country should be afforded some protection against vicious exploitation by either the independent owners in the drug business or chain and corporation stores. I was tempted to write this to you my dear Mr. President because the Supreme Court decision relative to the Wagner Act according to the newspapers does not apply to druggists. After all to become a Registered Pharmacist one must have a H. S. education or its equivalent, then 4 years Pharmacy School and a possible 2 years before one receives the coveted certificate from his or her Pharmacy Board. Then a corporation comes and compels us to work from 60 to 80 hours a week for a meagre pittance of a salary that the average steelworker would scorn to accept. Of course, I realize our tragedy: lack of organization. But that is not our fault. We would be black-balled by all the employers were we to even think of an organization to ameliorate our condition.

We are College men and that's why we must not mix with labor organizations. That is the Dictum of the employers, corporations, chain stores and independent drug stores alike. The N.R.A. did help a great deal while it lasted. However, it did not last very long. Please Mr. President, my family who sees me only once in two weeks because of the exploitation that I am subjected to and also in the name of the countless thousands who are exploited by chain stores and corporation outfits alike, do something to alleviate our miserable condition. In some states there are laws governing hours for Pharmacists but the state governments either favor corporations & chain outfits or are helpless to do anything about it. I have campaigned for your re-election as to me you are the Redeemer of the Working Class.

My wife did her bit to the Democr. Party in the last campaign among the women's organizations. Now do something for us druggists and we shall everlastingly bless the name of F.D.R. from morning til night.

Please Mr. President: "Do not pass us Pharmacists by."

M. F., PhG

Bloomington, Illinois, May 21, 1937

[Dear Miss Perkins:]

Quite Sometime ago I wrote you regarding the office working class of people who are forced to work long hours with small pay.

Just yesterday I read in the paper where Pres. Roosevelt (The greatest President of them all) was considering New Labor and Wage Legislation but only for those firms engaged in Interstate Commerce.

If this information was correct I wonder if he doesn't already know these workers are being taken care of with their various Unions while we cant unionize due to the fact, there aren't any Unions for this class of people nor for store clerks.

You, with your position as Secretary of Labor could do something about this if you only will do so and many thanks in advance if you do.

A TIRED OFFICE WORKER

Brooklyn, New York [May 28, 1937]

Dear Mrs Roosevelt:

Under the date of May 27th., I noticed in the press notices that you favored, quote, "equal pay for equal work" unquote.

May I at this time take the privilege of bringing to your attention a situation that, tho, small in a National sense, is I assure you extremely important to the thousands who are affected by the conditions I shall mention, i.e.

I speak of the "White Collar" clerk in Wall Street, who welcomed the N.R.A. as a chance to get home for supper once in a while, or who at least received fair compensation for his hours of work.

We, of the "Street", either work untold hours or when we get a chance to go home by 5.00 or 5.30 P.M., are laid off, and in most cases after years of service. The majority of the men in the "Street" have worked nowhere else, are fully qualified in their experience in the Brokerage business, yet they are hardly, if ever, treated as worthy of their hire.

We realize that with such an erratic thing as the "markets" can, and have been, that it would be impossible for any firm to set a definite quitting time but on the other hand, it does not make sense, when a firm pays out an average of $70. per week for 12 to 14 weeks to 8 men as "supper money" ($2. per man, per night, for a 12 or 14 hour day). When one or two men at $25. or $30. per week would alter this continual over work, improve the standard of the men's work, and without a doubt, make a better working spirit.

Speaking from nine years experience in one of the largest Wire Houses in the Street, I have never seen the equal in downright "plugging" yet, these conditions are absolutely ignored.

All other trades, have a definite opportunity to establish themselves, to assure themselves proper renumeration for work executed, therefore I feel I can take it upon myself to state that, The men in the STREET are looking forward to the day when they may wear a "White Collar". . . .

R. E. L.

Clerks and other employees of national chain stores were victims of their manager's desperate maneuverings as they attempted to comply with orders from the firm's headquarters. The following two letters, from a clerk and a manager of such stores, tell the same sad story.

Attica, Indiana, October 26, 1937

Dear Madam [Perkins]:

This letter is a plaintive cry from a lone outpost among the corn rows of Indiana. Various groups in the past have called themselves the forgotten man but permit us to say that we, chain store employees, feel we are the forgotten man. For some time we have felt the urge to give some volume to our feeble and muffled cries in this wilderness but only until the recent discussion by the professors on the Chicago Round Table did we obtain sufficient impetus to our pen. The Round Table discussion informed us that there are from five to seven million people in the white collared class who are dependent on Labor and the farmer, yet are unable to avail themselves of possible benefits from the government because lack of organization or bargaining power prevents them. They said also that the degree of organization determines their degree of benefits. Where then, if any, do we have the chance to speak of evils in the business when the organization is scattered into fifteen thousand stores?

Quite recently, especially soon after the President of the United States gave his fire side address, the company (A&P Tea Co.) demanded a drastic reduction in selling hours. By this is meant a reduction in personnel which means a reduction in service to the consumer. The methods used to fall in line with the company's demands are varied: of two, one may put down the hours wanted by the company and work night and day or pay for help out of one's own pocket. To employ help enough to do the job expected of you would undoubtedly mean the loss of your job. During NRA, evidently a loop hole was sought and obtained whereby, calling a manager an executive the hour limit was null and void. This created a responsibility on the manager to get the work done, regardless of whether it took eighty or ninety hours per week. In fact we have on file the company's endeavors to evade the spirit of NRA. Only until a law, which like some transfer and motor bus employees have, (fines for over-time work) can we expect to have decent working conditions. It is not the company alone that is at fault, it is the evils boring from within also.

We have but partially written what we could have written but let me quote from J. T. Adams', "The Epic of America": "Steadily we are tending toward becoming a nation of employees—whether a man gets five dollars a day or a hundred thousand a year. To-day the appalling growth of uniformity and timorousness of views as to the perfection of the present economic system held by most "comfortably off men" as cor-poration clerks or officials is not unrelated to the possible loss of a job." You see our voice is after all very weak.

So we who are silently struggling to make a decent living for ourselves and our families do not demand a Shangri-La on earth but we would like to have a small bit of the good works created here. We pray that, and hope, before our backs are broken on the wheel that this humble letter shall not fall on silent ears.

As a parting thought it may interest you to know that on week ending November thirteen we are to absolutely show a reduction in hours on our weekly statement. Isn't it a coincidence that congress convenes the following Monday. And how nice the reports will look when presented by the lobbyists.

J. O. A.
R. C.
H. L. L.
R. E. S.

Paterson, New Jersey, October 7, 1937

Dear Madam [Perkins]:

We wish to call your attention to a grave situation!

In the City of Paterson, State of New Jersey there are two large retail dairy and grocery chain stores, Modern Dairy and Grocery, Inc., and Sunnyside Food Stores, Inc., who are impairing the health and intelli-gence of their workers.

Both chains consist of at least nine stores and employ approximately 100.

Their working week undermines the vitality and mental capacity of each and every employee. This degenerating week consists of *75* to *80* hours in stores *without heat* in *winter* or sufficient *ventilation* in *summer*. . . .

We, as citizens, wish to correct this misdemeanor so that we might enjoy clean, healthy, and normal lives.

WE WANT TO SEE OUR MOTHERS AND WIVES SOMETIME, TOO!!

> Hoping to receive your aid
> S. B.

> Boston, Massachusetts, November 12, 1936

Honorable Secretary [Perkins]:

This letter must necessarily remain anonymous for the reason that I am employed as an executive of the concern which I am reporting; and while I am torn between a sense of loyalty to this concern that supplies me with a reasonable living wage, I am I feel justified, because the lower priced store clerks, are the victims, in my opinion of a very grave injustice; and should have the support of some outside agency as we within the organization can get nowhere and are practically told that our positions are in jeopardy if we attempt to bring about or recommend any change.

The concern involved is the Great Atlantic and Pacific Tea Company. Right here in New England there are literally and truthfully hundreds of store clerks that within the past year have had their salaries cut from $17 to $12, from $15 to $10.

It is true that when these cuts were put into effect, the hours employed also were cut accordingly so that the hourly rate remained the same, and we were told that we must strictly adhere to this. However, the injustice of it all is that even though the hours were cut, the working hours of the clerk are fully monopolized. For instance there are many 20 hour per week clerks here in New England stores of this concern. These clerks work 8 hours on Saturday as this is the busy day of the week and 2 hours daily for Monday through Friday. These 2 hours daily are divided in most cases as follows: the clerk comes in between 11 and 12 noon daily and between 5 and 6 in the evening daily.

You can readily see that while the clerk works but two hours daily from Monday to Friday we practically monopolize his entire time. Many clerks also work three or four hours extra, not having anything else to do; and especially if they live far from the store in order to save the extra carfare involved in going home.

When we read of the benefits those men have who have unions and realize the benefits that could be derived from such a union, those of us who are really thoughtful of the clerks and other employees feel badly at their plights.

While nothing openly has ever been said, we do know that this company will positively never stand for unionization, and no one has ever dared take any step that would bring this about.

While it is no doubt beyond my capabilities to suggest a proper remedy, I do feel that you and your very capable bureau can devise some legal plan that can be put into effect and still not jeopardize the positions of the employees.

I like my Company and feel that I am perfectly loyal to them by giving them my entire cooperation as far as working hard is concerned. However, I am more and more becoming very much disgusted by their horrible policy with reference to store employees. Many of the older employees that are receiving high salaries have been replaced by younger men at lower salaries, and while I can realize that this was probably an economical justification, I can not bring myself to feel that the clerks who are working anywhere from 20 to 40 hours per week and brought in on "staggered hours" as we call them, can be considered as being treated fairly.

I do not know whether or not you disregard anonymous letters; if you do not, and insist on a proper name, I feel that I would willingly jeopardize my own position and come out in the open. In such a case, if you will write to me care of General Delivery, Boston, Mass., and address it as "Joseph Pacif" which of course is not my name, I shall take whatever steps you suggest in properly reporting this.

ANONYMOUS

This week the headquarters office of this Company sent forms to every store and had the managers list the exact hours each clerk worked, showing when he started and finished each day of the week. These reports will clearly show just what I have reported.

Washington, D.C., November 23, 1936

Dear Sir:

At your suggestion we are addressing you under the name you have given us, in order that you may have acknowledgement of your letter of November 12 addressed to the Secretary of Labor.

We appreciate very much the fact that you have made a frank report of the conditions existing in the great Atlantic and Pacific Tea Company. It is unfortunate that at the present time, as you probably know, the Federal Government can take no action on behalf of these workers. You have not mentioned the employment of women in your letter, but if you know of instances in which women are employed in excess of the legal hours and below the minimum wages established by Massachusetts law, we suggest that you report the matter direct to Mr. James T. Moriarty, Commissioner, Department of Labor and Industries, Statehouse, Boston. I am quite sure that an anonymous complaint would receive the attention of the Department. The problem of the part-time worker whose few hours of work are spread over a long period of hours during the day is one which should certainly be given consideration. The application of hour laws to men has been very limited in the past, but within the last few years there has been increasing interest, as evidenced by the number of bills introduced into State legislatures. We can only hope that as public interest becomes aroused to the need of conserving the health of workers and also to the need for spreading employment, more States will act to provide hour laws for men.

We are very glad to have your letter, which is valuable in furnishing evidence of the need for considering hour and wage standards for men, as well as for women.

VERNE A. ZIMMER

New York City, January 30, 1938

My dear Mr. President:

Please pardon me for the abrupt manner in writing you, but I would like to advise you of a condition that exists in the White Collar Class.

I am thirty-five years of age, have dependents and have been employed by the Johns-Manville Corporation for the past four years. My salary as an auditor is the most wonderful compensation of $125.00 a month. This salary is really no compensation, for all the schooling you go through preparing yourself for your life's work.

For the past month, they (Johns-Manville Corporation) have let about 40 men and women go. The remaining employees are being worked plenty with much overtime. In my case as in many more employed by the company, I am working until 10 pm, four nights a week and all day Saturday to the tune of 58 hours a week, without any additional compensation, except the customary $1.00 supper money. Why is it, Mr. President, the larger the company the less respect they have for their employees? Why should a condition like this exist?

I, as well as many others, know, to organize the White Collar Class is most impossible, but why shouldn't Congress pass laws to eliminate these big corporation sweatshops. Why not have a law that offices will be obliged to cease at a certain hour and if they wish to remain open for overtime to pay their employees a reasonable compensation for their overtime. I believe it will aid a great deal in reducing the unemployed among the White Collar Class. It will insure the happiness and fair returns for our labor giving us a right to live — not exist.

I humbly ask of you to keep this letter confidential until I can make the necessary change to give me happiness and a right to live.

J. P. P.

"Help Us the People Who Work Underground": Miners

Mining has always been the most dangerous of occupations, but the conditions faced by miners in the United States have been especially harsh. At the turn of the century, the death rates of miners in England, Germany, and France hovered around 1.5 per 1,000 workers; in the United States during the same period, more than 3 miners per 1,000 lost their lives every year. Between 1902 and 1915, more than 200 American workers lost their lives every year in mine disasters, and in one year, 1907, 920 miners were killed. Between 1922 and 1930, an average of 282 miners died in accidents every year. While several states enacted legislation designed to stem the flow of blood, mining maintained its reputation for danger. The federal government entered the mine safety field in 1910 with the creation of the Bureau of Mines. Rather than seeking to regulate the industry, however, it acted as a research, educational, and training agency for the mining companies. The law establishing the bureau specifically denied it any right or authority in connection with the inspection or supervision of mines in any state.[9] It was not until 1941 that the Bureau of Mines received authority to inspect mines without securing the permission of the owners.

As the production of coal and other minerals declined during the De-

[9]William Graebner, *Coal Mining Safety in the Progressive Period* (Lexington: Press of the University of Kentucky, 1976), p. 32.

pression, the average number of mine deaths fell to 52 a year. With increased demand for war production in the early 1940s, the number of miners did not increase but their hours and output did, and so did the dangers of the job, especially after experienced miners entered the armed forces and were replaced by inexperienced workers. Between 1940 and 1945 the average number of mine deaths increased to more than 136 a year.[10]

Even though conditions in the mines had supposedly improved by the 1930s, the following letters reveal that miners lived in terror of underground disasters and management intimidation.

Minnesota, April 8, 1937

Dear Madam [Perkins]:

I live on the Missabe Iron Range in Minnesota and must write you some facts as industrial conditions are getting worse. We have nearby the Vermillion and Cuyuna iron ranges. These three produce nearly all of the country's iron ore. The miners have no unions on any of these ranges, therefore, no protection from the unscrupulous employers. These employers are mainly the Oliver Iron Mining Co. and the Pickands, Mather Co. These companies have shown themselves to be antagonistic to our government, and care nothing for progress. We were expecting unionization of the miners this spring, but late reports from our state legislature are that no assistance toward unionization will come from the legislature. Therefore our mines are again working six days a week and may work Sundays also during the active ore season. They did last Fall.

Now, here is a strong point. For three years, until last Fall these mines worked five days a week. Last Fall during the heated campaign they again began the six and seven day week as of old, working the men like machines. They became more hostile to the government. They worked the six day week all winter. They also scared the men to vote for six days. When these non-union men hear that the company wants a six day week they dare not say a word against it, as they would be fired. The last two summers the men felt they were safe and voted strong at the mine for the 5 day week. 90% of the miners are for a 5 day week. These companies may now tell Congress a different story as the men have been intimidated and

---

[10]Daniel Curran, "Dead Laws for Dead Men: The Case of Federal Coal Mine Health and Safety Legislation," Ph.D. dissertation, University of Delaware, 1980, pp. 41–42.

may vote contrary to their own wishes. That is the way the companies
fooled the Government in 1917. Here are the facts as we workers understood them. President Wilson proclaimed the 8 hour day throughout the
land, as we working ten hours. We did like to get the 8 hour day. The
companies did not want to grant the 8 hour day then any more than they
want to give the 40 hour week now. So they sent a report to Washington
that the men want the ten hour day, because they will pay the men time
and a half for overtime. We did not know the men were asked at all. They
never asked us. I am sure they lied to Congress or the President. They
paid time and a half for the overtime but everything went sky-high in
price and the ten hour day stayed for another 15 years or so. They are now
doing the same thing to get away from the 5 day week. They are working
six days here and paying time and a half for the sixth day. They are probably telling Congress the men want the overtime to get more money
which is false. The men know wages don't mean so much as prices soar
accordingly and all we get is a bare living. With the 5 day week we have
a chance for recuperation and recreation. We need these as much as
money. We are worn out at 45 and perhaps you are aware these companies will not hire a new man over the age of 45. These firms apparently
are no longer afraid of either the Government or unionization. They intend to work six and seven days a week. $5 per day is the minimum wage
and the time and a half scheme is again in play. This brings the lowest
pay to $135 per month. If there is anything we can bank on it is that the
dealers will boost prices in accordance with this $135 per month mini-
mum earning power of the miners. Where will this put the W.P.A. workers earning $60.50 per month? The W.P.A. workers here out-number the
mine workers. If the miners are to get $135 low per month, W.P.A. work-
ers will need to get at least $100 per month, to live.

The only way out is to force the Oliver Iron Mining Co. and Pickands,
Mather & Co to abide very strictly by the 5 day week plan, by cancelling
all Government orders for steel products put out by these firms. No orders should be given them before they discontinue the 6 day week. Did
they tell Congress or the President that the men want the 6 day week?
When did they start complying with the wishes of the men? I've worked
30 years at the mines and never realized they were so eager to abide by
our wishes.

The local Pickands, Mather open pit mine last season put out 670,000
tons of high grade iron ore in 7 months with 65 men. No cooperation
with the Government. They will not keep a single worker above absolute
necessity, lay men off for several days and have them on a day as badly

needed. In the old days this was not done, when a man was hired in the Spring he worked steady thru the ore season. Now, every work counts with the company, their profit system is highly developed. The men are laid off about Nov. 20 and stay off 5 months to live on relief. The men drawing $25,000 to $1,000,000 yearly salary get a big bonus for a good ore season after the workers have sweated blood. Their bonus is starvation for the winter. How is that for the old U.S.A. And the only way to get at them is not to give them orders. Money talks with them. All they can see is money. Their system will bring a shooting bee if not checked. They bring in new labor saving devices yearly thus relief ranks will swell. If we have the 5 day week, more of the steel these companies sell will be used. The 5 day week gives the workers time for recreation which will use up more steel products. Don't they see this or don't care. Seems to me they are just hostile, get that way worse last fall. The 5 day week was going along fine until the campaign. The Oliver I. M. Co. and Pickands, Mather will fire a worker, have done so, if he isn't a good Republican or belongs to a union. Are these the fellows who bellow so loud for the Constitution? They make profits with the 8 hour day and can make plenty with 5 day week. No excuses there on grounds of seasonal operation. A shorter week is the only way out, or there will be shooting. I'm in U.S.A. but can't sign as the Missabe range isn't Americanized yet. I do not know who will get this letter first and I have no right to sign, as these companies have spies, even underground. They are playing their own game. They do not seem to need to care for the country or the people. Only profit. Sometimes I wish it would come to a shooting match. They don't want W.P.A. and they don't want to give the people work. They are millionaires, still very foolish. Which goes to prove that wealth doesn't mean sense.

Would like to sign, although a worker's signature has no weight. Have given the bare facts which should be all that really counts. Perhaps this letter should go the rounds. Hope the Government will investigate the Minnesota iron ranges. Why did these mines have the 5 day week for 3 or 4 seasons and now start the 6 day week again, and perhaps 7 day, with more labor saving devices than before? These mines are now adopting a new conveyer system of loading ore which will increase output with still less men.

It now seems clear these mining companies will not cooperate with the Government. For 3 years they had the 5 day week and now they are again working 6 days just when the 5 day week is more imperative than ever. They will work the 6 day week all season unless stopped.

About 9,000 men will work on the three ranges. To date they have hired no men off W.P.A. although half have applied. The mayor went to see about this and was told that W.P.A. men already have jobs. They hire single men and reject married men who are on W.P.A. If these mines are permitted to work the 6 day week and their men earn a minimum of $135 a month, prices will soar and W.P.A. workers at $60 per month will suffer. These mining officials seem prejudiced against W.P.A. workers and the Government. They should be taken to task. These companies will drive the men one hard season, including Sundays, then lay them off for another 2 years.

New Deal Booster

Mahanoy City, Pennsylvania, January 30, 1940

Miss Perkins:

I am trying to find out something about the Workmens Compensation Law that was signed by Gov. James concerning the Occupational disease law. I am one of those sufferers from working in the mines over 30 years and my case is the one that they have up for a test case and was awarded twice already. Now I do not know what it is gone to, the last award I got was in Sep. 1939. they have awarded me up to Sept. 23, 1939, and signed by the commission board and it was affirmed by them so I wish you would please try and find out for me and the other suffers whether we will get anything out of it I do not see if it is a law and the state set up a 100,100 fund towards it and the law came into affect Oct. 1, 1939. I do not see why the state does not take some action on it and try and help us men out and pay there share for we have reaped the cream for the Coal Co. and they are trying to get out of it now if they do not abide by the laws that are made why should we abide by them. I think it is soon time that the American people sit up and take notice and see that they put people into office that will make all good Americans abide by the laws that are made so please let me know if you can and give me some information so that I know something about the law.

F. M. S.

Beech Creek, Kentucky, October 29, 1940

Dear Miss Perkins:

Flocks of miners are being thrown out of employment and added to the relief roles by mechanical loading machines. Not because of modern progress, but modern "barbarism."

Mechanical loaders are out of place under the ground. With the noise they make it is impossible for the top to give you any warning. Whereby a handloader can hear it break and has a chance to get out of the way.

At the mines of the Pacific Coal Co. Central City, Ky., since the installation of mechanical loaders (which has been a very short time) one man's lifeless body has been brought to the surface. No telling the ones that have been injured, broken limbs etc. It's really pitiful that a man can't earn a living for his family without his life being at stake from the time he enters the pit until he returns. Not saying anything about the almost unendurable and unbearable hardships he has to endure.

. . . I have good explainable reasons to believe that most of the mechanization of the mines is done to throw the employees on the W.P.A. to try to fight President Roosevelt's Administration.

This letter has the endorsement of this local union and I believe that an investigation will prove that it voices the sentiment of this entire district. We are giving you the facts about mechanical loading in hopes that there might be some procedure that you could make against it.

BEECH CREEK LOCAL UNION #188
W. C. R.

Blaine, Ohio, November 14, 1940

Dear [President Roosevelt]:

I feel that it is my duty to write and let you know how things are here. Our Governor hasn't done one thing for us. The day after election the Mine went dead the bosses made the coal loaders take their tools out of the mine and they are letting the machines do all the work. The people that has families they won't give them their jobs back and the ones that are single they give them work. And the houses that we have to live in they are not hardly good enough for a dog to live in. The company won't just won't come right out and fire the men they have the doctor to turn them down and the men are getting hurt and killed by these machines. We feel that you can help us. So many men have been getting hurt and killed they stop putting it in the paper. The way you can find out these things just send someone out here to investigate and find out for yourself. So we are depending on you to help us. . . . I wouldn't like to have this published because they might throw us out. So we are looking to you.

MRS. M. T.

Reliance, Wyoming, March 2, 1941

My Dear Mr. President:

The miners are notified that they will not give us six hours. That is what Mr. McCaulix President of the Union Pacific Coal Co. Reports. We don't want long hours when we work 2 days a week. Besides its all machinery in the mines. It also kills the people which work in the mines. We live like dogs two days and three days a week. In short words a Miners Life is a Dog Life. We all the miners supported or voted for Mahoney he promised to discard the Machinery from the mines & every day they're adding more. Every five men have 1 pusher, and they sure do push us for the solid seven hrs.

Please Mr. President help us the people who work underground.

I am a supporter of yours & a very respected American citizen.

A RELIANCE RESIDENT

I don't want to sign my name because the minute they hear of me writing to you Mr. President they'll fire me. I mean the company I work for.

Pana, Illinois, January 26, 1942

Dear Miss Perkins:

The Penwell Coal Mining Co. employing about 250 men has been closed for the past ten months. Several buyers have tried to purchase this mine but each time the deal did not succeed. The mine members here have had many meetings and offered the best propositions that could be offered but everything went without success for some strange reason.

This mine is what we call a hand loading mine while the other mines in the state are mechanized. This mine could be semi-mechanized. The mechanized mines can produce coal much cheaper than the hand loading mines. Therefore the markets we held in the past gradually slipped away from us so that the operator had to close his mine. This Penwell Coal Co. is in a good and safe condition.

This mine when in operation will produce fifteen hundred tons of coal daily and if we could get this mine to reopen it would mean a great deal to the miners and their families. It would also mean a payroll of several thousands of dollars that the miners would spend with the merchants, thereby helping the city in which they live in.

A good many of the miners are at the age of 40 to 65, where they can not go out and seek other employment. They can work as hard as any of the younger men but they are doomed to idleness because of their age and finances. Many of the men have their homes here, too.

Now with the country at war I thought there might be some way found to reopen this mine giving the miner the right to work in order to provide for his family and not be forced to go on relief, which almost seems impossible to secure.

This town, of 6000 population can be saved if something can be done and we hope, Miss Perkins, you can in some way, by the aid of the government, help to reopen this mine.

Each and every member is a loyal citizen of the United States. We could help so much in buying Defense Bonds, etc. if we could work in this mine.

We shall appreciate anything that you can do for us and also an early reply.

Thank you.

V. V., Pres. of Local #56
J. K., Financial Sect. of Local #56
Progressive Miners of America

"The Farm Laborer, They Get Nothing"

Like workers in the cotton textile industry, American farmers rarely shared in the prosperity of the 1920s. As one scholar has recently pointed out, there were "too many small inefficient producers who lacked the capital, equipment, and talent needed to farm in a society subject to sudden changes."[11] Throughout the 1920s, farmers faced shrinking markets as the birth rate declined, food habits changed, and foreign markets dried up. The problems created by a declining birth rate were exacerbated by the reduction in demand for corn, barley, and rye during Prohibition. The use of barley, for example, declined by 90 percent between 1922 and 1927. The consumption of lamb and chicken fell in those years as well. The conservation campaigns during World War I and the growing emphasis on a "healthy diet" led to an increase in consumption of fruits and vegetables as substitutes for grains and meats. At the same time, the development of rayon and other synthetic fabrics caused hardship for cotton growers. By the beginning of the Depression, the farm sector of the economy was in disarray. The inability of small farmers to adapt quickly and efficiently to the changing demands of the marketplace led to over-

---

[11]Theodore Saloutos, *The American Farmer and the New Deal* (Ames: Iowa State University Press, 1982), p. 14.

production and dropping prices. Many farmers found themselves on the brink of bankruptcy even before the stockmarket crash of 1929 threw the entire economy into a tailspin.[12]

When the Depression hit, farmers were pushed over the edge. Between 1929 and 1933, farmers' incomes declined 50 percent while farm prices dropped nearly 60 percent. At the same time, an onslaught of natural disasters—drought, locusts, erosion—staggered the farm belt. Between 1930 and 1933 nearly one third of all farms in the country were sold or auctioned off. By 1935 more than 3 million farm workers had been forced into mass migration.

The New Deal sought to ameliorate this agricultural crisis through the Agricultural Adjustment Act (AAA), which provided for payments to farmers who agreed not to grow certain crops in order to force prices up. Prices did rise, but the country was aghast to learn that millions of acres were being plowed under and that 6 million baby pigs were slaughtered while much of the nation went hungry. In the end, the AAA benefited the large commercial farmers and hastened the decline of the family farm. Many displaced farm workers went to work for large producers and faced the problems vividly described in John Steinbeck's *Grapes of Wrath*. Others worked for a bare subsistence in smaller, specialized operations. The conditions they faced were appalling, as these letters testify.

Plaquemine, Louisiana, July 27, 1937

Dear Miss Perkins:

I am writing to you because I think you are pretty square to the average laboring man. but I am wondering if anyone has told you of the cruel and terrible condition that exist in this part of the country or the so called sugar cane belt in Lousiana. I am sure that it hasn't made any progress or improvement since slavery days and to many people here that toil the soil or saw mills as laboring men I am sure slavery days were much better for the black slaves had their meals for sure three times a day and medical attention at that. but if an American nowadays had that much he is a communist I am speaking of the labor not the ones that the government give a sugar bounty too but the real forgotten people for the ones the government give the sugar bounty too are the ones that really don't need it for those same people that has drawn the sugar bonus for two years has

[12]Edward C. Higbee, *Farms and Farmers in an Urban Age* (New York: Twentieth Century Fund, 1963).

never gave an extra penny to their white and black slaves labor. I will now make an effort to give you an idea of the terrible inhuman condition.

I will first give you the idea of the sugar cane tenants and plantations poor laboring people. The bell rings at 2 a.m. in the morning when all should really be sleeping at rest. they work in the summer until 9 or 10 a.m. the reason they knock them off from the heat is not because of killing the labor from heat but they are afraid it kills the mule not the slave. Their wages runs from 90¢ to $1.10 per day. Their average days per week runs from three to four days a week in other words people that are living in so called United States have to live on the about $4.00 per week standing of living in a so called American Community which is way below the Chinese standard of living for the Chinese at least have a cheaper food and clothing living but here one has to pay dear for food and clothing because these sugar cane slave owners *not* only give inhuman wages but the ones that work for them have to buy to their stores, which sells from 50 per cent to 60 per cent higher than the stores in town still these same people that are worst than the old time slave owners or yelling and hollering for more sugar protection, why should they get more when they don't pay their white and black slaves more. It is true they give the white and black slaves a place to live on. But Miss Perkins if you were to see these places they live on you'd swear that this is not our so call rich America with it high standing of living for I am sure that the lowest places in China or Mexico or Africa has better places to live in. These Southern Senators which are backed by the big shots will tell you it is cheaper to live in the South but have you investigated their living condition. Sometimes I don't wonder why some of these people don't be really communism but they are true Americans only they are living in such a low standing of living that one wouldn't believe they are living in the good old U.S.A.

Now regarding the saw mills of this town and other towns in this section but most particular this town they pay slightly more than the plantation but they get it back by charging more for food & clothing which they have to buy in their stores.

I am writing you this hoping that you will try to read it and understand the situation which if you think is not true you can send an investigator in this section of Louisiana that has American freedom of speech for some hasn't that speech in our so called free America and if you can get in touch with people who are not concern about it I am sure you will see that I am right and I do hope that you are kind enough to give this your carefully attention and I am sure that President Roosevelt nor Mrs. Roosevelt nor you would like to see this terrible and inhuman condition go on worst now then old slavery days for I know you people believe in the real American standing of living.

Again I will call your attention if you don't believe of the slave wages condition in this lost part of U.S. investigate and you will find out. Thanking you for humanity sake.

R. J.

Weston, Ohio, March 2, 1937

Dear Miss Perkins:

In hope that there is someway out of the situation in which we find ourselves, I'm sending you a letter. Please read & consider it.

There is help for men in almost every walk of life in America but the lowly farmhand. The farmer has his from the government, the shop worker, the rail-roader, in fact every working man but the farm laborer. They get nothing.

My husband works from 6 to 7 a.m. doing chores from 8 a.m. to 12 noon takes his hour then works till 6 p.m. gets $35 per mo. a very poor house to live in a garden 200 ft. sq. and 1 gal. of scimed or separated milk a day.

On this we must feed & cloth 4 children. Understand this is for 10 mo. The first of Jan. he is out of work completely.

How can this be a land of opportunity for our children if they must grow up under conditions like that? It seems to me there should be some better way for the Farm Laborer.

You see, this is only one of many cases throughout the country.

Farmers have their swell cars, their fancy meals, their nice cloths But the man who makes their money gets scarcely enough to eat.

How can we give our children a decent chance on such conditions?

Maby you, I hope you Miss Perkins sees this instead of one of your staff looking at it and tossing it in the waste basket, can see if something can be done.

Please do something for the Farm Laborers.

In hopes of better times

MRS. J. B. T.

Andover, Massachusetts, March 5, 1935

My dear Miss Perkins:

I am uncertain as to whom I should address this letter, but since it is a labor problem, and the N.I.R.A. group is so involved, I am sending it to you.[13]

There are several questions I wish to ask, for although I am certain of the wrongness of the situation, I am not quite sure of some of the legal points.

I am giving the name of the company, for I think if inspectors do come through the district, the company is worthy of consideration.

I now present the case, my questions will follow its presentation.

Mr. William Kroemer of Hicksville, *Long Island, New York* owns and manages, with the aid of his two sons, a *small retail seed business*. Although his headquarters are in Long Island, his activities are not *confined* to that section of the east. Up to ten days ago he had not signed any N.I.R.A. code. He employs eight to ten men as laborers, the number varies. They are *non*-union. Their supposed hours of work are from 7:00 A.M. to 12:00 noon, and from 1:00 P.M. to 5:00 P.M. for six days a week. The men work overtime nearly every day—sometimes until 10:00 P.M. without supper and without extra pay. Those men who take their luncheon do not get a full hour at noon. Occasionally they have to work on Sunday. They are not *asked* to work overtime but *commanded* and they dare not resist the command for fear of losing their jobs. There is no whistle gong or time clock for the laborers. (There is a clock in the company's office, but the laborers do not work in that part of the building.) The managers of the company give the time signal and that comes when the job at hand is completed. Frequently a new task is begun at 4:30 P.M. making its completion impossible by 5:00 P.M. Frequently the hardest jobs, such as loading potatoes and the like, are given at the end of the day.

Potatoes which come from northern Maine are covered with a powdery clay. The men shovel and sort these potatoes in an unventilated basement. One man opened a window one day and the manager promptly closed it. The men suffer from heavy colds caused by this dust. No respirators are given them to use.

There is irregular "docking" during illness.

[13]On May 27, 1935, less than three months later, the National Industrial Recovery Act was declared unconstitutional by the Supreme Court in the case of *Schecter Poultry Corp.* v. *United States*.

One laborer for this company, in order to retain his job, was forced to move from northern Maine to Long Island. He did not receive his traveling expenses, nor his pay for the week he moved.

Conversation with two men revealed that the company induced them to leave jobs which paid them better for the ones they now have. Better positions and chances of promotion were the inducements. Because jobs are scarce they dare not leave. They are so afraid of their jobs that if questioned by inspectors they would doubtless say they were satisfied.

The company presents a nice appearance.

Now for my questions:

Is there at this time any code for the *small* seed businesses?

Are there any laws which state how long the laborers in the seed business shall be required to work? (that is how many hours per week)

Are there any laws pertaining to this peculiar situation of sanitation, that of inhaling dust unnecessarily?

I have given a Massachusetts address as I am about to move from Long Island to Massachusetts.

Mrs. C. H. R.

Farmers, forced by the seasons and the demands of agricultural production, worked from dawn to dusk. As this letter indicates, sometimes they did not understand the problems of industrial wage earners.

Jerome, Utah, April 19, 1942

Dear Miss Perkins:

As I read the pros and cons on the Labor Situation, I can't help but feel very indignant. We people that have had to put in 16 or 17 hours a day on a farm working hard with no vacations feel that the demands of labor are far too great. They talk about increase in the cost of living. Why this increase? It is mostly the increase of labor wages that increase the cost of living. And we who have watched the labor unions and know what they are doing have seen for many years what we were coming to. Labor rules our nation. A good many of the administration members are afraid to do anything for fear the unions will rebel. 48 hours a week is short enough day for anybody and at regular pay for all over time. We can not afford to give labor so much. They get extravagent wages anyway and it is enough for overtime too. If they wont work put them in the army and then there would be as much work done as there has been with so many strikes.

Good wages for all, coal diggers miners and so on but not extravagant wages for any should be the rule and it should be fixed up *now* while there is a chance *for all time* not just until the duration of the war. Farmers need increases in price of products raised for they have raised crops below the cost of expense for the past several years. Men are charging $1.20 an hour and we can't afford to pay that we old people who have just a little to live on can't afford such prices for repairing homes, etc. and as I think of it there was the Townsend Bill that was such a splendid idea for recovery.[14] The people seem not to grasp the main point in the bill. It would have given employment to close to 8,000,000 people besides the help we old people need to do things we can't do anymore. It would take care of the W.P.A. I wouldn't have been needed at all. Taken care of most of charity and stopped petty thieving and made so many happy why wasn't it passed? Politics. I wish the men and women in high office could see and live for a while the struggles of the poorer class.

E. G. H.

[14]The Townsend Plan, originated by Dr. Francis E. Townsend of California, would have provided a monthly pension of $200 to every American citizen over age 60, with the proviso that the entire amount must be spent each month. The funds for the pensions were to be provided by a 2 percent tax on all monetary transactions. The plan won many adherents.

3. *"Very Dangerous to Humanity"*

Health and Safety on the Job

In its most basic form, the struggle between labor and capital for control of the means of production has set the context within which safety and health programs and policies have developed. The great labor struggles of the late nineteenth and early twentieth centuries revolved around wages, hours, and working conditions. Labor organizers understood that an underpaid, overworked, and poorly fed worker was more likely to be injured or incapacitated on the job: a machinist who worked twelve to fourteen hours a day could not stay alert enough to avoid injury from unguarded machinery in unlighted, noisy, humid factories; miners found their lives under constant threat from speedups, explosions, dust, and suffocation. Nearly every major strike in modern American history, from the railroad strikes of 1877 through the Flint auto workers' sitdowns of 1937 to the United Mine Workers' strike of 1977, has sought to eliminate conditions that jeopardize workers' health and safety. Employers, fearing loss of control over production and the costs of improving work conditions, have traditionally resisted concessions and placed the blame for accidents and disease on the workers themselves. As the letters in this chapter reveal, workers were not blind to the life-threatening conditions in which they labored. They argued that management had the power to improve those conditions and the primary responsibility for doing so.

Concern over working conditions reached a peak in the first decade of the twentieth century, in the wake of the revolutionary social and economic changes the United States had just undergone. Speedups, monotony, and exposure to toxic chemicals, dust, and unprotected machinery made the American workplace among the most dangerous in the world. The enormous wealth produced by the new industrial plants was achieved at an inordinate social cost.

In the early twentieth century, unions and middle-class reformers based their campaigns to protect the work force on the proposition that cleaning up the workplace and keeping workers healthy benefited the public as well as the worker. The prevalence of contagious diseases among the working class—diphtheria, influenza, tuberculosis, typhoid—spurred middle-class consumer groups to take up the issue of health conditions on the job and in the home. The appeal was based partly on the fear that middle- and upper-class consumers might be infected by goods tainted by sick workers. The garment industry of New York City became a focus of such fears. As many dresses, shirts, and trousers were sewn on a piecework basis in workers' tenement apartments, what was to prevent the diseases prevalent in the slums from being transmitted to the people who bought and wore those garments? It was this fear that led the National Consumers League to become active in tenement reform and antituberculosis campaigns. Its label on goods, along with that of the International Ladies' Garment Workers Union, came to be recognized as the mark of clothing manufactured under hygienic conditions.

The campaign took a conservative turn in the 1920s as the National Safety Council, a coalition of professional and business groups, assumed the leadership of efforts to reform working conditions. Its general proposition was that "safety pays": employers would benefit economically by taking the lead in accident prevention. Industry argued that improvements in plant safety required two major programmatic changes: first and most important, workers had to be educated to avoid accidents; second, the responsibility for educating them should be assumed by experts in the newly emerging field of industrial medicine who understood the overall needs of industrial production. "Safety first" advocates no longer saw the workplace as part of a larger social and economic environment, nor did they see it as in need of the substantial reorganization advocated by earlier generations of progressive reformers. The task of protecting the work force was to be entrusted to people knowledgeable in the emerging field of occupational medicine and specifically to the company physician. An article in *Scientific American* predicted in 1917 that "the physician will . . . be confessor, advisor, priest. Through him the employee may learn that it pays to be healthy, steady, and of good habits. He does not hesitate to preach the 'Sober First' campaign."[1] During the 1920s, hundreds of companies hired physicians, nurses, and engineering personnel to oversee workers' health and safety. As the control of workplace hazards came to be dominated by experts in industrial hygiene and engineering, the workplace lost its central place in the broad perspectives of progressives and labor reformers.

Until the New Deal, nearly all governmental regulation of occupational health and safety had been carried out at the state and local levels, and safety codes and enforcement practices varied widely. They were more stringent in the urban North than in the agricultural South. States that were not receptive to labor unions were equally unreceptive to efforts to protect workers' health and safety.

Except for the insights we may gain from union pronouncements on workplace conditions, most research on workers' health and safety before the New Deal must rely on documents generated by management and by state and local governments. With the coming of the New Deal, however, workers began to voice their concerns directly to the federal government. When we begin to hear from workers themselves, we find that safety and health issues were central to their lives. Unionized workers translated their concerns regarding safety and health into contractual terms. A survey conducted for the U.S. Department of Labor in 1939 revealed that about 25 percent of the 7,000 union contracts on file contained clauses dealing expressly with the prevention of accidents and industrial diseases. Of the contracts covering iron and steel workers, 85 percent contained such clauses; of the twenty-eight contracts covering workers in asbestos plants, in contrast, none contained such provisions.[2]

"A Cripple for the Rest of His Life": Accidents and Compensation

Before the twentieth century, workers were offered a minimum of protection by a variety of statutes that addressed very specific workplace conditions. The Progressive era brought demands for a more systematic approach to curbing the excesses of industrial capitalism. Perhaps the most important legislative effort in this regard took the form of workers' com-

[1]Otto P. Geier, "The Human Potential in Industry," *Scientific American Supplement* 84 (December 22, 1917): 386.

[2]Dimock to Secretary of Labor, May 26, 1939, National Archives, RG 174, Department of Labor, Office of the Secretary, "Labor Standards, General, 1939."

pensation laws. In the decade after 1911, twenty-five states passed laws that guaranteed some form of financial compensation to workers injured on the job and to their families. Employees gave up the right to sue an employer in return for prompt and sure compensation for an accident incurred on the job, regardless of who was at fault. Proponents argued that the trade-offs for labor and management were equal: labor would not have to bear the burden of industrial accidents and management would not be faced by unpredictable and possibly extremely high costs. Furthermore, experience-based insurance premiums would give management an incentive to improve working conditions. Opponents argued that workers' compensation was unfair to laborers, who would be denied redress through the courts for life-threatening conditions at work; that the premium incentives were not sufficient to induce managers to clean up their plants; and that significant plant improvements would be so costly that they would not be carried out. Statistics on workplace accidents during the 1920s and early 1930s tend to bear out the latter argument. During the early years of the Depression, as companies sought to cut costs in the face of falling profits, safety improvements were among the first casualties. As our letters indicate, unscrupulous employers blocked efforts to protect worker's safety and health and evaded compensation payments. Even the steel industry, which had claimed to have made the greatest progress in the "safety first" campaigns of the 1920s, sought to undermine the compensation system.

When we think of the hazards that workers face, we often think of chemicals or unguarded machinery. As the following letter shows, speedups also constituted a severe hazard. Along with unsafe conditions went management harassment and disrespect for workers. The letter is neatly but not very accurately typed.

Muskegon, Michigan, February 3, 1935

To Whom it may concern:

I wish to draw your attention, to the some of the most terriblest conditions, that prevail here, in the foundry of the Company known as Campbell, Wyant, and Cannon. These conditions certainly must be looked into, one very dangerous feture of this foundry is that the men's lives are in constant danger of being burned to death or by a heavy load dropping and crushing them to death, sinse all heavy loads of iron flask's, sand, and core's and ladle's of molden metal weighing a ton, pass over the men's head's by crane, this dangerous operation is going on all during the working hours, this is very dangerous to humanity and certainly ought to be stopped. I have worked under these conditions, and have been burned from spark's of iron, when these crane's would pass over our head's and in regards to working conditions, in this foundry they are awful, for example, I will illustrate some of my own experience, myself and another man, were working on a job, which required about twelve finished mold's in eight hours this job I worked on several month's ago, when we made twelve in eight hours, recently the same job came in, the two of us were required to make twelve, then rushed us until we had to make twenty, with the addition of one more man, I was advised by the forman that the Superintendent, expected the three of us, to make twenty mold's in eight hours, he allso advised me if we made more than twenty we would get piece work rates, which would be more than, the hourly rates we were receiving, finally we were forced, to make twenty five mold's for three of us, with the aid of the forman hurrying us up and after making twenty mold's each day the job was rushed out, we got no extra pay, no piece work, but was laid off, this kind of business will not help labor conditions, or bring back prosperity, but it is a menace to humanity, please do something, and try put a stop to such working conditions, and the dangerous conditions the human being's work under in this factory, I returned to work after being rushed out of a job, and being idle for one week, but this time, after returning to work, I found conditions much terrible, I started work again Monday morning February 28th, and therefore the week was over, the new forman I was working under, was hitting and pounding me with his fists, this forman who's name is H. C., had been cussing me from the very first day I started to work under him, Monday, February 28th, about the first thing he told us, was that we had to get sixty mold's a day, there were two men making the molds on the machine, which was allmost impossible for them to do, to make sixty in eight hours, there was three of us men, to set all the cores, and close the molds, and move the molds by crane, onto the floor and get them ready, for the metal, but the first day, sixty was out of reason, it could not be done we made about forty four, the second day Feb. 29th, we had to speed up to fifty molds, these two first days were eight hour days, these dates should read January, as per my mistake Feb The third day January 30th, we were forced to work nine and quarter hours in order to push out sixty molds, On Thursday morning January 31st, I was going about my work as usal, when a cussing voice came, and a jerk at my cloths, it way this forman, C., he cussed me, and said, come

out here and look at the scrap, he took me alone, out to see the scrap, out
in another department, I was shown one scrap casting, which was a small
four cilinder motor, I tried to explain to this brute that it may have not
alltogether, been the fault of mine, while he was cussing me something
awful, I mentioned the fact that it was the first defect, in any casting but
my explaination was of no avail, while this brute, was cussing and damn-
ing me, and telling me to get the hell out of here, I could not stand that
abuse, and I resented his remark's, I in no way abused his feelings as he
did my feelings, but when I told him to use reason, he without warning
struck me in the mouth and beat me, on the back as I seeked to avoid
trouble, I went to the Superintendent, to explain what had happened, the
Superintendent, V., told me if I could not get along with the forman,
they didnt want me around, whereas he told me to get my time, and get
out, which I did I took the case up with the Justice of Peace, and was advised to see the Prosecuter which I did, the Prosecuter advised to start a
civil suit, it seemed he did not care to issue a warrant but he did advise
me, to get in contact with the Labor board, I have contacted several authorities, and have finally been advised, to write the Dept of labor an
industry at Washington, these certainly are deplorable conditions to
work under, and to have officials uphold such brutality as this, this same
forman who hit me has the name for that kind of business, I have heard
him cuss and swear at others, to speed them up, if this is fair justice, we
certainly are drifting back to slave day's I wish to allso state that one of
the men that was working with me, when I was on the former job, of
twenty five a day, when this job was out he was fired out for good, for
the simple reason he had a little hard luck with a mold, I further wish
state, that this job, where we used to make twelve for eight hours, and
then with one more man was forced to make twenty five for eight hours
work we were finally forced to make the twenty five molds in seven
hours, how on earth can such conditions as these, help Mr. Roosevelt
recovery plans in regards to labor, if your Dept, can really only moderate
to some extent, these outragous conditions, if your men would go in
these shops here, and not pay any attention to the shop's owners, just because they are the money side, investigate their selves, see with their own
eyes, talk with the men and then make true reports, to the government, I
know the situation could be remedied a whole lot, I am at your service at
anytime, providing I am living to prove these facts, in regard's to what
I have mentioned, can there not be something done, about this mean
brute of a boss, striking me, when I weigh [one hundred and] twenty
and that tough forman weigh around one hundred and ninety pounds,

we need civiliseation in these shops, and untill the government investigates, and lay's the law down to their owners, things will be no better but will get very bad, I have now been kicked out from this shop, therefore have nothing to lose, but those human beings, remaining there to toil, have lots to gain through government efforts, this certain shop is known as, Campbell, Wyant and Cannon, foundry, Company, located at Stanford Street, Muskegon Heights, Michigan, I wish to remark, that its a question as to weather the respected owners of this concern are aware of these prevailing cruel tactics, used by some of the forman's to force the men to work, allmost beyond their working capacity, but to my estimation, to safe guard the lives of others, I think this advise ought to be worthy of consideration, and if good advise is truthfully handled it may be the means of preventing a great disaster in the future, and may even save the Company great trouble and money, In all fairness to justice, I beg of you an early reply, I again urge you, to see that justice is done in this case.

H. S.

P.S. I wish to state that a man does not ever know how much wages he is going to get, untill he receives his pay check and for the lack of heat in this shop men I know have constantly had colds, I have been down in bed myself working under these conditions.

In the following letter we see the effects of accidents and injuries on the worker's family, especially in a company town where the loss of a job usually meant the loss of a home, medical care, and credit to buy food and other essentials.

Windber, Pennsylvania, June 28, 1939

Dear President:

I have never gone as far as writing to a person of your rank in office however in a case of my own and speaking for my mother & dad also my sisters and brothers which in all does number (8) people now at home.

My brief but very sad problem is one that has me guessing always and I have done all within the requests of the Berwind-White Coal Minning Company and every thing was done as they wanted it done so I am now writting to you and telling you and all persons in these beloved United States my most and a very, very sad matter which has confronted us sometime ago already and a week or more has taken effect upon us with no out-looks at all and my sole reason of writting to you and all of our

law makers or amenders is to show definate but honest proof of unfair labor practices and how they injured employees of this same company are
treated while the remainder are those that are taking strong interest in
union activities and as I see and not often read the "Wagner Law" I see
where it is a violation to these said people and as we have a Labor Relations Board set-up I would very much like to have my case brought-up
and bring results because I can honestly say & swear the truth that you or
probably others out there do not hear of such things or that they are doing so many things that are unfair such as having (thugs) or Company
police. I do know that the law does not allow any person or company to
have these men in disputes or do as the Company tells them to. Well they
do it here and the Company police are paid $125.00 a month by the said
company and doing what they want or please with the people mostly
persons who are injured or those who are taking interest in union affairs.
As soon as they found out that a person knows something in the interest
of the laboring class they bought him out and give him good positions
while others were spied upon from all angles by persons unknown and
later "blackmailed" for even a (simple-reason).

Now regarding my dad: Dad had worked for this same company for
(34) years continuously never moved or worked elsewhere since 1904. He
had a house rented for (27) years and has rented it since 1912 December
15th and never moved elsewhere. He has always paid his rent and never
back a cent. On May 12th 1937 he was injured in the Company's coal-mine
and was injured very badly. The cause of his injury was a punctured lung,
splintered breast bones and other small bones in his chest. This accident
occurred at Eureka mine #36 Windber, Pa where he has worked all this
time while he was discharging off holes and blasting solid rock in heading with dynamite. After his admission to the hospital the doctors had
little hope for his recovery and gave him 72 hours to live. I watched and
witnessed the whole operation as the doctors were going about his chest
and often the doctors put their whole arms inside of his chest. It was bad
to look at and dad was in an unconscious condition for several days.
Whenever he would breathe he would breathe through his wound in the
chest. The would-be dead (meaning my dad) had a wound and a hole
about (8) inches round in his chest. As the operation was done the doctor
asked me whether dad belonged to any church insurances or societies. I
asked why? He answered me in this manner quote: He (meaning my
dad) hasn't a pint of blood inside of himself and I'll have to call the priest
or pastor of his church which the doctor did do and the priest came at
once. It was a sad moment however they did what they could for him and

used so many different items to ease his breathing & pains and little by
little he came through but he isn't able to do any hard work any more as
long as he lives.

We had a compensation case hearing before a union referee at Pittsburgh. Pa and won out. The State and company . . . doctors proved that
he was unable to do any hard labor but maybe could do work of light
character such as a watchman. The doctors advised dad to go for a job of
this type which dad did at once.

The Company made a definite promise that they would secure him this
job as watchman but he had better wait a while till they can place him on
it. Dad didn't want to have any compensation if he got this (watchman's
job). He went for it the week he left from the hospital. They promised
him they would do all they could to suit my dad and promised him this
job as soon as a vacancy occurred.

The Company turned around differently and cut his compensation out
altogether and he didn't get any for a while. We again filed a petition for
another case and won out (300) weeks. The Company got very angry at
this and dismissed me from work without reason or cause. They came to
dad at home and told him (neither he nor I even belong to the Company
anymore) and told him to get out of town at once. I would like to know
if they can do a thing like this without reason or cause. We had trouble right along and still have. On Monday June 26, 1939 they threw my
brother-in-law's furniture outside on the highway and dad's also. My
brother-in-law was living together in dad's home and was willing to pay
rent because he worked and still works for same Company. They refused
him entirely and he made his home with dad for the time being until he
could get a vacant home somewhere now we are all out without any food
or shelter. My sister (my brother-in-law's wife) is expecting to give birth
to a child any moment but the Company didn't care at all of her condition. We are all outside, no home, shelter or food to eat. Our furniture is
being ruined by the rain and will not be fit for use again. The furniture
alone amounts to over $1,000.00 which was bought new in the Compa-
ny's store also. They took my automobile out of the garage. The Company said they don't want cash money customers but (only their employees). We were down for aid and help from the American Red Cross but
they refused us altogether and felt sorry because they could [not] help us
any. My sister is in a critical condition now and from the strain of all this
is taken sick and may give birth to a child (right in the street mind you.)
The Company don't care for this at all. We can't get help or anything at
all from anybody. Is it fair to treat a human being this way. I don't think

so. It is a worse treatment then for a dog. We haven't done anything wrong for the Company nor do we owe them anything at all and I don't think they could (in the name of the law in this land) ever do a thing like this at any time. I say this for the sake of human-life. Do you think that is justice. I don't but I can't do anything myself and I want the government to step right in here at once without any delay and if possible I want to go to the highest court of the land together with the Company as a whole and do as the law states for humanity sake! and the human side of life. I want this done and I'm asking you most heartily to do this. We are all born American citizens and I never neither one of us (10) persons in all ever did commit a crime, arrested or in jail at any one time and further more we are not cattle but should be given some respect and be respected in a human way not treated like a dog. Just because I am a strong fight-ing member in unionism is not saying that I and dad are to get out of town because of that they (Company) hasn't anything to lose in regards (why I am dismissed and why they moved (throwed us out whatever and I am seeking the law and truth of the land.

Today is a different story from the Company they reversed it now. The Company said they (may) but do not promise for sure) that they (might) give my brother-in-law a home (sometime) but dad and mother also 6 children mostly small have to get out of town. I want to know why, rea-son or cause? We are not trespassing on the Company's ground. How can they say this anyway? In closing my dear president we (6) children, mother, dad, sister and brother-in-law are faced with destiny and have only the bare sky for our roof with no shelter or food or medicine on hand. Can you do something? I would like to have this case brought in the highest court because I know its impossible & unfair to do a thing as this. Unfair to labor and unfair as the law is concerned itself. I would like a reply very soon. Thanking you for your time in reading this letter.

I look forward to you to success. Thanks you very much.

J. S. K.

The Company branch office here is Berwind-White Coal Mining Company, Corner 15th street, Somerset Avenue, Windber, Pennsylva-nia—Main Office:—Berwind-White Coal Company Exchange, Chest-nut Street, Philadelphia, Pennsylvania.—Berwind-White Coal Mining Company, 1 Broadway, New York City, New York.

Many companies hired doctors to screen potential employees for dis-eases or injuries that could interfere with their ability to work. Workers injured on the job were often required to pass a physical examination before they could return to work. Such examinations were often manipulated to block the return of workers who could be replaced at less cost to the company.

Linwood, Pennsylvania, January 30, 1940

Dear Miss Perkins:

In 1916 my husband went to work in the Jet room at the American Viscose Corporation, Marcus Hook. That has been just twenty years ago. In 1919 his eyes became infected from the fumes: the working conditions at that time were terrible. He had the doctor tending his eyes and at the same time lost a lot of time from work. When they got better he went back to work in the same department. His eyes became infected the second time.

After this they transferred him to the Wash department: he worked there until the strike was called. He was out for three months this time and one of the very last to get back. When he went back they put him to work on the Dryers in the Finishing department. He worked there up until the last lay off in April 1939 and been out of work ever since. The Company sent for him this time but the Doctor would not pass his eyes, then they sent him to Dr. C. to have his eyes examined. He has never heard a word since then about a month ago.

Mr. J. has also had a dose of Chlorine Gas which caused him to lose time from work. He is forty-six years of age and most certainly not disabled by any means. There are lots of jobs in the Viscose plant that he can do, no other plant will give him work on account of not being able to pass the Doctor's examination.

Miss Perkins don't you think if they were going to do something for him they would have sent for him by now. He has spent twenty four years, the best part of his life, with the Company; that is a long time to work in one plant. The Company knows his eyes are bad and the cause of it, yet they don't seem to do anything for him.

If there is any way you can help him or any information you can give, will you please let us know as soon as possible? I assure you it will be greatly appreciated. Expecting to hear from you soon.

Mrs. C. B. J.

As early as 1910 the steel industry initiated a "safety first" campaign after its high accident rate was exposed in the popular press. Throughout the 1920s industry spokespeople claimed that this campaign had resulted in a dramatic reduction in injuries on the job. As the following letter suggests, however, such claims had little basis in fact. Steel production remained among the most dangerous occupations, and from 1927 through 1933 the frequency of accidents in the industry actually increased.[3]

Aliquippa, Pennsylvania, March 16, 1943

Dear Mrs. Perkins:

I am writing to you concerning my husbands case, he worked for J&L [Jones & Loughlin] in Aliquippa since 1925 up until now, and with a good record. Then in 1930 an accident happend in the department where he worked, he was hurt very badley, had his right ankle broken, so spent 18 months in the hospital, well all he got during that time was $15.00 a week compensation, outside of that nothing else.

His foot had healed but not until they grafted part of the muscle from the left foot on to the hurt ankle, and after that the ankle is stiff, and will be stiff for the rest of his life, it also pains him when ever we have any change of weather, now this is our problem. When he went back to work, he was not put to work in the same place where he worked before he got hurt, as he could not do that sort of work being his ankle was stiff, he asked to be put on an ingot buggy, for he knew that was the very job suitable for him, so after some time he got put on the buggy, and stayed on that job for some time, doing his job well, then about 3 years ago, the Co. had every electrical operator have his eyes examined, well my husband failed that examination, so the doctor said, even after he went to the expense of buying a pair of glasses.

So then they took him of the buggy job and put him in the labor gang and has been there now for the last three years, they told him when they put him there that just as soon as there is an opening in something better they would give him first choice, well he received those promises now for 3 years and still doing labor at $5.80 a day, you can just imagine us, him, myself and two girls age ten & twelve getting along on that, and lately it has been so tough my oldest girl has to be under a good doctors care, as her eyes are very bad, so with my husbands income I am unable to do so. I am desparet, there ought to be some law to protect men under such circumstances, I am fearful that a day may come, when the Co. will do their best to get rid of him altogether, what are we to look forward too.

---

[3]U.S. Department of Labor, Bureau of Labor Statistics, *Handbook of Labor Statistics* (Washington, D.C.: Government Printing Office, 1936), pp. 6, 290.

My husband is only 37 years of age, and has to be a cripple for the rest of his life J&L does not give this a thought, if they put him out where can he get another job? no other firm will take him being he was hurt in J&L but through no fault of his.

Please Mrs. Perkins send me some information as to what I should do, I will forever be grateful to you, to know that I can raise my two daughters and not have to worry how I am going to do it. I myself should be under some Docters care, but have to get along with out it.

Mrs. Perkins I will be anxiously waiting for your reply.

Thank you very much.

MRS. W. E.

"I Got Some Asbestos That Lay in the Lung": Dust Diseases

An environmental and occupational disaster of major proportions has come to light in recent years as tens of thousands of workers have begun to show the effects of massive exposure to asbestos dust during World War II and earlier. Even minute amounts of asbestos inhaled into the lungs can lead to slow, painful death from lung cancer, asbestosis, or mesothelioma. The asbestos industry, having for years required workers to handle this deadly material without adequate protection, has sought by legal and legislative means to evade its responsibility for their suffering. Other occupationally caused diseases, too, have plagued America's workers since before the turn of the century. Silicosis, brown lung, black lung, white lung, and other job-related pneumoconioses have been identified among textile workers and miners for decades. Poisonings from lead, phosphorus, benzene, carbon monoxide, and many other industrial chemicals have also been widely recognized.

The legal system has offered little help to workers in their efforts to prevent industrial diseases and to secure compensation for those afflicted by them. Legislation passed by the various states during the first few decades of the twentieth century provided for compensation for accidents that occurred on the job but rarely covered job-related diseases and never covered illnesses that developed years after initial exposure at the workplace.

During the 1930s the problems of job-related illnesses became especially severe. The tremendous expansion of the American economy and industrial base during the previous decades had brought millions of workers into contact with thousands of new health hazards. As the growth of the auto industry spurred the development of new rubber and petroleum products, workers were exposed to substances whose dangers were barely understood. Rather than test new chemicals and hold them off the market until they had been proved safe, industry sacrificed workers to its own needs. Although some limited attempts were made to control immediately recognizable effects of industrial poisons, almost nothing was done to protect workers from the long-term effects of substances encountered on the job.

Silicosis, a disease of the lungs that slowly chokes its victims by destroying the ability of lung tissue to absorb oxygen, brought the dangers of industrial production to national attention in the 1930s. Silicosis was widespread among granite cutters, tunnel workers, miners, steelworkers, auto workers, and glassblowers, among many others, but most people knew little about it until the bodies of nearly 200 black men were discovered crudely buried in a field at Gauley Bridge, West Virginia. Investigation revealed that the men, employed to build a tunnel, had died of the effects of the silica dust they had been forced to breathe as they drilled through a mountainside. National media attention made the dangers of silicosis in industry the occupational health topic of the day. A government-sponsored colloquium in 1935 brought together technicians, consumers, and representatives of labor, industry, and local governments to discuss for the first time the prevention and treatment of silicosis.

The following letter indicates the difficulty that workers encountered when they sought information regarding the hazards they faced on the job. The swift response from the Department of Labor demonstrates sensitivity to the worker's concerns at the same time that it indicates the government's inability to improve the conditions of which the worker complains. During the 1930s the federal government had little authority to force companies to improve working conditions. The Walsh-Healey Act (1936) authorized direct federal regulation of working conditions only in companies working under contract with the federal government, and its provisions were not widely applied to safety and health regulation until World War II.

Minneapolis, Minnesota, July 26, 1936

Dear Madam [Perkins]:

Am writing in regards to some information in regards to *Silica* in tunnel work. We are working 67 ft underground, and in sandrock which in one place near us tested 98.3 per cent silica. We are also faced with the problem of damp air which is blowed in to us by a fan which is connected to an airphole pipe drilled from the top of the ground. We have one man who had to lay off because of loss of weight, he went to the City Hospital, and they said he had what they call *sandrock poison*. I understand there is no such thing as that, and that is nothing but Silicosis and are afraid to tell him. I would like to know whether there is a poison such as sandrock poison. Would also like to get some information regards to combating the damp air and first aid treatment for Silicosis so we can fight them conditions. I myself carry a first aid certificate from the Bureau of Mines No. 703925F. Any information on this we would like, by all who are working with me as I am the only one which has a first aid card.

A. E.

P.S. Would like an answer as soon as Possible.

Washington, D.C., July 30, 1936

Dear Mr. E.:

Your letter of July 26, addressed to the Secretary, requesting information regarding "sand rock poisoning" affecting tunnel workers; means of controlling the health hazards incident to the exposure of such workers to damp air; and first aid treatment for silicosis, has been referred to this office for a reply.

As regards "sand rock poisoning," it is a new term to us, but often such terms are well understood by the profession in a given locality, being used to denote a condition often known in other localities by an entirely different local name. For instance, silicosis as it develops among potters is sometimes called "potters' rock;" "miners' asthma" is the term used among miners; "stone cutters' phthisis" is used among granite cutters, etc. It is quite possible that physicians in your locality may speak of the disease which results from the inhalation of sandstone dust as "sand rock poisoning."

Exposure to damp atmospheres may affect workers in many different ways. The individual with neuritis or a tendency toward arthritis (disease of the joints) will probably have the condition aggravated. Likewise, those with chronic respiratory disease will experience an increase in this trouble. Workers with no physical defects may develop trouble if proper attention is not given to the type of clothing worn and to personal hygiene.

If the tunnel where you are now working is naturally wet, any air furnished and distributed by fans to the face would be damp air. If the workings are dry, it would seem that the air supplied could be furnished with no marked increase in humidity. In some instances, such as in wet mines and in spinning and weaving departments of textile mills, the dampness cannot be eliminated. Of course, where it is possible to control the humidity practically, such measures should be adopted, and as a matter of fact we usually find these steps taken, if for no other reason than that they increase production.

When we think of what the individual can do to increase his tolerance for exposure to a wet working environment, and to protect himself, if normal, from such exposure, there are two chief factors to consider: First, if the worker must accept such employment, he should correct and watch over any physical defects he may possess. If there are removable foci of infection, such as diseased tonsils or chronic upper respiratory infection, the tonsils should be removed and the infection treated. Excessive use of tobacco and alcoholic beverages should be avoided, since this would increase the susceptibility and lower the resistance. Much benefit can be obtained by wearing proper clothing. Light woolen underwear is much better than cotton or none at all. Sturdy, wind-breaking outer garments, such as the common overall, and lightweight woolen underclothes make for very satisfactory protection from harmful drafts in a damp atmosphere. Such underclothes control the rapid evaporation of perspiration. Taking warm baths and keeping the skin healthy helps it to function normally, so the practice of good personal hygiene is important.

Workers exposed to abnormal temperatures and humidity naturally require more fluids. They should not drink ice water; cool water is as effective for relieving the thirst and is much less liable to cause digestive disturbances.

The only treatment known for silicosis is prevention. It is a chronic disease, and the question of first aid has no direct relationship to its control. The first consideration should be given to the elimination of the dust hazard. This may practically always be accomplished by controlling the dust at its source, thereby preventing it from gaining access to the breathing atmosphere. Where local exhaust measures are not practicable or possible, workroom ventilation must be such as to keep the dust concentration within permissible limits. When the worker must work in atmospheres which are uncontrollable to this extent, he should be furnished personal respiratory protection, and that which is furnished him should be of an approved type. Engineering or mechanical control is mentioned first because without it individuals without defects and in good physical condition will be injured.

Of second consideration in the field of prevention is proper placement of men with physical defects in occupations for which they are physically fit, and in which they may carry on without danger to themselves or fellow workers. It is not necessary to refuse employment to men with simple pulmonary fibrosis as the result of inhaling silica. If conditions are controlled, most of these men may continue throughout a normal working life without suffering from a disabling silicosis. Those men, however, who either upon application for work or during their employment are found by physical examination to be suffering from pulmonary tuberculosis should not be given work in, or continued at work in, surroundings which would expose them to even minimal concentrations of silica dust, because if they are, their condition will be aggravated and their fellow-workmen exposed under conditions which make even the well more susceptible to tuberculosis. Workers in any dusty environment should pay particular attention to infections of the throat, sinuses, bronchi, and lungs. They should have adequate medical advice and supervision, since such conditions are aggravated by dust and also make the individual more susceptible to the effects of dust inhalation.

I am enclosing herewith several copies of Safety and Health leaflets which discuss the cause and prevention of specific occupational diseases. Should you have use for additional copies of these leaflets, for distribution among your group, they may be obtained either through your State Labor Department, or this office will furnish you with a limited number without cost.

I hope that this information will be of assistance to you, and that you will feel free to call upon us for any further advice we may be able to furnish.

ROY R. JONES, M.D.
Division of Labor Standards

The writer of the following letter clearly recognized the dangers of the asbestos with which he worked. When he asked for alternative work, however, he was refused. The investigation referred to in the letter to Verne Zimmer indicates that the government recognized the hazards of asbestos in this and other plants but lacked the power to force the company to reduce the hazards of its operations.

Ambler, Pennsylvania, February 1937

Dear Mr. Franklin D. Roosevelt:

I am V. P. and please excuse me if I am abusing to write you these few lines, because you are in head of the United States of America.

I wrote to other offices and nobody answered me. Mr. President I notify you that I came to Ambler Pennsylvania in the year 1905 and from that time I been working in Keasbey & Mattison Co. and after working a pretty long time in that mill I got some asbestos that lay in the lung that has been exsamined by Dr. Philip J. Lukens 540 Butler Avenue Ambler Pa. in date 10-3-31 then I learned to work in the garden. Now I asked again for the job to the employment man of Keasbey & Mattison Co. . . .

I asked him about more than 100 times for the job and he send me all way down the seller where they work with the masks of the face. I told him again to give me the job to some other departments and he says that I refused that job in the dust, and he never want to give me work again.

Now I owe him two months of rent and I can[not] even pay it because I work only in the summer. I am an honest labor and my trade is for working in the flour mill, in the factory, and in the garden, all of my life. I am of 47 years of age I was born April 30–1889 also I am an American citizen. Excuse me if I disturb you. Thank you.

V. P.

Harrisburg, Pennsylvania, April 5, 1937

Dear Mr. Zimmer:

The inclosed copy of recommendations to the Department of Labor and Industry are a result of your letter of March 4 to Mr. Ralph M. Bashore, regarding working conditions in the Keasbey and Mattison plant in Ambler, Pennsylvania.

WILLIAM B. FULTON, M.D.
Chief, Industrial Hygiene
Department of Health
Commonwealth of Pennsylvania

April 2, 1937

The Keasbey and Mattison Co.
Ambler, Pennsylvania
Dr. Edith MacBride-Dexter
William B. Fulton, M.D.

Following a survey of the asbestos industry by this division which included the above mentioned plant, the cards in the Keasbey and Mattison Company have almost been completely hooded, with marked reduction in the dustiness of the card room. The company has requested a second determination of the dust concentrations in the card room, which will be done in the near future. In addition to the installation of exhaust ventilation equipment in the card room, additional steps should be taken by the management to reduce their dust concentrations in other operations, not exceeding ten million particles per cubic foot of air.

Recommendation:

1. The shaker screen in the preparing room, which is located in the basement of the fabrication plant, although used only at intervals, should be covered and exhaust ventilated.

2. The bagging operation of screened fibers should be provided with exhaust ventilation, which would insure removal of dust in a manner that could prohibit exposure of the operator.

3. A method should be devised for the batching operation that could be exhaust ventilated and which would prohibit exposure of the operator to dust produced in this operation.

4. Local exhaust ventilation should be provided for the feeding end of the mixing picker.

5. Local exhaust ventilation should be provided for the looms in the weaving department. Wet weaving, if possible, is highly desirable.

6. Local exhaust ventilation should be provided for the asbestos crusher in the paper plant. Ventilation in this department should also include the bagging operation.

7. The plant management should insure proper maintenance of their ventilation equipment. Good housekeeping of the entire plant should be maintained at all times. The floors, walls, ceilings, machines, benches, rafters, etc., should be cleaned periodically with a vacuum system.

West Nitrona, Pennsylvania, April 26, 1937

Dear Miss Perkins:

In regards to some Information on working conditions we have to put up with is unreasonable this line of work is Sand Blasting Plates and Sheets in Allegheny Still [Steel] Co At Brackenridge Pa there is a State Law on this kind of work on how long a man is suppose to work in side of a Unit and how much time he is suppose to be out in fresh air after he leaves the Unit in which he is working we have no place that is fit for a man to rest we come out from a unit after taking our Mask of Sweating and the only place there is that is out side of the Sand Blast Unit which we might as well be resting inside with out our masks I do not call this kind of working conditions good for any man or beast every once in a while we have to go down under neath of the Unit or in other words in the cellar to clean the sand out when It plugs up this place is full of Sand dust that is Impossible to see what you are doing no place to connect your mask to Is there any way that we can Compel this Company to make Decient working conditions If there is kindly let me know and I will take it up. . . .

E. L.

Please do not let no body know who is doing this or I will be out of a job.

Los Angeles, California, May 17, 1937

Dear Miss Perkins:

I am a strong New Dealer and wish to do all I can do to assist our President in his effects.

For the past four years I have been employed by the Calif. Consolidated Water Co. which is owned by the Standard Oil Co.

During the N.R.A. this concern violated in many ways as many others did. At present we all feel that something will be done to protect labor in the near future so I am giving you some of the latest moves of this company. For the past year they have discharged all old men that had years of service without reason or notice. They have cut the forces in all departments demanding the balance to get the work out in the same time or some one else would. I as janitor have worked 8 hours six days a week and got extra help every week for major operations this was cut off later more duties were put on and last I was given all windows to wash which was over 30 hours per month by other men. I was not allowed any overtime and told it must be done and in 8 hours. . . .

Every man working for this concern must stand an examination by the Standard Oil Dr and pay for it.

They had one man working on a sand blast machine in a small room in the basement with a helmet on and when they kept him on that class of work much longer than they should they had him examined by their Dr and then changed his work and made it so miserable for him he had to quit. After finding another job and was examined for sand blasting he was turned down on account of his lungs being full of sand. In less than six months this man lost 38 pounds and at present is on his last leg. Every man is forced to take out their group insurance at $1.55 per month and we do not get any insurance if we are hurt on the job and draw compensation. We must be sick one week before we draw $10.00 and that for a limit of 13 weeks only.

I hope this information will help the New Deal in its future efforts.

L. M.

Altoona, Pennsylvania, November 23, 1937

Dear Miss Perkins:

Would you kindly inform me about the doctors that examined those silicosis victims in the West Virginia tunnel case. I have silicosis from rock tunnel work in the Anthracite fields the Dr. here has taken x-rays and say they can not do anything. Must a fellow just wait to die or can someone do something. I am forty seven years old, is there any compensation for same when the company busted up or quit operating but has holdings in other parts of state.

Any information will greatly apreciated.

J. T. O'D.

East Chicago, Indiana, December 1, 1939

Dear Secretary Perkins:

I am writing you concerning a situation that has arisen in connection with a strike of Local 12120, District 50, United Mine Workers of America, against the Harbison-Walker Refractories Company plant at East Chicago, Indiana. Recently when you lectured before the university at Bloomington, I know you spent most of the day examining the industrial safeguards against silicosis in the limestone mills and quarries there. I know, too, that you have given much of your life to agitating for industrial health laws and safety measures. That is why I bring to your personal attention the situation that has been uncovered here. I believe it is quite as serious, comparatively, as the Gauley Bridge incident . . . , which a few years ago shocked the whole country.

In the first place I wish you to know that I am in no way connected with Local 12120, the United Mine Workers, or the CIO. I am an instructor in the Indiana University Extension here, and my only connection with the labor movement is as a rank and file member of the AF of T, an AFL affiliate. I am not being remunerated in any way, and I am acting only as an impartial and disinterested citizen. My only personal bias in the situation arises from the fact that I have a prejudice against industrial murder, and I don't like to see young men die needlessly and before their time.

Local 12120, U.M.W.A., went out on strike November 2 when the Harbison-Walker Company refused to bargain collectively with the union on: (1) a 5 cent hourly wage increase; (2) vacations with pay; (3) adequate machinery to eliminate the silica dust.

In replying to the last of these issues, S. M. Gamble, plant manager and company spokesman, gave a press release in which he asserted that the dust eliminating equipment at the plant was "the best and most modern known to science." Incidentally this equipment was installed only four years ago. Before that time there was no dust collecting system in the plant.

A week later Mr. Gamble's statement was effectively refuted by the death of E. J., a colored worker, who had been ill since the preceding May. After the death of J. was reported in the press, Mr Gamble still insisted that the dust machinery was adequate.

It was at this point that my wife and I entered the controversy. Determined to get at the truth about the working conditions at Harbison-Walker plant, we interviewed the striking men to secure the names of all employees who had died during their memory. We then checked these names in the death files of the East Chicago Public Health Office.

Here are the facts we have uncovered to date:

1. 35 men have died at the Harbison-Walker silica brick yards in the last 12 years from silicosis or coincident diseases. For these deaths we have the testimony of the diagnoses on the certificates.

2. 8 of these deaths are listed as due directly to silicosis. The remainder are listed as pulmonary TB, lobar pneumonia, acute broncho-pneumonia, etc. The high incidence of deaths from pulmonary diseases among those suffering from silicosis has been attested to by medical authorities and roentgenologists everywhere. We have medical statements to back our contentions that these deaths are due primarily to the fact that the men were silicotics and in weakened condition. (See particularly *Pneumoconiosis* by Henry K. Pancoast and Eugene P. Pendergrass, both professors of roentgenology at the University of Pennsylvania, especially the chapter entitled "Coincident Tuberculosis.")

3. Of the 35 proven deaths only four men lived to be beyond 50 years of age. 18 of the men died under 35.

4. This list is by no means complete for: (a) we have had to depend on the memory of the men for the names of those who have died; (b) the death records in East Chicago were burnt in 1927, and for records of

deaths prior to that time we shall have to investigate the vital statistics at Indianapolis; (c) we have yet to check the death records of nearby Whiting, Gary, Hammond and Chicago; (d) most important of all we have a list of between 30 and 40 names of men who were sent to other cities and states to die when the company discovered they were dusted. We are writing to these cities and states for the death certificates.

5. When the lists are complete—though they will never be completely so—we shall have between 70 and 80 deaths attributable to silicosis and coincident diseases and all attested by death certificates.

After compiling this list, we began to interview the widows and dependents of these men to discover whether the company had been paying compensation for occupational diseases and deaths. Here is what we found.

1. Before the passage of the Indiana Occupational Diseases Act of 1937, the company's policy was:

    (a) To pay no compensation whatever, no doctor's bills, no hospitalization fees, no funeral expenses. Or,

    (b) To send the dusted men away to other states to die—Mississippi, Alabama, West Virginia, Missouri; to pay their way there, but to pay no or a very small compensation subsequently. No compensation was paid to widows after death. Or,

    (c) To pay a nominal compensation—varying from $6.25 to $10 a week, but in no case over $10—for the period immediately preceding death, usually three months to a year. After death no compensation to widows or dependents. In such cases the company usually had the employee sign a release, a typical example of which we have in our possession.

In March 1937 the Indiana Occupational Disease Act went into effect. This act provides for 55% of the average weekly wage for 500 weeks for total disability; 55% of the average weekly wage for 300 weeks for widows and dependents in event of death.

2. Since the Indiana Occupational Diseases Act went into effect, the policy of the company has been:

    (a) To pay no compensation at all to men diagnosed as having silicosis; to pay no doctor's bills, hospital fees, or funeral expenses—all required under the act. And,

    (b) To pay no compensation as provided by law to widows and dependents. Or,

    (c) To pay in a few cases a nominal weekly compensation—never over $10 a week—while the man is sick. In no case but one to my knowledge has the company paid the compensation required by law. In no case has the company paid compensation for more than a year. No doctor's bills, hospital fees, or funeral expenses were paid in these cases.

(d) To pay in some cases a nominal compensation—never more than $10 a week—to the widow and dependents for a year. After a year these payments were stopped, as the widow no longer had legal right to file a claim under the Occupational Diseases Act because of the clause of limitations.

(e) The only cases in which the company has observed the law in regard to compensation for total disability or death were two; in the case of E. J. who died three weeks ago, the union forced the company to pay the compensation, but was unable to force the company to provide hospitalization; in the case of F. W. who is no longer totally disabled, the company is paying 55% of the difference between his present and former salary as compensation.

I am fully aware that the law does not require a company to inform a totally disabled man, or a deceased worker's family of their rights. The fact is, however, that many of these employees are colored, many are foreign. Most of them have not had the advantage of schooling and are semi-illiterate. In no case have we been able to discover a sick man, or his family after death, who knew their rights under the Indiana law. In no case have we discovered that the company ever informed them of their rights—even when the diagnosis was stated to be silicosis on the city records.

In many cases, on the other hand, we have discovered that the company knew that the man was sick, and had the man sign a release, which it is doubtful he understood. In many other cases the company has protected itself against the operation of the law by paying nominal compensation to a widow until it was too late for her to file a claim under the act.

Three years ago the company had X-rays taken of all the men in the plant. Not one man was informed of his condition by the company, though subsequently many men were discharged, or sent south with no, or small compensation, until they died.

In those cases where the men have died in the last year and the limitations clause is not yet in effect, of course the union will prosecute the rights of the men, or their widows and children.

Last week in order to clinch its case, the union sent a sampling of 17 men into Chicago to be X-rayed—this time not by a company doctor. The results of that X-ray show that out of the 17 men 6 were definitely dusted and several of these seriously, so that the doctor advised discontinuance of work.

May I briefly describe the dust elimination system which the company asserts is adequate. In the main building are located the crusher mill, drypans, sifters etc. Here the dust is worst. This building has a volume of roughly 400,000 cubic feet. It is served by one small fan. The fan is in a casing about three feet in diameter. The blades of the fan are 12"–14" long. The fan is manufactured by the Clarage Fan Company of Kalamazoo, Michigan; it is Type W, Design No. 4, Size 2, Serial No. 56814. The motor attached to this fan is an original 15 hp motor, which has been stepped up to 25 hp, and the rpm increased to try to make it do a job for which it is not designed.

There are, according to the men, 13 intakes served by this fan. The conduits are old and second hand, having been taken from an old factory. They are worn and full of holes, which have been stopped with paper and cloths. Often the concentrated dust blows back into the factory. Some intakes are clogged and do not work. There are no hoods over the individual processes.

When the system was put up four years ago, there was no study made of the needs of the plant by ventilating engineers. Yet ventilating engineers state that every job requires special study to meet the requirements of the task. Studies must be made of specific gravity of the dust, air velocity over the processes that are to be cleared of dust, etc. This system was erected by the contractor who sold the fan and the plant's regular maintenance men.

The plant manager has refused to allow accredited newspaper men to photograph the dust collecting equipment.

These are my conclusions from an impartial and as yet incomplete survey:

1. Harbison Walker Refractories East Chicago plant is a death mill, and a constant hazard to the health of the employees.

2. The death files of East Chicago and other cities prove this.

3. The recent X-ray photographs of 67 men prove this.

4. The equipment is not adequate for clearing the dust.

5. The company is wilfully evading, if not openly violating, the Indiana Occupational Diseases Act by not paying compensation due.

6. The men are entirely justified in refusing to return to work until a study has been promised by the company, and adequate machinery installed.

Knowing your work for health standards in industry and your sympathy for workers condemned to such working conditions, I beg that you will give this your attention, and if we cannot get action from the state health office, that you will order a federal investigation.

E. W. K.

Reading, Pennsylvania, August 1, 1942

Gentlemen:

I wish to report a very important and serious matter to you. We have a foundry here in Reading Pa called the Birdsboro Steel Foundry and Machine Co, *Reading plant*. They have a molding dept and they are committing wholesale murder there. The conditions in that molding dept are terrible the men that start to work there are healthy and strong and in a short time they become sick, short of breath cough and spit up substances we think it is that terrible Silicosis and it is the company's fault. Sand and dust all over that dept. Men work in sand holes shoveling sand, molding jobs other things done around sand and no respirators are used at all for the protection of the working men. They breath in air containing dust and inhale dust and sand in their lungs. Iron is also melted in that department and when that is done the sulphur is so terrible that the men almost pass out the danger of that is terrible. it is something like a poison gas. There are no lunch rooms the working men must eat their sandwiches right where they work with sand and dust accumulating on their food and that is swallowed. No dinner hours to rest, the shower room is full of sand the place where they change clothes is full of sand. You should see some of the men they sit down to get their breath they can hardly breath. Soon the boss will tell those men they are to sick to work and they ought to quit their jobs they obey them they do not know what sickness they have because the company's doctor does not tell them. When they quit their jobs they are out of compensation. That company treats their men in that dept like the slave was treated years back, a master has more love and pity for his dog than this company has for their workingmen. My cousin worked in that dept for a short time and when I heard what was going on there I begged him to quit and I am very thankful he did before it was to late. I am sure when you will send an investigator he will even see more than I can explain to you. He will be surprised at the conditions in that molding dept. No protection for the workingman's health at all. The bosses of that firm know what a dreadful disease Silicosis is and they should be compelled to protect the workingmen from it. Last week the firm gave a report to our local newpapaer of the profits they made in 6 months was $152,656,10 can't they use some of those profits which the men help them to earn to equipe the dept in a way that the men should not become sick and helpless and perhaps ready for their graves It is a crime Hope you will look into this matter immediately every minute counts. Please do not notify the bosses you are coming make it a surprise they are very tricky Thank you

B. B.

The following series of letters, stretching over a four-year period, stem from the efforts of a militant mineworkers' union to force mine owners in Oklahoma, Kansas, and Missouri to protect their workers against silicosis and lead poisoning. The letters indicate the differences in the approaches to safety and health issues taken by the Labor Department and the U.S. Public Health Service. Lead mill owners preferred to work with the Public Health Service, which they considered to be friendly to management; organized labor sought the aid of the Labor Department. With no power to intervene directly, the department's Division of Labor Standards publicized the plight of these workers by organizing a landmark conference on silicosis in 1940.[4]

Salt Lake City, Utah, May 23, 1935

My dear Miss Perkins:

In what is known as the Tri-State District, which consists of a portion of the states of Missouri, Oklahoma and Kansas, and where the principal industry is mining of zinc and lead ore, a condition exists which I believe should be called to your attention to be seriously considered.

Realizing as I do your sympathy with the trials and tribulations of the real wealth producers of the nation, I am requesting your cooperation in alleviating to some extent the deplorable conditions under which the employees of the various mining companies of this district live, move and have their being. The enclosed communication will give you some idea of the conditions, but from a recent visit that I have made to this district, I realize that the author of the enclosure has been very conservative in his

[4]David Rosner and Gerald Markowitz, "Research or Advocacy? Federal Occupational Safety and Health Policies during the New Deal," *Journal of Social History* 18 (Spring 1985): 365–77, discusses the differences between the approaches of the Public Health Service and the Department of Labor to occupational safety and health.

summing up of the situation as it really exists. You would have to visit this community to realize the poverty, squallor and disease existing there.

According to the report of the census enumerator for the City of Picher, Oklahoma, in a visit to 544 homes he found 205 cases of Silicosis. This, as you perhaps know, is a disease peculiar to the workers who come in contact with and breathe air laden with silica dust. It has been proven that with ordinary precautions as to ventilation and the use of water to lay this dust, this disease can be largely controlled. The mining companies in this district make no effort to alleviate this condition, with the result as indicated by the census enumerator.

These people have been patient and have tried by every peaceable means to remedy the existing conditions, but in final desperation have resorted to the strike. The companies have completely ignored their requests for conferences, and the Eagle Picher Lead Company which dominates the situation is dictating to the smaller operators.

These employees are 100% American, the majority with a background of several generations. The thing I am interested in is adequate relief for these workers while they are fighting for themselves and their families. Will you use your influence with the Relief Administration to the end that these people will at least be assured of the bare necessities of life during their struggle to establish something at least resembling a decent standard of living?

I will sincerely appreciate any assistance you may be able to render.

JAMES ROBINSON
Secretary-Treasurer
International Union of Mine,
Mill and Smelter Workers

Oklahoma City, Oklahoma, June 3, 1935

Dear Doctor Zimmer:

This will acknowledge your letter of May 29 relating to certain written complaints received by Secretary Perkins relative to hazardous and unhealthful working conditions in the lead and zinc production area of Oklahoma and in which part of a complaint is quoted relating to the lack of ventilation and the failure to use water to lay the dust in various mines of the district, etc.

I doubt very much if the reports have been exaggerated as there always has been a serious condition in that section of our State but if you will refer to the State Mining Laws, the State Health Laws and the laws affecting labor, you will find that they are administered by three separate and distinct departments of state government.

All laws relating to mines and mining, which include safety, the hours even for labor in mines, is specifically placed under the authority and administration of the Chief Mine Inspector. Health and sanitation come directly under the State Department of Health. The authority of the State Department of Labor does not seem to enter into it in connection with the operation of mines, although through our Bureau of Factory Inspection we have issued many orders relating to the safety of mining equipment at and around the top of the mines and have received reasonably good cooperation, regardless of the fact that under the law our authority to do this was seriously questioned.

If the State Department of Labor was to interfere with health and safety in the mines, we would immediately meet opposition by the authorities having jurisdiction in the premises and in case we did not receive opposition from that source, the mine operator could easily ignore our orders due to the fact that it was a matter over which we had no jurisdiction. Hence, you can readily see that the present over-lapping of authority in matters that should come directly under the Commissioner of Labor is the cause of a very serious situation.

I shall be very glad to get in touch with the State Health Commissioner and the Chief Mine Inspector and also the State Industrial Commission, whom I am sure will be interested in a survey along the lines stated in your letter and shall be glad to advise you in the premises.

During the present acute stage of the strike, it would not be advisable to undertake any kind of a survey until such time as conditions have become more normal. However, for my part, I am very anxious to know the true situation but shall advise you further after conferring with other authorities.

> W. A. PAT MURPHY
> Commissioner of Labor
> State of Oklahoma

Flat River, Missouri, February 24, 1936

Dear President [Roosevelt]:

The attached petition signed by some of the persons of St. Francois County Missouri who feel that working conditions of the lead mines of this (The largest lead mining district in the world) should be investigated by Congress.

Hundreds of men in this section allege that their lungs have been affected because of the dust, gas, smoke, improper ventilation and failure of the mining Companies to properly protect them against these damaging causes as set forth in petition.

Damage suits have been filed in many instances for several years but are delayed from time to time for various reasons and in some cases claimants have died with cases yet unsettled. Some of our attorneys who have been most active in these cases have disbarment suits started against them, which causes other attorneys to be afraid to take these cases for fear they will meet the same fate, and this leaves at present the men hopelessly in the hands of the mining Companies to take any small sums they may offer.

We therefore beg of you to have this matter taken up and feel sure many startling facts could be revealed similar to West Virginia tunnel situation if properly investigated, by Congress, which seems to be our last hope as we cannot get it locally.

Assuring you of our fullest cooperation in all matters and anxiously awaiting a hearing from you.

Committee. L. K.
Committee. C. B.
Committee. M. K.
Chairman. R. F. B.

Flat River, Missouri, April 16, 1936

Dear Miss Perkins:

On Feb. 24th, we mailed a petition to President Roosevelt asking for a congressional investigation into working conditions (past and present) of the lead mines of this county, as well as court practices against lead miners.

This petition was signed by sixty miners and represent about 600 ex-miners, who testify that their health has been damaged by dust, gas, smoke, improper ventilation and failure of the mining companies to properly protect them against these damaging causes.

We were informed by the President that the matter was being referred to you for consideration but to date have had no hearing from your office.

Within less than one week from date the petition was mailed to you, two of these men had died of silicosis and several hundred in this district are on Federal relief because of said damages, in fact more than 90% of these men are on the relief rolls.

Many of them have had damage suits in the courts for three years but big industry seems to have combined their forces and funds to defeat us, poison the minds of the public against us and prejudice the courts.

Therefore Miss Perkins we beg of you to use your influence to see that we get consideration for our legislature here ignores our situation for reasons of their own, and we feel sure an impartial investigation will show that our problem will compare with that of West Virginia.

We have letters from our Senators, Congressman and others pledging their support if the matter can be brought up that this (the largest lead mining district in the world) be included.

Assuring you of our support in any matter and anxiously awaiting a hearing.

Committee   R. F. B. Chairman
Committee   L. K.
Committee   C. B.
Committee   M. K.

Columbus, Kansas, August 21, 1938

Dear Ma[dam Perkins]:

As you probably already know, the International Labor Defense and the Committee for Defense of Peoples Rights are now raising funds to conduct a tuberculosis and silicosis clinic in the Tri-State district of Missouri, Oklahoma and Kansas this fall.

This is the district where no safety measures are enforced in the lead and zinc field that produces 38 percent of the worlds' output of these two minerals and men die like dogs.

I am writing to you to impress upon you the necessity of your department cooperating with these two great organizations in holding this clinic.

I have lived in this district all my life, served as union president and organizer and I can furnish you any information you desire in regard to the terrible working and living conditions here.

Would it be possible for the U.S. department of labor to make a health and hygiene survey of the tri-state area of Missouri, Oklahoma and Kansas in order to focus national attention upon this district and secure federal legislation to compel the companies to install ventilation systems and safety devices. The average life of a miner in this district is from 7 to 10 years. Many die in 2 or 3 years. The health hazard here is silicosis, caused by breathing particles of silica dust caused by drilling and breaking by dynamite the ore bearing rock containing lead and zinc. Silicosis is the most dreaded industrial disease known to medical science. There is no cure, the only remedy is absolute perfect rest. There are absolutely no facilities for taking care of the thousands of miners who have contracted this dreaded disease. Please give this matter your immediate attention and let me hear from you. It is a matter of life and death to the thousands of workers in this district.

E. C., Secretary
Cherokee County Central Labor Body

Columbus, Kansas, September 4, 1938

Respected Madam [Roosevelt]:

Please forgive me for having the courage to write a letter of this nature to Americas' No. One Lady.

However, after reading your daily column I feel sure you would welcome a letter from the grass roots of "Landons?" Kansas.[5]

This letter comes to you from the Tri-State, (Mo., Oklahoma and Kansas) lead and zinc field of southeastern Kansas. Thirty-eight percent of the entire world supply of lead and zinc ore is produced in this district. We have here health hazards known as "lead poisoning" in the smelters and "silicosis", the most dreaded industrial disease known to medical science.

Silicosis is contracted by workers in the mines breathing the fine particles of silicate dust caused by drilling and breaking the ore by the use of dynamite. These small particles of silicate although microscopic have razor sharp edges that cut the lungs of the workers like emery dust cuts soft iron. Nature causes an incrustation to form over the affected area of the worker's lungs which destroys the cells. There is no cure for this terrible disease.

However, these health hazards can be eliminated if the mining trusts

---

[5]Eleanor Roosevelt's newspaper column, *My Day*, was widely syndicated. Alfred M. Landon, Republican presidential candidate in 1936, was governor of Kansas from 1933 to 1937.

will install air cleaning devices. This, of course, costs money and the greedy, grasping employers apparently haven't any extra money except to buy tear gas, munitions, and to hire thugs and gunmen to terrorize union men and women who demand their right to join a union of their own choosing.

You remember this is the district where Alf. M. Landon then governor of Kansas in June of 1935 sent the national guard into the district to crush the workers and establish fascism, which exists here today. The workers live in one room shacks with the boards running up and down, many with dirt floors.

Why don't the labor department make a health and hygiene survey of this district?

Will you add your voice to our's in requesting that this be done. Will you please answer this letter and send a copy to Ma Perkins.

We will immediately send plenty of factual and documentary evidence that men are dieing like flies and that 8 out of every 10 women in this district are widows, 75 percent of the children orphans.

We haven't written the president, we feel he is too busy keeping us out of war with Europe to bother with us 18,000 miners, but we appreciate the progressive legislation he has fought for like the Wagner act.

The boys tell me it won't do any good to write you, but after reading your column I feel like you are something substantial, something solid. I feel that you are really close to the working class, one of the family.

If the mine operators who control our school districts, our Republican sheriff, our newspapers knew I was writing a letter of this type to you they would do like they have in the past, have me thrown in jail on framed up charges on which I always have come clear, so don't give this letter any publicity under any circumstances.

E. C., Secty.
Cherokee County Central Labor Body

October 25, 1939

To: The Secretary [of Labor]
From: V. A. Zimmer
Subject: Tri-State Mining Area Problem

Since dictating the attached memorandum Evan Just, Secretary of the Tri-State Zinc & Lead Ore Producers Association, of Kiani, Oklahoma, came into the office to see me about this matter Tuesday afternoon, October 24. He wanted to discuss what he termed the "unfair publicity of the Committee for Peoples Rights" and doubtless his principal object was to find out whether this Department was fostering the investigation or just how we tied in.

I made it clear to Mr. Just that we had no connection with the investigation although we had correspondence from the Committee requesting factual data and certain information pertaining to dust control measures. I told him frankly all we knew about the matter. I also told him with equal frankness that this Department had received frequent complaints about the conditions in the Tri-State area, as well as in the entirely separate area of southeastern Missouri. . . .

I told him that our most frequent complaint was that the Association, through its clinic, systematically and cold-bloodedly eliminated every worker found to have actual or incipient silicosis. He denied this unequivocally as being "a damn lie." He said frankly, however, that the companies in his Association naturally wanted to protect themselves by refusing to employ workers who had contracted silicosis or any early fibrotic conditions elsewhere. He maintained emphatically that the members of the Association were adopting every proved preventive measure, including wet drilling. He stated that they have as consultant Dr. Max Gardner of Saranac.

The Association is obviously extremely concerned about the forthcoming publicity. Mr. Just tells me that he has contacted the Committee on Peoples Rights and requested them to hear and consider the employers' side of the story. He stated that it was unquestionably true that in 1914 this area was the outstanding hell-hole of the United States. He admits too that the living conditions are still very bad and indicates . . . that the Health Departments of the States have been able to do very little in bringing about an improvement. He thinks the principal difficulty is that this type of worker—unlike a "foreign element"—will not take orders. Further, he indicates that because of their ignorance it is almost impossible to educate them in a sanitary way of living. He feels that the operating companies should not be blamed for these housing and living conditions as the companies do not own the shacks or dwellings and hence have no control.

Mr. Just gave me two significant pieces of information. First, within the past two weeks the Association has hurriedly contact Dr. Lanza of the Metropolitan Life Insurance Company and Dr. Sayers of the Public Health Service and got them to undertake an immediate investigation. Second, in the course of our conversation he said that if the United

States Labor Department "wanted" the opportunity he would arrange for our representative to have entry to all the companies in his Association. When I immediately showed some interest in his suggestion he rather hesitantly suggested that it would perhaps be more desirable if we did not come into the picture inasmuch as "the employers in this section feel that the Labor Department is radical and definitely prejudiced, and that any investigation by us would be in the nature of a star chamber proceedings." I told Mr. Just (1) that I was not at all sure that we wanted to come into the picture, and (2) that if we do so it would be with absolutely no commitment and that he need not expect a white-wash. I put this to him bluntly because of his previous statement that the employers in his Association had more confidence in the Public Health Service. To this I rejoined that while this was doubtless true, it was equally true that labor had more confidence in the Department of Labor. This latter thought was borne out by the several complaints we have had to the effect that the previous investigations resulted in no permanent improvements in the area from the standpoint of the worker.

I also discussed with Mr. Just the possibility of persuading the employers to support occupational disease coverage under workmen's compensation in Oklahoma and Kansas (under the Missouri Act employers may elect to cover for occupational diseases). He was quite interested in this matter and thought that he could persuade the operators to agree to a "reasonable" compensation act for occupational diseases.

While our discussion was very frank on both sides, it was on the whole pleasant and agreeable. In conclusion I told Mr. Just that I would confer with you as to the possibility of accepting an invitation to go into the field. My present thought is that we should wait at least until this story breaks. Otherwise it might appear to the workers that we were hurrying to the scene with a white-wash brush.

"Fumes in the Place Where We Work": Miscellaneous Diseases

The problem of industrial lead poisoning has been recognized for centuries. It was not until the early decades of this century, however, that it was brought to wide public attention, through a series of studies conducted by Dr. Alice Hamilton, a pioneer in industrial hygiene. In the 1920s, when spray painting came into wide use, particularly in the auto industry, painters' unions organized studies to investigate the effects of lead in the paints used by their members.[6] It was also in the 1920s that lead was introduced into gasoline, and its threat to public health became the focus of intense debate and controversy.[7] The following letters reflect the ongoing concern of individuals, unions, and public health advocates with the problem of industrial lead poisoning.

Chicago, Illinois, November 23, 1935

Madam [Perkins]:

About two weeks ago we had the honor and pleasure of meeting Dr. Alice Hamilton at the Hull House in this City.

By our request she attended the regular meeting of the Central Organization of our trade in this City: Painters' District Council No. 14 of Chicago, Ill., located at 1446 W. Adams Street. She spoke on the subject of "Protection of the Public Health". This favor on her part was highly appreciated by every one present at that particular meeting.

The following Saturday at a conference with her, attended by Mr. John A. Runnberg and the writer, we discussed some of the modern methods of applying paints, lacquers, varnishes, stains, enamels, etc., and also the use and nature of certain kinds of solids, solvents and diluents now being used as substitutes for white lead, turpentine and linseed oil, and the gums of copal and damar etc., as formerly used in manufacturing fine varnishes, now being replaced by synthetic substances, the base of which being principally cellulose products skillfully treated with tung oil, and where a high luster is required in enamels, by the addition of perilla oil.

We also spoke of our difficulties of obtaining proper protection for every one engaged in the daily use of materials containing benzol, carbon tetrachloride, amyl acetate, methyl alcohol, acetone, also many highly volatile hydro-carbons too numerous to mention here, and other chloroform-like substances, such as trichloroethylene, contained in so-called varnish-removers, in adulterations of floor-wax, and in so-called dope for aeroplanes and so on.

---

[6]See David Rosner and Gerald Markowitz, "Safety and Health on the Job: The Workers' Health Bureau of America in the 1920s," *Science and Society* 48 (Winter 1984–85): 466–82; Angela Nugent, "Organizing Trade Unions to Combat Disease: The Workers' Health Bureau, 1921–1928," *Labor History* 26 (Summer 1985): 423–46.

[7]David Rosner and Gerald Markowitz, "'A Gift of God'?: The Public Health Controversy over Leaded Gasoline in the 1920s," *American Journal of Public Health* 75 (April 1985): 344–52.

To protect our health we introduced in the Illinois State Senate Bill No. 297. A BILL for AN ACT to regulate SPRAY PAINTING.

It was read and referred to the Senate Committee on Industrial Affairs. We withdrew this bill a few days after April 17, 1935 on which date the Illinois Supreme Court rendered a series of decisions invalidating Section 1 of the Occupational Diseases Act of 1911 and Sections 12 and 13 of the Health, Safety and Comfort Act of 1909, as amended in 1915.

They also decided, that the exact meaning of such words as adequate, reasonable and approved, as applied in these different sections is not definite enough; also that the Department of Labor of this State has no power to enforce any rules and regulations contained therein, because the Legislature has never authorized or granted such action to be assumed.

In other words, we are now without any protection in this State and Senate Bill No. 297 has to be re-written to contain a detailed scientifically defined description of safety-devices, approved by a recognized authority, as for instance, the U.S. Bureau of Mines.

This applies to respirators, masks, etc. We received through the courtesy of Mr. W. P. Yant, Consulting Engineer of the Pittsburgh Station a copy of Schedule 21 and the laboratory tests of dust respirators, also the promise, that as soon as the tests of pressure respirators are concluded, we will receive a copy of the report as soon as it is printed. Our trade is vitally interested in pressure respirators, while miners and others demand the other kind to be protected against dusts.

The words: Adequate illumination in our bill have to be defined in foot-candles, according to the academic standards.

Exhaust ventilation has to be defined by the number of changes of air per hour, according to the size of the room or rooms and the potential of the most dangerous substances used.

Another very important matter is the chemical analysis of the materials used by our trade in the line of painting, decorating and hardwood-finishing. Such data would be of no value, except when perfected and approved by a recognized authority.

This question caused Dr. Hamilton to make the suggestion to request your advice and possibly obtain your assistance in this vital matter.

Therefore I was instructed to write this letter.

If I am correctly informed, the U.S. Bureau of Standards, the U.S. Department of Public Health and the Department of Agriculture have the use of a chemical laboratory of their own and the necessary staff of experts.

It is for obvious reasons, such as the close relationship of the medical profession to the study of occupational diseases, that the laboratory of the U.S. Public Health Service would be the preferable agency, though this is my private opinion only.

This matter would involve the question of labels, which I presume would be an issue for each separate State to take up, with the State of North Dakota at the head of the list (I have a copy of the excellent label law of that State before me), though we introduced Resolution No. 154 for a "Proposed Federal Industrial Poison Act" at the Convention of the A.F. of L., held in San Francisco in 1934. To my knowledge no action has been taken up to this date.

In conclusion I will say that we all agree that the spraying processes as applied in the different lines of industry without any safety devices is a constantly growing menace, when in normal times thousands of young girls and women are engaged in spraying lacquers, enamels, cosmetics, using the sandblast to remove the sand from castings, instead of pickling them as formerly in fluoric acid to prepare them for machining, engage in soldering processes, die-casting, when as a rule they are more susceptible. We fully realize the efforts of a determined opposition to make a beneficial change and know that it took twenty years to inaugurate the parcel-post system, the pure food act and others. In spite of that, we do not intend to quit now, until the employers put their feet under the same table with the accredited representatives of Labor to agree on effective inspection-laws. I hope you pardon us for taking up your valuable time. We consider Dr. Hamilton's suggestion as a very important matter.

R. GRONEMANN, Correspondent
Painters' District Council No. 14 and
Illinois State Conference, Brotherhood of Painters
Decorators and Paper Hangers of America

Cleveland, Ohio, January 15, 1936

Dear [President Roosevelt]:

Hope you will pardon my adding one more problem to your now to many. but I don't know whom else to turn to and it is important.

For the past two years I have been employed by a Brass & Copper Co. in the manufacture of wich they use lead, arsenic, zinc and other things wich cause fumes in the place where we work, they get by the law by having hoods to carry fumes outside but do not enforce their use, also they have muffels or furnaces fed by Natural Gas they have no way for these fumes to escape except through the windows in the roof wich in the winter are closed.

The other night I was caught opening a window and was threatened with discharge. I have spent everything I have earned for the past year over and above living expenses, for Dr bills I am married and have two children, this Gas causes Gastritis and eventually ugly ulcers of the Stomach.

My only reason for writing is it may help some one else from the same fate as I and several others.

Also while they are figuring a way out of that terrible happening in W. Va. they might be able to do something about this condition.

There are a couple of other things I would like to mention, one is where they are drawing one tube on a draw bench now, they are working on a patent to draw two tubes wich will mean same amount of men double amount of work.

Also I worked in Sheet & Tin mill's several years ago; they worked 8 hrs a day then 5 days a week about all a man could stand as it's hot and heavy.

They are still working the same, if they could be forced to work 6 hrs 4 shifts they would still make plenty as they get better pay than the average person.

Thanking you for your interest in reading this and hoping and praying for your continued success.

                                                               R. R. N.

As the American auto industry grew, its workers responded increasingly to the organizing efforts of the United Automobile Workers (UAW). In December 1936, in an effort to force General Motors to recognize the UAW as their bargaining agent, workers in Flint, Michigan, refused either to work or to leave the plant. The first sitdown strike lasted through February 1937 and led to the recognition of the UAW by the auto industry. Health and safety issues were of great importance to the Flint strikers, for only three years earlier the most serious outbreak of lead poisoning in ten years occurred in Detroit's auto factories. As many as 4,000 workers were found to have acute symptoms of lead absorption. Of the workers' seven initial demands, five were related to health and safety conditions on the shop floor. The following letter from the secretary of a St. Louis local expresses the workers' concern about lead poisoning. Lead, used in car batteries, paint and rubber production, power grinding and welding, rarely killed workers outright, rather, its accumulation in the blood and bones resulted in a wide range of physical and neurological symptoms: kidney failure, mental retardation, convulsions, "insanity." The letter also reflects workers' suspicion of company health programs and policies. The honesty of company doctors was universally suspect, for they communicated the results of their examinations not to the workers but to their employers. To protect themselves against possible lawsuits, managers then shifted contaminated workers from one job to another before firing them, in order to obscure the role played by a particular work site in the illnesses identified by the company physician.

St. Louis, Missouri, May 3, 1937

Dear Friend [Perkins]:

I have been instructed by my organization to write you requesting any or all data regarding information on Industrial Disease. We in the Ford Motor Co. are confronted with a very serious problem, in regard to lead poison.

The Company Doctor who examines the workers in our plant seems to keep the news from the workers when he finds such a case, and it is no time until the company shifts them from one job to another, and are finally let out.

It is then they realize they are saturated with lead poison. Hoping to hear from you immediately and thanking you in advance.

J. L. C., Rec. Sec'y.
Ford Local No. 325, UAW

McKeesport, Pennsylvania, November 16, 1938

Dear Mr. President,

I don't know whether this letter will get to you or not, but I am in hopes that it will.

Mr. President I am one of great many in Uncle Sam's service and proud of it. I am now serving my country at Ft. Geo. G. Meade. This is my place of service till my three years are up, which is not until Jan. 24, 1940.

My main reason for writing is in an interest of my dad's, and a few other men as old as my dad and even younger. My dad has been working in the steel mills, and tin mills now for at least 27 years. Lately the mills were closed because there was no work. Just recently they've started to work and many a man fell out completely because after such a spell the work was too heavy. Some were suffering with cramps, others with sore backs from lifting, still others, like my dad, who work at the picklers, were felled by heat and acid solution. Dad has not been able to work since.

Upon my arrival at home the first of November I've set to find out why they must completely kill one man and then discharge him after he is half dead or so crippled that they can work no more.

These men also belong to the C.I.O. They've paid their dues and for what. None of them get any returns. After you fall out from your work then you are through. They won't give a man any sort of lighter work. This I know for I've went to the head committee to find out why dad was through. He was one man that kind of got angry at the remarks of the other foreman. I couldn't blame him, for he was one of the many men that saw dad double up. After calling Mr. J. F. on the phone to ask why dad was [not] back to work this was his remarks, "We are not obligated to Mr. B. so why should we put him back to work." (Mr. F. is one of the McKeesport Tin Plate headsman. Just what his position is I can't say.)

What are we supposed to do. There are 5 other children (all younger than myself) to be clothed, fed, and some need medical care. All this runs into money and I can't help them but very little from a soldiers pay. Dad has been the only one working and now that's gone.

Mr. President I hope this letter was one of the many of yours that you've received and listened to them. This I had to do as my last choice. Nobody else will listen so I'll close thanking you for reading this and I pray this letter is not in vain.

P.f.c. P. E. B.

Birmingham, Alabama, October 12, 1940

My Dear Miss Perkins:

A number of years ago Labor was very much pleased with a fight you made in an effort to eliminate the dread curse of grinders, sandblasters, etc., silicosis.

Recently I have run across a condition wherein the victims are not so numerous, nevertheless it is causing serious suffering to workers, namely, cancer, due to spraying casters, structural steel and pipes with coal tar.

During the past few months there have been called to my attention four different cases of men having skin cancer, allegedly due to this work in the Central Foundry Company in Bessemer, Alabama.

I believe that a study should be made of this condition since, perhaps, it is prevaling in other plants and that something should be done to force employers to furnish proper clothing and equipment to prevent this chemical continually coming in contact with the flesh of the men.

> N. R. B.
> Executive Director
> Steel Workers Organizing Committee

Washington, D.C., October 16, 1940

Dear Mr. Zimmer:

The letter from N. R. B. is very interesting and calls for an investigation as he suggests.

There are varieties of coal tar which produce cancer of the skin while other varieties are free from this property. It should be possible to substitute the safe kind for the cancer producing kind as was done by the Carbide and Carbon Company some years ago.[8]

If there is anyone in the Labor Department or Health Department in Alabama to whom the question may be referred, I think it would be well to call his attention to the situation.

> ALICE HAMILTON

[8] In continuing correspondence, Zimmer brought to the attention of union, state, and company officials the fact that even Union Carbide's own doctor questioned whether any coal tar derivative was safe.

4. "We Are Human and Not Work Ox"

Women and Black Workers

As the economy collapsed between 1929 and 1933, millions of women lost their jobs. Later, however, as employers sought to reduce their labor costs, they turned increasingly to women to fill jobs formerly held by skilled men. The percentage of women in the census category of craftsmen, foremen, and kindred workers rose 27 percent between 1930 and 1940, while the number of men in this category declined 2 percent. Among manual workers, women again experienced a 27 percent increase while the number of men increased only 4 percent.[1] Overall, however, the proportion of women in the work force grew very showly, from 24.3 percent in 1930 to 25.1 percent in 1940. A large number of these women were married. The proportion of all wage-earning women who were married climbed from 28.8 percent in 1930 to 35 percent in 1940.[2]

The Depression caused women's wages to fall, but not so rapidly as those of men. Before the 1930s, women's earnings averaged between 55 and 63 percent of men's; during the Depression, they tended to hover at the higher end of this spectrum. As the historian Alice Kessler-Harris notes, "the data suggests that women may have been pulling men's wages

[1] *Historical Statistics of the United States: Colonial Times to 1957* (Washington, D.C.: Government Printing Office, 1960), p. 74.

[2] Alice Kessler-Harris, *Out to Work: A History of Wage-Earning Women in the United States* (New York: Oxford University Press, 1982), pp. 250–72.

down, but for a change, [women's] own wages were not tumbling quite as quickly."[3]

The letters from women workers bring home to us some of the effects of these changing employment patterns on the families of women wage earners. First, the increasing number of women in the work force provoked a reaction from others, men and women alike, who felt that working women were taking jobs away from men. Second, many people believed that working married women were sacrificing their main responsibilities as homemakers and mothers. Several states and the federal government passed legislation that prohibited married women from holding jobs if their husbands were working.

Despite the apparent progress women made in employment, our letters make it clear that their work was often demeaning and oppressive. Women were generally forced to take low-paying, entry-level jobs. It is not surprising, therefore, that we find descriptions of women working "75 to 80 hours in stores without heat in winter or sufficient ventilation in summer." A worker for Illinois Bell complained that "they keep a girl under constant observation from the time she starts to work until the time she goes off duty." The strain caused one operator to have "a nervous fit right at her switchboard." Conditions were equally oppressive in factories. The secretary of the YWCA of Monroe, Louisiana, after fruitlessly complaining to the state factory inspection department, wrote to the Y's national board of the plight of a worker in a paper bag factory who packed and carted more than 500 tons of 16-pound bags in an eight-hour shift for wages of less than 35 cents an hour. This young woman and her co-workers were all but chained to their machines, unable to eat or go to the bathroom.

Black workers experienced even more difficult conditions than white women. At the beginning of the Depression, 39 percent of the black labor force were engaged in agriculture; 26 percent had jobs in industry; 26 percent were employed as domestics; and 9 percent worked in the trades, professions, or the service sector.[4] Some New Deal programs aided black workers but many others did little to alleviate their suffering. The Agricultural Adjustment Act, for example, had a particularly deleterious effect on black sharecroppers and tenants. The National Recovery Act, aimed at establishing minimum wages and maximum hours, systematically excluded from its provisions job classifications in which black workers were

[3]Ibid., p. 258.
[4]See Horace R. Cayton and George S. Mitchell, *Black Workers and the New Unions* (Chapel Hill: University of North Carolina Press, 1939).

heavily concentrated. In the textile industry, for instance, most blacks were classified as "cleaners and outside employees"—categories excluded from the NRA codes. Antagonism toward the administration of the NRA was so strong in the black community that some black newspapers sarcastically dubbed the NRA the "Negro Removal Act."[5]

Other federal programs were more beneficial. The Works Progress Administration (WPA) and federal relief agencies provided much-needed support for the black community. By 1935, 40 percent of the black population were enrolled in either a relief program or the WPA. But even on WPA projects, expecially in the South, black workers earned substantially less than white workers. Under pressure from southern politicians and industries, the WPA abandoned its original minimum wage of 30 cents an hour and allowed wages to be cut in half throughout the South. A prominent black attorney estimated that the lower rate covered "71.5% of the [southern] negro working population but only 26% of the white working population."[6]

It is also clear that the craft unions in the American Federation of Labor blocked the entry of black workers into the skilled trades. The Congress of Industrial Organizations made a major effort to organize black workers in such industries as steel, autos, textiles, and rubber, but occupational data indicate that blacks continued to be concentrated in the lowest-paid, least-skilled jobs within those industries. Our letters suggest the harsh environment in which most blacks worked. A tobacco worker in North Carolina complained that unskilled white labor was earning $12 a week while most semiskilled black workers were making between $7 and $10 a week. Very large numbers of black women continued to work as domestic workers. One such worker in St. Louis begged the president to urge employers to "give us some hours to rest in and some Sundays off and pay us more wages. Let them know we are human and not work ox." Seven-day workweeks and low wages spurred some early efforts at organizing domestic workers, as we saw in Chapter 2.

☏ Section 213 of the Federal Economy Act, passed in 1932, provided that when the staffs of federal offices were to be reduced, the first employees

---

[5]Raymond Wolters, "The New Deal and the Negro," in *The New Deal*, ed. John Braeman, Robert H. Bremner, and David Brody, vol. 1, *The National Level* (Columbus: Ohio State University Press, 1975). See also Gavin Wright, *Old South, New South: Revolutions in the Southern Economy since the Civil War* (New York: Basic Books, 1986).

[6]Wolters, "New Deal and the Negro," pp. 188–89.

to be fired were to be those whose spouses were also employed by the federal government. Throughout the country, citizens reacted strongly against the hiring of married women. More than three-quarters of the nation's school systems, for example, refused to hire such women.[7] The following two letters express the widely held sentiment in opposition to the employment of married women.

January 11, 1936

Dear Mr. President:

Congratulations on your re-election and we're looking for better conditions this coming year.

I know that something can be done about the married women who are working in factories, department stores and offices. They have no right taking the jobs and positions of single girls, single men and married men.

It's all well for a married woman to work if she has become a widow or if her husband is in ill health, but she has no business holding a position if she has a husband working. Some husbands are not working but they will be soon and the majority of them have been working all along.

Their place is at home after they are married and have no right taking other peoples jobs and positions.

You are surely going to bring back the N.R.A. and am trusting you will see that something is done about this married woman business of working.

If the married woman is put out of business, it will make room for many unemployed men and women in factories, department stores, offices and numberless other places.

Together with the "Townsend Plan" and your other good ideas, our country will be back to a better basis of living socially, morally and otherwise.[8]

Wishing you success in your many endeavors.

A GOOD CITIZEN OF THESE
GRAND UNITED STATES

---

[7]Kessler-Harris, *Out to Work*, p. 257.

[8]Apparently this man is ready to give Roosevelt credit for any proposal he considers a "good idea." Roosevelt was not, of course, responsible for the Townsend Plan.

Dayton, Ohio, February 1, 1937

Frances Perkins:

I am a girl 23 years old have to make a living and can't get a job. I wonder if they don't think we got eat or if we are supposed to live off the air. We have to eat just like those who have a job.

I think our government should pass a law so that married women can not be employed in factories or stores, that would give the single girl a chance to get a job.

I think the single girl is entitled to make living more so than the married woman who has a husband to support her and mostly they work so they can buy a lot luxuries.

Furthermore we unemployed girls get very discouraged to walk every day looking for a job and then get turned down just because we haven't the experience. How in the world do they expect us to get experience when they don't give us a job. Sometimes I feel like I am at the end of my rope that's just how disgusted I get.

It's about time that our government pass 30 hour week working law and also enforced it.

VERY DISGUSTED

The statistical increase in the number of working women should not obscure the suffering experienced by married and unmarried women alike in the industrial work force.

Boston, Massachusetts, November 20, 1936

Dear President Roosevelt:

I want ask one favor of you not for myself but for a great many other poor, honest & good citizens. There is A factory here in Roxbury Mass., The Name of it is the Graham Corp., they employe at least 75 to 100 help. There is know heat in the Building not Even to sit down & have a decent place to eat, the wages is very small the wimen get $9.12 a week the men $13.26 now when you by coal 300 lb. a week, milk, for baby, food, lights, Rent $14.00 a month, will please tell if you think it is a fair living, of cause I am just asking if Graham can't fix it so the people can have a little better place to work it is a slave shop, from the Boss down they use you just like dogs it is the most unhealthiest place in U.S.A. the place was inspected about two yrs ago (but the inspector got rake off) and that was the end, it is only a trap for your death. I worked there myself & almost met my Death. The main office is 104-126 Ward St. Roxbury Mass, he also has an office in Fitchburg Mass. I am not employed there anymore as I could [not] stand the cold & exposure. but it is very hard for those who are there. I hope I have not done any harm as asking your help in regards to the poor employees there. We are all thankful to God that you were reelected because God knows you certainly are good to the people God wont let us suffer for the right man to Father our Country the ought not ever to take you from the White House until you die you are a God send to the People of America & may God Bless you & your family.

Wishing you a Happy thanksgiving.

P.S. Please excuse writing & withhold name.

M. B.

The following letter graphically describes the harsh life of an elderly hotel worker. Significantly, she is writing to Mrs. Roosevelt on behalf of younger women.

Atlanta, Georgia, February 19, 1937

Dear Mrs. Roosevelt:

Since Congress is in session again, and our wonderful President is also again on the job, I am begging you to help assist the women working in hotels in this country, especially in the South. I have been in the work since I was 32 years of age, and I am near 61 now, and on a hard job in one of our best hotels here in Atlanta, in the salad department.

I leave home at 10:30 A.M. to be on the job at 12 o'clock. I work like fighting fire, until 10 at night, and more than that. We have late people, and very often, it is 10:30 before I leave the department, and I must then dress for the street, get a [trolley] car, and transfer to my home car. I look over the daily paper, then to bed, and it is almost all I can do to get up and do some little things and leave for my work.

Often I go a little ahead of time to get a cup of coffee, and a bite to eat, before 12 o'clock. But it is no use, the waiters call for things, and where is the man in the dept. he has slipped out to smoke a cigarette, and I must leave my dinner, and go on the job. My coffee gets stone cold, and the only dinner and lunch I get is a bite at a time, for I must do all the cleaning behind the 18 year old boy, that they keep at a smaller salary, and help serve the lunch and then get everything ready for the night meal, and most of the time several parties. We had a party of 150 last night, and a good regular run, and some overtime to stay. I grab a cup of coffee, as I am closing up, and swallow a bite of something, as the manager is hurrying to close.

Well . . . what do I get per month for this fast hard work seven days per week and overtime and to 12:30 on Saturday nights. I get $35 per month, and 60 cents out of that on the Old Age Pension. So you see they rate me at $60. I wear some old ragged uniforms that the coffee shop girls have discarded and an average of three per week are run through their house laundry. My top aprons are brought home and put in another laundry at my expense with my caps and so on.

Yesterday . . . I had given to me for lunch a spoon of mashed potato, a little dumpling, made with something, and a spoon of collard greens. I just go ahead and eat a little ice-cream behind the backs of the managers, or I would go hungry, with $25 taken out of my salary, and me eating breakfast at home.

I am an old experienced worker, and fast and clean and give full satisfaction, but that is the life of a Southern hotel woman worker. Young men soon get better pay while the poor women are made the goat on and on. Me and the colored help scrub at night. Me in my dept., and the negros for the cooks and cold meat counters. The men smoke cigarettes and laugh and talk.

Mrs. Roosevelt, is this fair to women in any section of the country, and can you not influence the President to make laws that will stop it. Laws — with six days and 48 hours per week. . . .

We are not fighting for a 30 hour week, we are breaking in health under 10 to 12 hours a day of fast hard work in a hot hot kitchen (will not let cold air in during serving hours) and only beg for 8 hours in a straight watch (not a split watch) and one day to lie in bed, and rest.

If you think I am telling you wrong concerning our work, you will find on looking over the work that I am right, and it is even worse than I am telling you.

I am so old that you cannot do me much good, but for the younger ones it can be a blessing in the coming years. What do I get out of life, and on pay day what do I have, and we all give to Red Cross also.

I am hoping that Dr. Townsend will sometime bring a better pension than we have so far. Capital will not pay us a living wage, so it must come some other route. I am opposed to Coughlin and all those crokers, but I believe that Townsend himself means well.

Thanking you for reading this petition, and hope you may see just what we live under while men are fighting for six hours and more pay.

Give the forgotten women in Southern Hotels a chance to eat, and a day to lie in bed and rest from the hard work.

Yes I am in favor of enlarging the Supreme Court, and I know that all that President Roosevelt advocates is right, or he would not advocate it to start with, and I know you are extremely proud of such a husband for he is even greater than any that has ever been in our country. We love him, and know that he is for the working man and woman.

M. W.

Washington, D.C., March 16, 1937

DEAR MR. [*sic*] W.:

The president has referred your recent letter to the Department of Labor for reply since his own correspondence is so great that he is not able to answer all of it personally.

We know, unfortunately, that the conditions you describe exist in many establishments throughout the South, as well as in other parts of the country. The Department of Labor is making every effort to call the attention of the people throughout the States to the need for legislation limiting the hours of both men and women. A number of hour laws have been introduced in the southeastern States and we hope that continued public interest will insure their passage and prevent such conditions as those you describe.

I know that the President appreciates your interest in writing.

V. A. ZIMMER

The following series of letters reveals the plight of women factory workers in Louisiana. These women were clearly engaged in heavy labor in appalling conditions. Despite the common view that the New Deal expanded federal power, the response of Clara Beyer, acting director of the Labor Department's Division of Labor Standards, makes it clear that the department had no jurisdiction is such cases, though she sought to intervene on a personal level with the state's labor commissioner. It is significant that Beyer did not simply counsel patience; she urged labor and other organizations to agitate publicly for enforcement of the laws and proper working conditions, though she recognized that such a course "takes courage."

Monroe, Louisiana [n.d.]

Miss Elsie Harper
National Board, Young Women's Christian Association
600 Lexington Avenue
New York, N.Y.

My dear Miss Harper:
  This will serve as a reminder of the conversation you had with Mrs. Tisdale, Pres. of the Y.W.C.A. Board, of Monroe, La., and with me, in regard to some of our Factory girls.
  The factory is Terminal Paper Bag Co. Inc., West Monroe, La. with headquarters at 146 Broadway, New York, N.Y.
  The girl I have interviewed today goes to work at midnight and works until 8 a.m. Sometimes, when they can spare a worker they send across to a cafe and get food, the cafe opens at 5 a.m. But many mornings they do not get an opportunity to send over until 6:30 a.m. or 7 a.m. Many mornings they cannot spare a worker to run across and get the food. So they do without. If, and when the sandwiches are brought to them, they operate the machines and eat at the same time. They are not allowed to leave the machine unless it breaks down. There are no relief operators on the night shifts, so they cannot go to the rest room—and in case of emergency if they shut their machines down—they "catch the devil" as the kid explains it.
  This girl is considered one of the "big girls"—height five feet two inches, weight 125 pounds—so she handles 16 pound bags—largest made in the factory.
  There are 100 bags to a bundle
  There are stacks of five bundles
  With 11 [stacks] on one board and 3 boards on one truck
  This girl runs 4 trucks in eight hours unless there is a breakdown. If there is extra work she has to stay on for sixteen hours—or double time with no more pay or "time over time".
  For her labor—and it is just that—she receives $2.74 per day for five days. 18 cents per month being deducted for Social Security and some State Tax.
  I believe that covers the case for you on that "grave-yard" shift, as it is called. The eight hour shift from 4 p.m. to midnight works under identical conditions. The day time shift from 8 a.m. to 4 p.m. have things a little easier—but the pay is the same, and so are the hours of course. The whole system seems cruel and uncivilized and one that needs to be investigated.

We did enjoy you at Conference at Hot Springs, and when I discard my scrub brush and Old Dutch Cleanser I hope I can attend the Seminar in Atlanta next month.

If you need further data, please do not hesitate to write me for it.

JULIA M. ARNOLD
General Secretary, Y.W.C.A.

New York, N.Y., July 27, 1937

My dear Mrs. Beyer:

When I was in Louisiana a short time ago I came across a number of rather terrible conditions, but no worse than that which you will find reported in the attached letter. This case, as I understand, has been reported to the Factory Inspection Department of the State of Louisiana but there has been no redress of grievance. I have just had another letter from Miss Arnold in which she says that she does hope something can be done. Is it a forlorn hope to wonder whether the Division of Labor Standards can put any pressure on the State Factory Inspection Department?

I need hardly say that under no circumstances whatever must it be known that the information came from the Y.W.C.A.

ELSIE D. HARPER
Secretary, Laboratory Division
National Board, Y.W.C.A.

Washington, D.C., July 28, 1937

Dear Miss Harper:

I wish that I could be encouraging about the Louisiana situation. Ruth Scandrett was there recently and her report indicated that there was little hope of getting improved working conditions or even enforcement of existing laws under the present set-up of the Labor Department.

I believe the only hope is for groups like the Y.W.C.A. and the labor organizations to publicly demand that the laws be enforced and proper working conditions be observed. This takes courage, but it is essential to improvement in conditions. The Governor, I understand, is young and generally sympathetic. It might be very well for a delegation to wait upon him and ask him why the Labor Department is not functioning in accordance with the new legislation which he sponsored.

Should the Black-Connery Bill be enacted, it would give the Federal Government a leverage that might be used in building up standards in the State.[9]

I shall write the Labor Commissioner and see if I can get him stirred up about this particular situation. Of course I will not bring the Y.W.C.A. into it.

I am glad you have written me and will be glad to hear from you at any time when you think we can be helpful, or you have information that we might use to advantage.

CLARA M. BEYER

P.S. We are now preparing a study course for groups on factory inspection in the States. While intended primarily for organized labor, I believe it might easily be adopted for use in Y.W.C.A. groups. It seems to me that if information could be obtained along the lines we have mapped out, it would tend to jack up administration by labor departments. I shall send you a copy of this study outline when it reaches a more finished stage.

This remarkable letter reveals that in 1939, after nearly seven years of New Deal reforms, families were still being torn apart by the Depression. This third-generation American expresses pride in her family's role in building the country with their labor, but she fears that with war already raging in Europe, the working class will be unwilling to "fight . . . to make more wealth for men that never had to labor and never appreciated where the real source of their wealth derived from." This woman has a firm grasp of the class structure of American society and its role in the plight of her country and her family.

Detroit, Michigan, November 27, 1939

President Roosevelt
Dear Honorable Sir:

I am living in a city that should be one of the prized possessions of these United States of America but it isn't only to a small group of chiseling money mongers.

I and my husband are and have been Americans for three generations and we are proud of what our parents did also our grandparents to help

---

[9]In 1938 a weaker bill, known as the Fair Labor Standards Act, was passed.

America progress. They were builders of our country not destructers as is now going on to make the rich man richer and the poor man poorer in fact try and starve them in a land of plenty. We have six growing children that are all separated each one pining for each other and our hearts nearly broken because we cannot keep them all together.

We have tried so hard these past seven years we lost our furniture twice lost our car our insurance even my engagement ring and finally the wedding ring to buy groceries pay rent and for illness. Neither one of us are lazy he worked in steel mills auto factories painting dishwashing and anything he could get. I worked at waitress janitress selling to make a few dollars now my health is slowly ebbing. I was a widow when I married my present husband my first husband died shortly after the world war having served as a submarine chaser. I received a check for $1.00 for each day he served he died leaving me two lovely children. Why should descent American people be made suffer in this manner living in an attic room paying $5.00 per week and if its not paid out you go on the streets. Welfare has never solved these problems as there are far too many inefficient social workers also too much political graft for it to survive or even help survive. We are one family out of 100,000 that are in the same position right here in Detroit where the ones we labor for and help build up vast fortunes and estates do nothing but push us down farther. They cheat the government out of taxes hire foreign labor at lower rates and if we get discouraged and take some groceries to feed our family we must serve time.

They have 40 to 100 room houses with no children to make it even like a home while we are denied a small home and enough wages to provide for them. Barbara Hutton has herself exploited that she pays $650.00 to have one tooth pulled and the girls in her dime stores slave all week for $12 or $14 and must help provide for others out of it. I'll wager to say that the poor class were lucky to have roast pork @ 13¢ per lb on Thanksgiving Day while the rich people in this country probably throwed a lot out in there garbage cans. These so called intelligent rich men including the Congressmen and the Senators better wake up and pass some laws that will aid labor to make a living as they would have never accumulated their vast fortunes had it not been from the hard sweat that honest labor men brought them.

We read with horror of the war in Europe and of the blockade to starve the people into submission and right here in Detroit we have the same kind of a blockade. Do the intelligent men of America think we are going to stand for this much longer. I alone hear a lot of viewpoints and it will be very hard to get our men to fight another war to make more wealth for men that never had to labor and never appreciated where the real source of their wealth derived from. This country was founded on Thanksgiving day to get away from the brutal treatment the British gave them and us real true Americans intend keeping it so. We need men of wealth and men of intelligence but we also need to make labor healthy and self supporting or our nation will soon crumble and it is head on to a good start. Even prisoners will balk at an injustice and we are not prisoners. God Bless all true Americans you have my permission to read this in the next session of Congress.

A true American mother & family

M. Q. L.

The fastest growing segment of the female labor force consisted of clerical and other poorly paid white-collar workers. The following letters describe the tension and harassment faced by secretaries and telephone operators.

Detroit, Michigan, July 11, 1940

Department of Labor, Lansing, Michigan
Copy to Department of Labor, Washingston, D.C.

I worked for [Contract Purchase Corporation] for four months and feel that I should report my case to you as an example of some working conditions.

I applied and got this job through an employment agency four months ago and paid exactly $33.33 for the position which was supposed to be permanent. The last installment was paid last June 29th. I worked every day with the exception of Monday and Tuesday of this week due to a throat irritation and inflammation of the left eye. When I returned to work on Wednesday morning neither Mr. A nor Mr. N. were there and I was referred to Mr. H., company treasurer, and told my services were no longer needed on my particular job, but there was a temporary job of three weeks I could accept or take one week's pay in advance and consider myself out of a job, which, considering the over time I put in, is very little and told him I deserved at least two weeks after the way I slaved, but my argument was to no avail. My own bosses couldn't face me.

Since I am single I need my job and it is not through inefficiency or wasting time that I'm out of work, but simply because of the slave-driving methods of the assist. to my boss, Mr. N., who is a terrible person to work for in any capacity. When I was hired I was informed my duties were secretary to Mr. A., Branch Manager, but his assistant gave me so much work (humanly impossible) besides relieving on the switchboard, which took two hours a day from my work, that I couldn't possibly do justice to Mr. A.'s work. Mr. N., who is a first class slave driver, constantly kept after me to see when I would have this out and that out—he nagged you so much one was hardly in a condition to complete anything. Finally I had to resort to working over time a few nights a week, then every night, then work over time and take work home, then work Saturday afternoons and then work at home on Sundays. The working hours were supposed to be from 8:45 to 5:00; Saturdays 8:45 to 1:00. I did not lose my job because of inefficiency or laziness, but because Mr. N. had the crust that he didn't think I had the health to continue—when he gets through with you you're lucky living. There was a married woman in the office with no responsibilities, whose husband has a steady job with the Bohn Aluminum, of whom, she (Mrs. F. B. or Miss H. in the office) constantly bragged about her husband working for ten years and making top money and how sure she is of her job. I hardly think it is fair to subject a capable, efficient single girl to the ordeal of job hunting—especially after having paid for the right to earn a living to the tune of practically $10 a month which I or any other single girl cannot afford—yet I noticed pressure was never used on her nor did she ever have to work over time.

It doesn't seem right they should "put the skids" on single girls who work so hard to keep a job. After what has happened I have no desire to be reinstated even though I need a job—I will look elsewhere—but if what they did wasn't wrong why didn't they face me instead of turning the dirty work over to the treasurer, whom I never worked with or hardly knew.

N. C. O'H.

Cicero, Illinois, March 18, 1942

Dear Miss Perkins:

After nineteen years of service with the Illinois Bell Telephone Company I suffered a nervous breakdown, and then they refused to take me back because I was ill.

I was ill due to the fact that they dog their girls around and do not treat them in a civil manner. They keep a girl under constant observation from the time she starts to work until she goes off duty. I happened to be one of them and I was only as human as the chief operator herself—so you see I could not take it.

The girls wanted a union and they had six women of the Company Federation question the girls and instead of straightening out the affair they threatened the girls with loss of their jobs.

I knew nothing at all about the girls wanting a Union and taking the matter too seriously I became ill. They, however, continued to deduct Federation dues from my salary which was as good as no Federation at all. My doctor's reports showed that I was suffering from a nervous condition, and when I returned to work I was again taken sick.

The girls in the South Division want a Union right now, which the company will fight against. An operator had a nervous fit right at her switchboard because they had been observing her board all the time, the very place I worked.

When I went to the girls on the Committee of Federation they informed me that the traffic manager had already told them that he was not going to take me back, and that they must see his viewpoint or he would dismiss them too.

I then went to the head chairman, Mrs. J., who is at the head of the Federation in Chicago. She made me promise not to hold a grudge against her if she could not do anything for me. She called me back three days later telling me that she talked the situation over the telephone with the Traffic Manager and that there was nothing she could do, asking me again not to hold a grudge against her and then said good bye.

I did not want to claim disability. I wanted a furlough. She said: "You are entitled to claim disability" and she refused the furlough, so I had to stay home as I was not able to work, and therefore got claim disability.

Please, Miss Perkins, can you tell me what a girl, almost 39, can do after giving the Telephone Company the best years of her life, and why Mr. M. should think I am not entitled to return to my former position. Perhaps with your help the company will take me back. Every employer wants a girl 19 years of age and not older than 23. I too was only 19 when they hired me, and when Mr. M. told me he wouldn't take me back, the company was hiring girls in great number. He told me I was a good worker and that he would give me a good recommendation—so you see it wasn't my work, it was only because of my illness.

I went to Mr. C., the head traffic manager, of Chicago and told him I was single and had no one to support me, and as I had spent all my money on doctor bills I must have a position. His reply was he knew nothing about my being dismissed and not to come to ask him anything about it. I told Mr. C. I wouldn't have a home, and after being so loyal and coming in whenever I was called for duty, giving up Sundays off, working holidays and taking all the assignments that were given me — vacations even changed on the last minute — would not justify a dismissal just because I was ill. He said he would have to think it over and would let me know. Later his secretary called and told me to go down to see Mr. S. (He is the man above Mr. M.). His first words to me were that they had decided to help me keep my health and that was for the better of the company. I told him it was the company's fault that I was ill, due to the uncivil treatment we were receiving, but he would not listen to this.

Since the Federation is as good as none, why do they deduct 50 cents every month for Federation dues from every girl's salary, and yet not do anything for them. I was dismissed last April 14 and it took them over 8 days to make it final.

Don't you think, Miss Perkins, I should have my job back since it was no fault of mine that I was ill? Isn't there something that you can do for me about it?

I am sorry I have had to write such a lengthy letter, but I felt I wanted to give you full details.

E. K.

The writer of the following letter, a dietician forced to accept any job she could get, describes her experiences as a factory worker.

New Canaan, Connecticut [n.d.]

Department of Labor
Gentlemen:

I wonder if your Department will be good enough to supply me with information re the following.

As I have been unable to secure adequate compensation in my own line of work (nutrition, foods, diets, etc.) I have for the past eight months taken up various types of factory employment from cementing to 30 different kinds of machines, hoping thereby to gain training to properly fit me for defense work.

1.—Due to lack of material in various non-defense factories many of us are having enforced "vacations" so I have been applying to other factories. Among them was the Manhattan Shirt Co., who offered to teach me how to run a power machine at a salary of $13.00 per week. I have always understood that $16.00 was the minimum salary for any type of machine worker, and have been told that the Manhattan people, being one of the big concerns, also being located in Connecticut, can "get away with murder, nothing can be done."

2.—If there is a holiday during the week, can employer force an employee to work an extra day to make this up, at the same rate of pay—no overtime? e.g. I was forced to take a Jewish holiday at my own expense. I feel that a legal or religious holiday should be paid for by the employer.

3.—This question may be out of your jurisdiction, but am not sure. Where I last worked—Nu-Made Handbag Co., Norwalk, Conn.—is located on the 3rd floor. The stairs are very steep, no lights in the hallways, & it needs only one false step to send one rolling down the stairs yet the "safety (or "unsafety") men" say "OK".

4.—Sanitary conditions in these factories are dreadful. Our Government is spending large sums to keep (or make) our people clean, we have blood tests, etc. yet our factories are allowed to have dirty & inadequate toilet facilities. It would seem that our local Board of Health members are woefully ignorant or the "don't care" kind. Something should be done.

5.—It is my understanding that women are not allowed to stand at their work for an entire day, yet I have been forced to do so until I ached all over, but again, nothing is done.

My former lawyer, now deceased, once told me that Connecticut had more loop holes in its laws than any other state in the Union. If this is so, why?

Then, too, in most of these factories, everything is quantity, not quality, & the two do not mix anymore than gasoline & alcohol—as for instance, 5000 new machine guns not fit for use. A little more attention to quality instead of quantity will save our country money, time & effort in the long run.

My 8 mos. in various factories have been most enlightening,—I could make this letter twice as long, still not have finished, but this will do for the moment.

Your comments, at an early date will be much appreciated.

C. A. P.

The following letters describe conditions that blacks were forced to endure in a variety of occupations.

Winston-Salem, North Carolina, January 27, 1935

Dear Miss Perkins:

Please allow me to state some of the facts concerning our wages paid in the Tobacco factories first I want to call your attention to the firm I am working for. The Brown & Williamson Co; We make 40 hours a week and we don't average $10.00 per week for semi skilled labor in my department where the *plug tobacco is manufactured* we that are doing semi skilled labor make less than those doing common labor. they make around $12.00 per week while we make from $7.00 to $10.00 and maybe some few of us might make $13.00 once and a while. Now how can we be considered in the Presidents spending program when we don't make enough to live on and pay our just and honest debts. Please take notice Meat advanced from 6 cents to 16 cents sugar from 5 to 6 cents flour has almost doubled and house rent and every thing but our wages the idea of men young and middle age making less than $2.00 while we are piling up millions for the firms we work and the sad part of it is the majority are afraid to make an out cry about conditions. Now I think our great trouble lies in the fact that no[body] ever investigates our working conditions and the greatest portion of us are colored people and I think every body hates a colored man. How can we support a family of 7 or 8 send our children to school and teach them citizen ship when capitalist choke us and make criminals out of some of us that might be a bit weak. Now Miss Perkins just think about our condition how hard it is to come up to the American Standard of living on less than $10.00 for 40 hours work and 7 or 8 in family or it seems that my race of people are not considered in the American Standard of living. Now most of my people are afraid to complain because some few years ago the R. J. Reynolds Tobacco Co. discharged every one that joined a union they were trying to organize here and for reason you can't find any union workers in the R. J. Reynolds firm among the colored people for better proof you can refer to the organized labor conference in Washington last August when S. Clay Williams represented the Tobacco Manufacturer there was no one to speak for labor for the colored workers. It seems that some investigations should be made. Now how can we pay our debts educate our children and if we have to call a doctor we don't have the money to pay him for his visit is

$3.00 at day and $5.00 at night and from that you can realize our condition then look at the chairman of the N.R.A. How can we get a square deal as our case is continued to be pushed a side. Please consider these facts Miss Perkins We are up against a hard proposition.

O. G.

Mobile, Alabama, January 7, 1937

Dear Mr. President:

I am a skilled workman in the saw-mill industry and am writing in the hope that you will please consider the plight of the people who work at the Southern saw-mills for a living.

The labor conditions in this industry are terrible, for instance I used to get in 1929 and for several years prior to that time, one ($1.00) dollar per hour straight time for my work, and now get sixty (.60) cents per hour.

About ninety-five per cent of the saw-mill work is done by negro common labor and they get in this section from 16 1/2 cents per hour to 20 cents per hour, and their work is plenty hard, which of course is to be expected, but I do not see how they live and work on what they are able to buy to eat. I notice the negroes eating their lunches around the mill and they usually have some white bread, syrup and potatoes or something on that order every day, and not much of that.

There has never been an opportunity for the Southern hardwood and pine saw-mill workers to organize as nearly all the work is done by negroes, and they have no chance to organize in this part of the country and demand a fair wage.

It would be a wonderful thing for the workers of the Southern lumber industry if the Federal governnment would conduct a secret and impartial investigation of our labor conditions. This is our only hope.

Most of the mills are operating ten hours or longer, shipping lots of lumber at a good price, but wages are very little better than during the worst part of the "depression."

S. E. M.

St. Louis, Missouri, November 29, 1942

Dear President:

This letter is to inform you about the jobs in these private home in St Louis. I wish you would set the hours to work in the home. We start to work at 7 o'clock in the morning and work until 8:30 and 9 o'clock at night don't have any time to rest they call my self giving us off days it be 4 and 5 o'clock in the evening before they let us off. don't give us time to have a half hour to eat and rest no days. And that way from monday morning until sunday on our feet all day. If we be sick they put that much more hard work on us. Dear President you know that we colored women got work. So please help us out they are rich people and don't want to pay us anything to work. 6.50 a week and we are on our feet all day long and part of the night. they want to treat us like they want us to treat them. So please Dear President publish or broadcast it over the radio that all the people will hear or see it. that they must give us some hours to rest in and some sundays off and pay us more wages. let them know that we are human and not work ox. So please Dear President help us out but we shall pray for your success in life. So please do something at once.

M. H.

Washington, D. C., December 14, 1942

Dear Miss H.:

The President has asked me to answer your letter of November 29.

State and Federal labor laws, which offer protection to workers in so many occupations, have so far not set up standards for working conditions in domestic situations. There is nothing that can be done at the present time to help you and others in this kind of employment.

I can only suggest that you talk with an interviewer in an office of the United States Employment Service and find out whether there is any other job open which will give you more reasonable working conditions.

V. A. ZIMMER

Milan, Tennessee, March 2, 1943

My Dear President:

I have attempted to write to you for several days but have been reluctant to do so. I am not unmindful of the tremendous task which devolve upon you as the head of our great Nation. You are one of the busiest men of all the world today. Too busy even to consider individual cases. Yet I feel that it is my duty to relate my case to you. This is why I am writing you today.

I believe I have done everything else that could be done in this matter, but it has been of no avail.

I am one E. C. C., Negro woman, and was hired by Procter and Gamble Defence Corporation, Aug. 8, 1942. And on Feb. 1, 1943 I was terminated for unsatisfactory work.

I was working in the laundry department, and because of the hay fever, the doctor recommended that I be taken from the job of pressing as it was definitely against me. This war recommended more than once. But my foreman, Mr. T., failed to do so. Miss B., who has the job of looking after the women, and who with Mr. W., have Charge of the personnel, went to Mr T. and had him to take me of the press. This seems to have made Mr T. angry, and from then on he seem to have had it in for me.

I wasn't notified at all concerning unsatisfactory work. Mr T. stated that I was one of the best pressers that he had and that he didn't want me to be taken from that work. I have never been fired for unsatisfactory work, and I have worked hard all my life. I was just snatched up on Feb. 1st, and carried to the Personnel, and was terminated. Mr. S., the Line Supt. said he knew nothing of it. Only what had been told to him. Mr. W. asked me had Mr. S. seen me and told me why I was terminated, but he never said anything to me.

I feel that the whole thing is simply a frame-up to get rid of me. I am just a hard working Negro woman, and want to work, and will work. I have talked to them all and they just shift me from one to the other. I am no more to be terminated than any one else, but I was not dealt with fairly in this matter. You have done much to help out our people, and if you will, please look into this matter. I believe you want all people that work for our country to have a square deal.

I regret that I had to bring this matter to you, but I don't know any one else to whom I can appeal. Your help will be greatly appreciated.

E. C. C.

5. *"Since He Took Over,*
the Atmosphere Has Changed"

Management Tactics against Labor

The history of the labor movement is filled with stories of management's attempts to intimidate and coerce its work force. Throughout the nineteenth century and well into the twentieth, companies hired spies, Pinkerton police, scabs, and thugs to enforce worker discipline and break organizing drives. Such efforts accelerated in the 1930s, as managers used every means at their disposal to maximize labor productivity in the face of declining profits and workers attempted to organize.

The passage of the National Labor Relations Act in 1935 did not halt efforts by business managers to stifle organizing activity. Between 1936 and 1940, the investigations of the La Follette Civil Liberties Committee, a subcommittee of the Senate Committee on Education and Labor, revealed that industrial firms routinely spied on their workers, and that when intimidation failed to stop union activity, they prepared for labor trouble by laying in supplies of tear gas, machine guns, gas bombs, and clubs. If labor strife did break out, industrial managers did not hesitate to use their weapons against workers. "Company police and hired strike-guards," an investigator reports, "constantly usurped the public police power by venturing away from company property, weapons in hand, to maintain 'law and order.'"[1]

Workers' letters suggest the variety of methods by which management

---

[1]Jerrold Auerbach, *Labor and Liberty: The La Follette Committee and the New Deal* (Indianapolis: Bobbs-Merrill, 1966), p. 105.

countered union activity. In addition to the tactics traditional in industry—spying, firing, intimidation—we find farm laborers in Arkansas
threatened with arrest and jail if they refused to work for less than the
union wage of 15 cents an hour. An Indiana woman complained to the
president about the conditions at the firm that employed her brother,
where the workers were "being paid with Script money" and were "afraid
to do anything about it for fear of losing their jobs." With work so
scarce, some companies actually made money by selling jobs to unemployed workers in distant communities, thereby undermining the cohe-
siveness of local workers and destroying a community's morale. "It isn't
fair," an anonymous correspondent wrote, "for people from Canada the
west south to take our jobs away and we have to go to other places for
jobs."

Another tactic used by some employers was to pay workers in common stock rather than cash. An Illinois woman complained to the president that the workers in a barbed-wire company were forced "to give half
their wages back to [the owner] & he would give them common stock in
the plant at 40 a share at present this stock isn't worth $10 a share if you
try to sell it."

In an exchange of letters about the displacement of coal miners in Alabama we see the devastating effects of technological unemployment. A
mine that had been closed for two years was reopened, but now it was
"more highly mechanized than formerly, and practically no unskilled or
semi-skilled labor" was to be used. The effect on the miners and their
families was catastrophic. One miner lamented, "We are coal miners and
some of us don't know anything else we have spent our lives working in
the mines."

The following letter shows us one employer's resistance to the NRA
codes and his threat to relocate his plant as a means of gaining concessions from workers. It is significant that the Labor Department's response actually encouraged the workers to organize.

Bronx, New York, January 17, 1935

My Dear Miss Perkins:

About eight years ago I obtained a job which was meant to be only
temporary, for the rewards for the services were very small. The employer succeeded to cajold me as the rest of them (three) for none of us
ever thought of associating with those desperadoes, the organizers.

Then came the depression. My employer was among the first to follow the vogue and reduce salaries by ten percent. Shortly after he repeated that twice, which made a grand total of thirty per cent. To anyone who objected to this needless repetition for business with them did not demand it, there was but one retort, "If you can help yourself, do so."

At the induction of the N.R.A., unlike the period of salary reduction, my employer refrained from signing the blanket code to the last minute, and then it was due to the association of which the firm is a member. When the cotton garment permanent code was signed, we as a children's cotton dress house were included. With pretended cheer one of the employers came marching in, and, taking advantage of our gullibility, announced that they have just signed the code of which they are the first, which in truth they were the last.

The bosses (of which are four) began to act differently in order to cover their animosity, for now we received the same salary for forty hours as we received for fifty-four hours before the code came in effect. These parasites could not see that, although they made money. They exhibited fear that we may take advantage of the 7A clause of the N.R.A. by repeatedly questioning us individually as to our opinion towards organization to which we replied that we have no intention.

At the outbreak of the strike last summer, our employer threatened us that should we join the strike he will move our department (cutting) with the plant of machines which is located in a small New Jersey town. He bribed us with a dollar increase, and called up the police department. Sergeants and patrolmen arrived shortly after for our protection, so the story goes. In spite of that assurance we were told to leave the shop about noon and were promised pay for a full day.

Early this month the New York department was moved to the New Jersey factory. The individual who is to supervise the entire dep. boasts of considerable popularity and influential in political circles, particularly in Trenton.

Three members from New York of which I am one, were asked to go along, and having nothing else on hand had to accept the proposition. Now, to our chagrin, we discover that we are to instruct the new hired help which receives from ten to sixteen dollars a week who are to replace us subsequently soon as we get them accustomed to the routine of the work. There is a bellicose attitude on the part of the employer and very threatening of dismissal. Would appreciate your information as to what steps to take in order to protect our present subsistence.

J. S.

Washington, D.C., January 21, 1935

My dear Mr. S.:

Your letter to the Secretary has been referred to me for answer.

As long as your employer is abiding by the provisions of the Cotton Garment Code, there is little that can be done by the Government. The improvement of conditions in general will probably only come through organization of the workers. I should think you would be justified in developing this possibility in your plant.

CLARA M. BEYER

Indianapolis, Indiana, October 23, 1936

Dear President:

The Employees of the Platter Furniture Company at North Vernon, Indiana, are still being paid with Script money, and seem to think they have to abide by these rules or are afraid to do anything about it for fear of losing their jobs.

Last winter this same company was operated without heat—causing injury to the health of many of the Employees.

I have a brother working there under these conditions—so would greatly appreciate any consideration you can give this matter.

I thought you would be interested in knowing of this case. Thank you.

MRS. H. R.

After workers had suffered repeated cuts in pay, mechanization deprived many of them of their jobs.

Chicago, Illinois, December 3, 1936

Mr. Martin P. Durkin, Director
Illinois Labor Department
Springfield, Illinois

Dear Mr. Durkin:

Have read your article in the Daily Times today, about improved working standards, bred under the NRA before the Supreme court death.

I have worked in the General Office of Armour and Company, U.S. Yards for years. I will give you a few facts how the big concerns are toward eliminating the depression. First of all, during the Depression in 1929 and 1930, the employees on the first floor of the General Office of Armour and Company, took a readjustment in salary from $2.50 up to $10.00 per week. On top of that, they took two ten per cent cuts in salary. To date, 1936 nothing has been done to reimburse the Office help.

Starting January 1st, 1937, they are to install a new system in the General Office on the first floor of Armour and Company, whereby, it will throw about 2,000 people out of work. This machine they are going to install, will throw employees out of work that have worked faithfully for years for this concern, not only in the office, but all through the plant also, anyone that has anything to do with, typing, printing, labelling, etc., this machine takes care of all that.

It is true that the Packers have given the people on an hourly scale a 7 per cent increase, but in order to make this up, they have cut down on the hours, or they either lay the people off after working one or two days the first part of the week, then they hire them again the latter part of the week for one or two days. Is this fair, with their 7 per cent raise.

During the NRA, they all worked forty hours, when the forty hours was up, the plant employees were told to punch their cards, then they had to work more hours in the same week, the only thing they received for the additional hours, was added to next week work. So you see they had some people working fifty and sixty hours in one week.

Right now at the present time, the people on the first floor of the General Office of Armour and Company, are putting in fifty, sixty and seventy hours, getting nothing for it, not even a cup of coffee or a sandwich, not mentioning anything at all about a raise in Salary. Is this Fair, they all claim the Packers are paying their employees so much, but these are true facts and all are open to investigation.

Armour & Company Office Employees

☏ Some managers tried to force workers to break their own unions.

Wellsville, Ohio, February 1, 1937

My kind friend Miss Perkins:

Just a few lines this morning hoping that these few lines will help us hot mill men.

I have been employed for the American Sheet & Tin Plant Co. since a boy of eleven years of age and I do not think that the employee has been treated as they should of been, i myself have had some pretty good jobs for the company but i have lost them fighting for my rights through strikes and now the company is asking its employees to donate to help fight the C.I.O. This is not our fight it is the company fight I did not donate and will not I am in favor of the C.I.O. and a six hour day hoping that you and President Roosevelt will see that the hot Mill men will get a six hour day through the hot summer months the hot Mill men can not enjoy any pleasure or show his family any or enjoy his home life. When he has done his 8 hours in the hot mill he is done lay down to get in shape for his next days work. The workers have backed this government to its full strength please help us to get a six hour day the understanding is if we do not donate we lose our jobs the company Representation plan does not help the employee any it helps the company so please Miss Perkins help us to a six hour day and some enjoyment in life and if you want to know any thing about the working conditions of the Hot Mills write me and I can let you know from A to Z. . . .

W. C. W.

The following letter indicates the variety of ways in which management pitted groups of workers against one another: young versus old, women versus men, native-born versus immigrant.

Inglewood, California, March 10, 1937
"Sharp practices and Malpractices—under the old NRA—will they be tolerated under new legislation?"

President Roosevelt
Honorable Sir:
    During operation of the recent NRA, termed "unconstitutional" by the self-appointed new 3rd House, Hattem's Markets (and others) of Los Angeles, reduced clerks earning $18 per week, to $15 per week—for a 48 hour week, so as to comply with the Hours, and Wages clause as applied to cities of over 250,000.
    These clerks, to hold their jobs, were compelled to work 60 HOURS PER WEEK, as formerly. On Saturday they were paid $15—then they had to sign a form and were paid $3 more—which brought them their original $18 per week.
    It is quite evident that manipulation of books had to be resorted to, so as to make it seem that the NRA was being lived up to.

The manager tore down the form relating to laws governing the new enactment (after a clerk had underlined the hours and wages clauses) —the while prominent posters announced the firm's intention to stand by the President.

Later, Hattem ordered the manager to "GET RID OF THE OLD MEN, PEOPLE DON'T LIKE TO SEE THEM AROUND THE CHECK STAND"

Ralphs—the cheapest selling grocers in Los Angeles, some time ago, commenced employing girls, who replaced higher paid, tax paying men.

Several wholesale grocery firms dismissed their warehouse and truck men, and employed cheaply paid Mexican youths, mostly weaklings, who, unaccustomed (and unable) to handling heavy cartons of canned goods, threw them, or dropped them down; more than tripling the original amount of spoils—a tremendous national loss.

Other retail grocery, fruit and vegetable firms were paying High School boys $1 and $1.50 for working 12 and 14 hours on Saturdays— thus doing many "OLD MEN" out of their miserable pittance earned ONE DAY WEEKLY.

Many bottling and trucking firms worked (and still work) their men 12 to 14 hours daily.

Trusting that the recital of these facts as practiced during your recent commendable attempt to "iron out" some of the inequalities that habit and custom had compelled the "forgotten man" to accept as HIS LOT, will make it possible to put teeth into a measure that will make the otherwise commendable "old gentlemen" hesitate about continuing in the Legislative field, and help erase the $ mark from the escutcheon of the American business man.

Trusting that the foregoing will at least, in part, reveal some of the inequalities that prompted your humane approach of the problems of men.

J. W. G.

Some bosses, like the manager of the firm that employed the writer of the following letter, believed they had the right to dictate their workers' personal lives.

Sylacauga, Alabama, May 10, 1937

Dear Miss Perkins:

I am writing you for information on what for us to do, we work for Danville Knitting Mill Co. Bon Air, Ala. The working conditions we have to work under are so bad we have no freedom nor rights, we are worked like slaves. I will outline to you some of the conditions we have to work under and you will understand better what I mean.

The company has had us on long hours ever since the N.R.A. was killed. We have to work from midnight Sunday night till midnight Sat. night and we have to work that way to hold our jobs if we don't we get fired, even if we refuse to or have anything to say about it.

We haven't had but one five per cent raise and no bonus this year and other mills around have given one five per cent raise one ten per cent and two bonus this year and are on 40 hrs. week.

The general manager A. A. K. is one of the hardest men on labor I have ever seen. He will fire the hands for anything they do outside of their jobs, in other words he is Preacher, Doctor, and Boss spelled with capital letters and the people have to take it or loose their job. We have hoped something would happen to straighten everything out, but we have just about given up hope. If Mr. A. A. K. was to know I have written this he would fire me before I could turn around, so I am asking you not to give me away. If there is anything in this world you can do to help us we surely will appreciate it.

I have been working for this company for about four years and the people have been treated so bad they are afraid to do anything for they know they will be fired if they do.

We have been hoping there would be a labor organizer come around and help us out but there hasn't been anyone yet. So, if you can do anything to help us in any way we will appreciate it very much. I wish you could come here yourself and just find out for yourself the condition of things for I can't explain to you how bad things are. This mill is on the Central of Georgia Railroad at Bon Air, Ala. and in Talladega County and employs about three hundred hands, it is owned by Danville Knitting Mills Co. in Danville Virginia. Mr. A. A. K. is general manager, he is the man we want you to straighten out, his address is Bon Air, Ala.

J. P. C.

Southern sharecroppers were subjected to intensive intimidation by both management and local officials.

Blytheville, Arkansas, May 27, 1937

My dear Madam [Perkins]:

The following is a truthful statement of facts relative to farm day labor in Eastern Arkansas, especially in Mississippi County.

For a number of years, farm labor has been forced to work twelve to fourteen hours a day at an average wage of 6½ cents per hour. About one month ago, the Southern Tenant Farmers' Union asked for 15 cents per hour, ten hours a day for cotton chopping. Landlords flatly refused this demand and are resorting to coercion through local officials, who are now threatening to arrest and jail day laborers and sentence them to terms on the county/penal farm when they refuse to work in the fields of planters for less than the stipulated union wage. In fact, landlords are using coercion through petty officers and threats of bringing about unbearable conditions to the laborer.

Such a state of affairs cannot exist quietly much longer. Any advice that can be read at a Tenant Farmers meeting concerning this situation will be most highly valued and appreciated by the laboring element of this community.

S. W. B.

The following two letters reveal a variety of tactics employed by managers to avoid paying their workers.

Sterling, Illinois, January 4, 1938

Dear [President Roosevelt]:

We listened to your talk yesterday over the radio and feel certain that you are in favor of the working men of this country therefore would appreciate a little advice.

My husband was a ladle Craneman at The North Western Barb Wire Co. of Sterling until Jan. first Then he and everyone else was let out of the mill who refused to sign a paper for Mr. D. who is the owner of the plant just mentioned.

This paper was to give half their wages back to him & he would give them common stock in the plant at $40 a share at present this stock isn't worth $10 a share if you try to sell it.

He made a drive in Nov. that the men had to buy stock or loose their jobs. So most of them bought 1 & 2 shares as they were able to make a living on the wages he paid them. But on December 1st. he gave them a 13 per cent cut in wages. and took their day rate away from them gave them only the tonnage they made. Then in a week he closed one furnace down cut their days from 6 to 4 a week.

Their salaries were cut in half. On Jan. 1st. He tried to force them to sign the paper to give him 50 per cent of their wages back.

Some of the men refused to sign this paper and went to the Post Office authorities how to find out if something couldn't be done according to the Wagner Act Bill that was passed.

The Post Office refused to give them any information as to who they should see to get a government man here to inspect this Mill Because Mr. D. belongs to the Chamber of Commerce here.

When the men went back to see if they couldn't reach some agreement without turning 50 per cent of their wages back were told they were only entitled to a piece of bread now & then. What does he think their families can live on & Who does he think he is that he can do this?

He still has some of the men working for him who signed this paper. He has set them on jobs that the men who refused to sign worked at.

Would sure appreciate if a government man could be sent here & have this matter looked into. If we as an individual were to break a law as he had done would be brought into court and tried.

Why does he get by with breaking such laws because he has a little money and industry because he belongs to The Chamber of Commerce.

This is supposed to be a free country but there isn't much freedom is it when a man like him can tell the laboring man what they should do with the wages they have earned because he runs the place where they happen to work. I as one am a tax paying citizen of this United States & feel as tho something should be done about him. I'm sure there are many others who feel the same way.

Mrs. S. C.

Norwalk, Connecticut, February 10, 1938

James Roosevelt, Sec. to the President
My Dear Mr. Roosevelt:

I'm writing this to you in reply to your letter what my husband L. T. D. got today from you. He wrote you last Monday complaining about my work. where I work I have been working over 9 years in the rubber Tire factory here in Norwalk Ct. not Norwich and my foster Daughter has been working their about 18 months the 20th of this month. Our pays was always up and down. So I couldn't stand it any longer, when you no you were supposed to get piece work, they wanted you to do extra work for nothing and last Aug. 1937. When they gave us our new rate they never included that extra work, if they did we wouldn't make so much and I thought I'd catch them so I made the efficiency man put all my prices I was supposed to get on a piece of paper. The last two wks what they give me was piece work. We didn't touch that work at all. and they were always threatening us about our job especially on the last day we work that was on Feb. 2, 1938 They told us then if we didn't do that work we could get our hat and coats on, and go home. I told them at the time, I wouldn't go home till I finished my work and the next day Thurs. was pay day. I forgot to tell you before, I asked them for my slip of paper cause I got fired. Now when I got my pay Thurs. I asked for my other pay, cause they hold back a week and they had nerve to say we quit and that made us angry as anything, for don't you think Dear Mr. Roosevelt we'd stayed home if we didn't hear them say that? Lo on the same week Friday I called up the Labor Department in Hartford Ct. and he was to our house in the afternoon. He went over to the factory, and told us go back to see if we could get our jobs back. We went back Sat. and the employment manager wasn't in we heard, and we went back again this past Mon. and he told us they have no jobs at all. They had others in our place. on Wed. yesterday we went down to the U.S. employment to see if they could do anything and I think they are going to do all they can for us. at the factory they have the Poor People terrible nervous, and up set long hrs, and barely any pay. Maybe they won't do that now when they see that they are getting checked on. We haven't anybody working in our house now. My husband was on Welfare, but was taken off of it, quite a long time ago and I hate to have him go down to the Welfare when you like to do the right thing always. my husband is older than I am and as long as I can work its my belief, to take nothing what we don't work for. I do hope you understand my situation.

Our job is inspectors on Tubes, Air Bags, and Truck Tubes. First we have to feel on sides to see if they are thin 2nd we have to inflate them, 3rd inspect them for defects, 4th put thru test tank to see if they leak and if they are a lot of buffing to do. When we are thru we have to wait, or do them next morning for nothing, and it makes you get long hrs. and they take out for bad tubes on our tubes and that's not right. When we go in next morning we have another day, on top of the work what was left the day before. They don't want to hire new help if they can get away with it they have been doing this for years.

I think your doing a fine thing for this country also your father Oh! how we would like to meet you people, you all take after our own hearts, an independent mind, and that's what you need now-adays. The time we was in they needed extra help. I mean the men, we were alright, cause when I told them about that they acted mad. Give our best wishes to the president your mother and family for you all are certainly doing a wonderful thing for the under dog. So with the happiest wishes, I remain Very Respt. yours.

Mrs. M. D.

P.S. . . . when I told them at the shops I was going to complain to the State about them, Mr. K. the Manager said what can the state do. I don't no if he really realized what he said to me. Thanks once again for giving this your earliest attention.

East Hartford, Connecticut, January 10, 1939
Dear Madam [Perkins]:
(Regarding United Aircraft Corp.)
East Hartford, Conn.

Some years ago J. C. W. came with the Aircraft as Asst-Gen Mgr. and later when Mr. C. W. D. resigned was promoted to Gen-Mgr. Since he took over, the atmosphere has changed. Throughout the whole Plant there has arisen a feeling of fear. Men once were happy at there work, most all were contented. Today through a spying system all men go around with sealed lips. Afraid to even talk about anything relating to their regular work. I want to go on record to say that the Administration is more overbearing, cold and grasping than in any period of their operating. One foreman told me that a few days ago that a larger output of work was demanded of him. And this was in the Assembly Dept.

He had men come to him trembling, complaining of headaches, asking to be excused to retire to the First Aid room for aspirin. His men are probably the pick of the Plant—or should be, for the final assembling.

Men who are interested in Aviation, yet are getting to the place where they cannot sleep nights. Afraid of their work proving un-satisfactory due to one reason only, working past the point that is safe for genuine efficient turning out of work. I have been a foreman in Maintenance Dept for 8 years, and most the time on salary. We had at the head of this Dept. a combination of father and son-in-law. And one great trouble in this Plant is the "CLICQUE" to the betterment of themselves, and to the detriment of the workers. Under the grasping, unfair tactics of Mr. W., my superiors grew more indifferent, more overbearing in their attitude and grew so bad that I could get no co-operation from them as I had some where about 60 men under me. To show the almost brutal indifferent attitude of my superiors is brought out in this incident.

A sand-blower was installed on the roof of the building, the sand after being used had to be shovelled out of the blower, placed in bags, carried to the edge of the roof, then by rope and pulley lowered to the ground.

This required 3 men. Now the framework comprising the wheel and pulley were poorly constructed. One day as a bag was being eased over the edge of the cornice the rope broke and a bag weighing about 150 lbs came down just grazing the shoulder of the man waiting to receive it. This might of meant death, or a total injury. Greatly disturbed I went to the Plant Engineer—my superior—urging him to issue an order to have it made safe. He laughed at my fears and made a real joke—as he saw it—out of the incident. I would not let it rest there and after a while I ordered the new parts. SEVEN months after, the parts were still lying on the floor in the stock room, not set up, and a carpenter told me he could fix it in 1½ hours. For over a year my men were compelled to draw out all the dirty grinding water and the rubbish by hand. We averaged about 60 lbs of rubbish and 20 of water. The officials would not give us trucks to do this with so we was forced to use trucks used for hauling heavy machinery.

The lightest weighed 990 lbs empty, the other 1650 lbs. for a year we had to use these trucks until complaints swamped the Front office. When the small truck was loaded it took 7 to 8 men to draw it out. There they went out through the snows and the rains and the mud, Egyptian slaves method for a full year. 500 men will vouch as to the truth of this statement.

They were supposed to work 7 hours per day, 5 days until Fridays, then 5 hours on Saturdays—40 hrs per week. Yet these men do not go to there Depts at 7, No! They have to go to the offices and clean them, 2 full hrs daily, leaving them actually 5 hrs to do their regular work. Let us still remember that with this work is the rubbish and water. And how about the extra moving of furniture—which occurs almost daily, they have that with the extra outside work, for they keep no man for this. Now they are going stronger against these men. And I claim it is impossible to do this work on the average 4 hours. They would not pay my men or hundreds of others in the Plant a living wage but, listen to this. The President, D. L. B., issued an order to all the foremen about April 1st that no new men was to be hired, ONLY REPLACEMENTS. Yet the highest one in the Plant and some others, while men were being laid off, brought their own children in and let them draw pay from the Company until school opened in fall. Mr. B. often has articles in the papers telling of the great heart the Aircraft has for the employees. How they pay the men more

than any one else. The social atmosphere rich and cheery. And no man
gets laid off without a personal study of the party and if humanly possible
they keep them. Let me state my own case. I have talked with Mr. R. and
challenged Mr. B., W., and other officials to face and deny the facts, to
date they are mum. I was a foreman for 8 years. In all that time I had no
complaints, nor was there anything to cause me to feel that the company
was dissatisfied with my work. As I have mentioned I had about 60 under my supervision. On July 15, I was called in and told without any reason, that I was to leave the job. If I wanted to stay could take a sweeper
job. It was work to hard for me. It called for a cut in salary of $60. per
month. Another man took my place, and I was told "Not to take it badly,
the new fellow was not yet hired."

I was in charge until the offices closed that afternoon, Friday. Saturday, the place was closed tight, yet on Monday following the new man
was on the job. This was an untruth. The man could not have been hired
on Sunday. Later I found that my Supt had a friend whose brother was
not working, and being lodge brother's this man was hired and me who
was on salary and worked many times 60 to 70 hrs per week for many
years and who never had one single complaint charged against in all that
period had this done to him. This is not a cry of one who had it coming
to him, but by one who can prove every statement made in this letter.
The year we built the large additions I was up all that summer to Dec 1st
at 4 o'clock looking after the cleaning of the offices after the night shift of
carpenters left. No overtime. They could do that as I were on salary. After a couple months of complaining and finally a demand for a show
down, they faced me and then, four months after, they then said, "Why
we did this was because you had fallen down on your work."

                                                                    A. W. B.

Management literature has often described the "scientific management" techniques propounded by Frederick W. Taylor as benign and
even beneficial to all. The following letter describes scientific management from a worker's point of view.

Baltimore, Maryland, August 25, 1940
Mr. President,
. . . I shall refer to the Efficiency experts or so called the Bonus men.
Those men tell the manufacturer that they can produce more work
without any extra help. So they go to prove their statement. They stay by
the man and time him as if he was a race horse or a piece of machinery.

And in a few weeks they speed up the conveyer and again they time him until every two men do the work of three men. For what little Bonus they give you the Bonus men with their ability and the authority given to them by the manager have that employee put forth all he has in himself whether it's dangerous to his health or not. They are not concerned. Just so they can work him like a slave and have Millions of People out of work with his skillful Efficiency.

The Efficiency experts are killing prosperity, bringing poverty to millions of families throughout America. They are the arch enemies to Humanity. It's a vicious sin that these men draw salaries to create poverty unemployment and sweatshops. The working man can't better himself. He has to work under such conditions.

Due to this recession we have today and the manufacturers take advantage of those conditions they want unemployment to exist. For it gives them the power to rule destiny of the working class of People.

For if the Manufacturer had any respect for the working men he would not work them like slaves.

S. K.

As most foremen had risen from the ranks of laborers, the people they supervised often saw them as traitors, turncoats who had allied themselves with management and took pleasure in exercising their power over workers.

Chicago, Illinois, April 21, 1941

Dear Secretary of Labor:

Since we are determined to give valuable aid to England and her allies resisting German and Italian aggression, we want to cooperate in a manner to speed production and maintain our honor at home.

One thing that will help us to get jobs and produce is the elimination of the hazing and swearing foremen, who are permitted to fire us and injure as they please; the kind that are employed at the Wabash freight house near 12th & State.

You see the checkers and all the older men line up the work on the floors, while all the new men are truckers. Truckers are compelled to load broken trailers that are dark inside. No lights are used in trailers. Older men cuss and boss as they please. They get so careless that it is easy to injure us. When the foreman comes around, he cusses so loud and mean, and if we don't like it the checkers do not like us. These foremen can fire a trucker as they desire.

One of the tricks used at the Wabash is to try and freeze a trucker in cold winter. Last winter the wash-room was nailed up, and the men had no place to get warm. The bosses gave orders to checkers to abuse truckers in a way so the truckers would not look for warm place. A very cruel practice.

Another cruel habit of the Wabash is to use broken trailers with a big hole in it, where a trucker might break his leg, and then the supervisors try to scare the trucker and make him run in trailers and break his leg. If trucker does not run in the trailer, he is subject to discharge.

Very little first-aid is given. Men work with bleeding hands. But they have won the Harriman Safety Cup for years. The safety board has not been washed in 11 years. Supervisors give safety talks, and if we try to execute a safety measure, the older men cuss us and call us no-goods.

The Wabash has not washed their windows in 11 years. Men work in dark. No spittoons are used. There are not lockers or clean place to eat.

One of the most cruel things at the Wabash is the manner in which all the truckers have to stand aside for a dozen of wicked supervisors. After the foremen cuss for doing right, some of us with pride do not feel so good. These supervisors are meaner than military officers. All the rotten checkers say, "Look out for these bosses", as if we were nothing but common trash. Please help us to get rid of these conditions. $100.00 at the Wabash is not worth $30.00, because we are so liable to become injured.

It looks like the big money men are trying very hard to get these cussing and hazing foremen in a respected position. But I don't care for them as much as I do for some rotten criminal. And if the big money men don't get rid of them and build freight houses and warehouse, that are fit to work in, we will have to do something.

All of this hazing is holding up defense because men do not like to work if they are subject to deliberate injury, and injuring men deliberately is un-christian and something that I am greatly opposed to. I hear that the Germans had control of the Chicago post-office, and that President Roosevelt discharged postmaster Kruetgen. Very good. That is one of the reasons for my writing; I do not want to see the Germans get control. I know we have a good President who is trying to help all of us enjoy peace and comfort.

You can see that about all the big trailers have no windows. Lights go on the bum, and men work in dark. This is getting to be a menace. I do not want to see this hazing go any farther.

I want to see the United States and the Allies win the war, establish permanent peace, and maintain the honor of truckers and American citizens.

Hoping that we may cooperate to eliminate this terrible menace.

T. M.

Cleveland, Ohio, June 18, 1941

Dear Miss Perkins:

The U.S. is a land of *slavery* brutal and merciless American workers are not "free". It's a mockery.

The methods used in 2 steel shops here in Cleveland are like the rack of middle ages.

Last month a man from Pittsburgh was at my house, found a job here, and was compelled all day to *lift* heavy steel masses weighing 85, 90 & 100 lbs! Naturally he couldn't stand the work & went back home, only had coffee to eat.

Yesterday, another man worked at Parker Appliance Co. (London rd. & Euclid) from 7–12, & from 12:30 to 4:30 in hot steam, lifting large heavy iron trays *all day* which burned his hands thru leather gloves with *No intermission no chance to go to the wash room, or get a drink.* This is a shop making air plane parts. in soulless brutal United States of America.

Such treatment in shops is just as bad as black-snake-whip slavery. Owner of such shop methods should be prosecuted. This is licking the men at home.

Can't you do something?

E. M. S.

The mechanization spurred by the Depression increased unemployment, especially among older, unskilled workers. Here a miner, unaware of the mechanization of his recently closed plant, finds that he and his fellow workers not only have permanently lost their jobs but are being forced from their homes. The first response indicates that the mine's management was segregating a work force that had previously consisted of "white people and colored to[o]."

Lubuco, Alabama, September 16, 1941

Dear Miss [Perkins]:

We are coal miners and some of us don't know anything else. We have spent our lives working in the mines. Now, the company that we have worked for is throwing us out. The mine here has been shut down for about 2 years and now it is starting up. But the boss wont let us go to work. They are going some place else to get men to work and wont let us. Now then we have 10 days in which to move out or be thrown out. We some of us have worked and lived here all of our lives and we can't possibly get any place to move to. We some of us are out of work and depending on Blue Stamps to live on if given a chance to we will work and support our familys like we have a right to. Some of our children can't start to school for the lack of clothes and nothing to carry in the lunch. We have a right to a living like every one some of these men that has come and are talking our jobs has got a job some place else, and because we have been working on W.P.A. since this mine shut down we can't get to work here. We are pleading with you to please do some thing that will keep us in a house this winter for this company intends to throw us out. We are not causing any trouble in the camp or at the mine. Just because we are old men with the company. Some of us have work all of our lives here and don't know any place else to go. We are not being treated half fair so we are leaving it up to you. We believe you will do all you can to save our homes and help to get us jobs at home like any other citizens. Hoping a quick reply we are yours humbly servants 76 families and children.

Chairman H. B. F.

P.S. This is white people and colored to[o]. Please come to our aid for if you don't by the 25 of this month it wont help us for they will move us all out in the road by then. God bless our homes and children for there are no houses in witch to move in.

Ensley, Alabama, September 26, 1941

Mr. C. F. Anderson, Director
Alabama State Employment Service
Montgomery, Alabama

Subject: Letter to: Judge Petree
From: Clara M. Beyer, Asst. Director
U.S. Department of Labor

Dear Mr. Anderson:

At the request of Mr. S. E. Greene, Field Supervisor, the following is a report of the condition at the Lubuco Mine of the Alabama By-Product Corporation.

The families referred to in the letter . . . will, in all probability, not be used since they have not had experience in operating machines or working around machines, and are too old and slow to be trained. The families will have to move if they are not accepted for employment.

The total number of men to be used at this mine will be approximately 150 men.

An order for 4 or 5 Mine Carpenters was received. An open order for several Coal Cutting and Coal Loading Machine Operators, white, between the ages of 20 and 40 was also received.

This mine will be operated on a closed-shop basis.

The above information was given me by Mr. F. J. Immler, superintendent at the Lubuco Mine.

> LLOYD W. TAYLOR, Manager
> Alabama State Employment Service

Birmingham, Alabama, September 26, 1941

Dear Mr. Anderson:

The actual operation of the mine, when started, will be more highly mechanized than formerly, and practically no unskilled or semi-skilled labor, such as coal diggers, miners, and coal loaders, will be used. The inside labor will be machine operators, cutting machines, loading machines, and electric locomotive operators.

Mr. Porter stated that when this mine closed down some two years ago, the Company offered employment, and absorbed most of the qualified workers then living in this area in other mines of the Company. He stated further that if there were any workers living in the houses referred to who were qualified to work for the Company in this mine that they would be given employment, although he felt that this number would be very few. He further stated that the houses owned by the Company had been leased to the present occupants with the distinct understanding that they would give them up within a reasonable time when notified by the Company to do so.

It is my impression after talking with Mr. Porter that the occupants of most of these houses are unemployables as far as this coal mine operation is concerned and that the Company is badly in need of the houses in order to move persons in who are qualified for their work.

Please advise me if there is any further information which you wish developed in this connection.

> S. E. GREENE, Field Supervisor
> Alabama State Employment Service

Corry, Pennsylvania [December 7, 1939]

U.S. Department of Labor
Dear Sir:

Please take some attention for two factories, in Meadville, Penna., which sell jobs for a very big price per person. These jobs can be bought through lawyers doctors and other high office job holders. These factories are: the American Viscose Corporation (silk factory) and the Talon Inc (makers of zipper fasteners). The employment manager of the American Viscose Corporation is Mr. B. He never does any hiring by the applications or hires anyone from the office.

He closes his office and goes after certain ones to come to work. He never hires any one from Meadville but hires only people from other states and Canada. These people who come in from other states never go to the employment office but go to a lawyer give the lawyer $50.00 or more. The lawyer keeps half and gives Mr. B. the other half and in a few days Mr. B. call them to work. But us local people can't get jobs there. Because he is afraid to sell jobs to local people.

These people from other states who go to a lawyers and buy the job have to swear that they won't tell or they will be fired. Most of the Meadville residents have had their applications in for 5 or six years and go to the office everydays. The out of state people who get jobs buy or rent the houses which are being built around the factory if you don't believe us send some one down to Meadville to investigate this big job selling racket.

This factory is a very large factory and is building more parts to the factory about 5000 people work there. He hires about 30 people every week. 50 × 30 = 1500. is a very large amount of money to receive for selling jobs. What is the use of having such a large factory when not a single person who lives in Meadville works there. It isn't fair for people from Canada, the west south to take our jobs away and we have to go to other places for jobs.

People around here have wrote letter after letter to the labor dept in harrisburg but they don't take any attention the main office of this factory is the American Viscose Corp.

[Anonymous]

6. "We Can't Get No Satisfaction from the State"

Federal–State Case Studies

The first secretary of the Department of Labor, William B. Wilson, a former coal miner, wrote that the department had been established "in the interest of the welfare of all the wage earners of the United States."[1] Its early interests included wages, hours, and working conditions, including what we now call the field of occupational safety and health.

When the Division of Labor Standards was established by Frances Perkins in 1934, its goals were innovative even in the context of the New Deal. First, it sought to educate workers as to the hazards they faced on the job. Second, it defined its role as that of advocate for labor, both organized and unorganized. Third, it launched programs that often went beyond narrow economism and sought to establish a safe and healthy workplace as a legitimate demand in collective bargaining. Federal involvement in such matters through the Occupational Safety and Health Administration (OSHA) is now so thoroughly established that this earlier effort to improve the health and safety of American workers tends to be forgotten.[2]

---

[1]"Annual Report of the Secretary of Labor," in *Reports of the Department of Labor, 1913* (Washington, D.C.: Government Printing Office, 1914), p. 5.

[2]David Rosner and Gerald Markowitz, "Research or Advocacy: Federal Occupational Safety and Health Policies during the New Deal," *Journal of Social History* 18 (Spring 1985): 365–82, and Gerald Markowitz and David Rosner, "More than Economism: The Politics of Workers' Safety and Health, 1932–1947," *Milbank Quarterly* 64 (Fall 1986): 331–54, provide fuller accounts of the origins of the Division of Labor Standards and the politics of safety and health during the New Deal.

When the Division of Labor Standards was established, the federal government took no part in regulating workers' hours, wages, or working conditions; each state and every industry had its own formal and informal methods for controlling conditions in the workplace. Some states had developed relatively extensive regulatory devices. The most highly developed mechanism involved inspection by representatives of the state labor and health department, who visited factories to check primarily on compliance with regulations governing child labor, fire codes, and public health hazards. This approach could claim some success in New York, and it is significant that Secretary Perkins and the division's two top administrators, Verne Zimmer and Clara Beyer, had been trained there. In the vast majority of states, however, regulatory activities were ineffective or nonexistent. "In general the functions of this new Service of the Department should be the promotion of desirable standards of labor legislation and industrial practices affecting labor," Beyer commented. In an internal memorandum she made it clear that her division—unlike most other government agencies, which sought to maintain an air of neutrality in the ongoing struggles between labor and management—was to be aligned with the interests of labor. The division "should be a service agency for labor, just as the Department of Commerce is a service agency for business," she maintained. Its goal was the improvement of conditions for workers, but Beyer and her colleagues did not see themselves as antimanagement. The division was to bring management and labor "into a harmonious working relationship, on the theory that more can be accomplished by coordinated than by independent efforts."[3]

By extending their efforts beyond the research and information-gathering activities to which government agencies customarily restricted themselves, the division's activists sought to put the interventionist ideology of the New Deal into practice. Unlike even its sister agencies within the Department of Labor, such as the Bureau of Labor Statistics, the division sought to promote *change* at the workplace. "This Service should be mainly concerned with promoting certain policies based on the firm factual foundation laid by the studies of these older bureaus. It should endeavor to translate these policies or standards into administrative realities," Beyer wrote.[4]

[3]Memorandum, "The Division of Labor Standards—Its Functions and Organization" (Clara Beyer, November 1934), National Archives, RG 100, ser. 1, 1934–1937, 1-1, Box 24.

[4]Ibid. A Labor Department official noted that the Bureau of Labor Statistics was "concerned with basic economic and statistical research" while the Division of Labor Standards was "engaged in adopting and 'selling' the end product of research to various governmental units" (Dimock to Secretary, May 26, 1939, National Archives, RG 174, Department of Labor, Office of the Secretary, "Labor Standards, General, 1939").

Working with a skeletal staff of only thirty employees in 1936, the division sought to expand federal involvement in the establishment of labor standards. We tend to think of the New Deal as imposing national standards of hours and wages, but the correspondence of the Division of Labor Standards indicates clearly that it sought to exert its influence at the state level, where regulatory activities were traditionally concentrated. Thus the division promoted "State labor legislation for the purpose of bringing about State labor laws more in conformity with an approved standard, so that the workers in one State will get the same measure of protection as the workers in another."[5] The division initially sought uniform standards through state legislative action and voluntary effort. Staff members prepared factual materials and information sheets to be used by groups promoting labor legislation; they provided standard bills for legislators and organizations; they developed safety codes in conjunction with such organizations as the National Safety Council; they gave out fact sheets on chemical hazards in new industries and proposed workers' compensation laws that covered occupational diseases as well as job-related injuries; they worked closely with state departments of labor to improve factory inspection, to develop services for handicapped workers and new apprenticeship programs, to organize adult educational and vocational programs, and to establish programs to rehabilitate and retrain injured workers. The division's efforts were often resisted by the states. As a worker in a northern industrial state observed in early 1937, "when a State inspector comes around everything looks rosy to him. An employee never gets a chance to talk to him." A Georgia worker complained that he had written to "Atlanta several times trying to find out something . . . but haven't found out anything . . . [they] haven't come so far."

The most radical thrust of the division, however, was not in its dealings with the states but in its effort to develop a constituency among workers themselves. Zimmer, Beyer, and their colleagues saw themselves as organizers. "The Department should be able, when requested," Beyer wrote, "to furnish advice to such groups [of workers] concerning how to proceed with forming unions for the purpose of establishing orderly relations in an industry in accordance with policies expressed in the National Industrial Recovery Act. The Department should also be able, when asked, to prepare and furnish material for use by workers' organizations in conducting negotiations with their employers, or in establishing various activities in which unions commonly engage." By working actively

[5]Memorandum, "Division of Labor Standards: Its Functions and Organization" (Clara Beyer, November 1934), National Archives, RG 100, ser. 1, 1934–1937, 1-1, Box 24.

on behalf of labor, they hoped "to stimulate [workers'] interest in labor legislation and enforcement."[6]

The following letter suggests both the importance of the educational efforts of the Division of Labor Standards and the limitations that restricted their effectiveness. Here we see an active, aware union trying to remedy an obviously hazardous condition. When the Kentucky Department of Labor ignored and undermined the union's efforts, the division had no power to intervene.

Louisville, Kentucky, May 7, 1942

Mr. L. Erskine
Division of Labor Standards

Dear Sir:

I am in receipt of your letter of April 15, 1942 with information, advice and booklet on Silicosis. We were very happy to hear from you and I have followed your advice of contacting the Kentucky Department of Labor on this dust situation. I will, however, point out that I sent the Commissioner of that department a 625 word telegram on the dust situation and one other grievance on April 8, 1942.

The Commissioner referred me to his Louisville branch office and on April 20th, I contacted his Local Branch Manager and again explained the situation. To date we have neither heard nor seen any developments at all. This, however, is nothing new to us, as we have had this question before the Kentucky Department of Labor no' less than twice before.

We are very much interested in conducting our own investigation on the analysis of the different kinds and types of clays, also to have the sil-o-cel powder, clays and sand analyzed to find out just what harmful properties they contain. Could you refer us to any department or laboratory outside of the State to whom we could send samples of these clays.

We are very anxious to do our part in the war effort, as we are now supplying the glass plants who manufacture bullet-proof glass, also the M. W. Kellogg Magnesium Plant, whom we are to understand are manufacturing magnesium for the government, but we cannot do so if every time we have a man examined the Doctor recommends that the man get

---

[6]Ibid. See also "The Division of Labor Standards," enclosed in Porter to Hodge, October 9, 1936, National Archives, RG 100, ser. 1, 1934–1937, 1–1, Box 24.

out of the dust. That is impossible in our plant as every department is exposed to some form of dust, either sil-o-cel powder, sand or clay dust.

We have approximately 200 men in our Union and everyone is up in arms over the hazard now that they have found out it can lead to Silicosis.

I will greatly appreciate any further advice or information you can give me on this question.

Hoping to hear from you in the very near future.

SHIRLEY MCGARY, Vice President
United Brick and Clay Workers of America
Local #782

It was not only southern state departments of labor that ignored workers' complaints; a northern Republican administration so effectively blocked the efforts of the Division of Labor Standards that the division representatives questioned the honesty of the state's investigation.

Nashua, New Hampshire, March 9, 1937

Dear Miss Perkins:

This is to let you know the condition in the Nashua Mfg co Nashua New Hampshire Nashua Mills the condition are very bad here the foremen are very mean to the help and driving us to death with speed.

the temperature in the spinning and Weaving Department are 90 to 95 degrees of heat.

they have signs on doors keep this door closed. we can't get no air at all. they are roasting us alive. we can't work in that heat and live. we can't get no satisfaction from the state they are republican and all in with these big company. for God sake Miss Perkins have these mills investigated so that we can get better condition and live.

A. LaB.
and the employees

Washington, D.C., March 12, 1937

Dear Mr. LaB.:

The Secretary has asked me to reply for her to your letter of March 9 calling attention to the conditions which you say prevail in the Nashua

Manufacturing Company. The Federal Department of Labor does not have authority to act in case of such complaint, but on behalf of the Secretary we are writing Mr. John Davie asking that he take any action possible under the law. We have not, of course, used your name in connection with this complaint.

V. A. ZIMMER

Washington, D.C., March 12, 1937

Mr. John S. B. Davie, Commissioner
Bureau of Labor
Concord, New Hampshire

Dear Mr. Davie:

May I call your attention to the following excerpt from an anonymous letter of complaint received by the Secretary with reference to conditions which are said to exist in the plant of the Nashua Manufacturing Company: [He quotes the bulk of Mr. LaB.'s letter.]

According to this report, the conditions offer a serious hazard to the workers and I know that the Secretary will be very appreciative of any action you deem appropriate in this case.

V. A. ZIMMER

Concord, New Hampshire, March 27, 1937

My dear Mr. Zimmer:

Acknowledge receipt of your letter of March 12 enclosing excerpt from an anonymous letter of complaint received by the Secretary with reference to conditions said to exist in the plant of the Nashua Manufacturing Company.

On March 19, 1937 I sent one of the Factory Inspectors connected with this department to make a special inspection of this plant. He reports as follows:

"Found thermometers at various points of several rooms of the weaving department showing temperatures varying from 77 to 80 degrees. The variation was caused by the opening of windows, which is left to the discretion of employees in the weaving rooms. No effort is made by the management to say what temperature shall be maintained. Some doors were marked 'Keep Shut,' but were in corridors leading to the outside and appeared to have been so marked by the employees. No regular notices were posted to that effect.

"In the spinning rooms thermometers ranged from 78 to 84 degrees, with an average of 80 degrees. Ventilation was similar to the weave rooms, some windows being open and some closed.

"Overseers of both weaving and spinning departments stated operatives opened and closed windows to suit their own convenience.

"Speed of machines appears to be comparable to other mills."

Trust you will secure the desired information from the above. Please feel at liberty to call on us again if you desire further information.

JOHN S. B. DAVIE, Labor Commissioner

Washington, D.C., April 3, 1937

To: Mr. Zimmer
From: Dr. Jones
Subject: Attached Correspondence.

I think here is an excellent example of the need for factory inspectors to carry out a program of health and safety among various industrial groups. They should be able in this instance to accomplish much in correcting some of the misinformation employees generally have concerning working under these conditions of temperature and humidity, and at the same time, should be able to impress the employer with the necessity of providing rest periods for those employees at monotonous tasks or speed-up operations.

Personally, I doubt very much the truth of the inspector's report that in the weaving and spinning department operators open and close windows to suit their convenience. This is certainly contrary to any procedures in textile plants with which I am familiar. If there is truth in the complaint we see from Mr. LaB., a physician trained in industrial hygiene methods should be detailed to carry out an investigation involving physical examination of all or at least a representative group of workers. I am sure the conditions described would be reflected in the defects found.

In the following exchange of letters we see the speed with which the Division of Labor Standards provided real and tangible assistance in response to a union's request for information.

Manchester, Connecticut, October 12, 1936
Division of Labor Standards
Dear Sirs:

We have a pamphlet concerning, Health in Industry, issued by the U.S. Department of Labor. As workers we are interested in any literature that will help us to safe guard our health in industry. We also have a safety council in the plants where we work, of which I am a member, anything that would help us in our inspections or conduct in the plants, would be appreciated by the group. Are there any routine measures that are to be followed in an inspection of a plant and what is the best way to go about this in order that the safest conditions possible can be had at all times. Since our Safety Council is something new, that the management of our company and the employees and members of this local have formed for the benefit of both parties, we are striving to carry our share of the undertaken in the best way we know. Any information that would help us would be appreciated.

MILTON YEOMAN, Secretary
Oak Lodge Local No. 43
International Brotherhood of Paper Makers

Washington, D.C., October 14, 1936
Dear Mr. Yeoman:

This will acknowledge receipt of your letter of the 12th advising of your interest and the activity of your local in an active program for safety in conjunction with management.

This Division is extremely interested in your plan, particularly because in the work of promoting safety and health in industry it has been our desire not only to disseminate information to workers in the way of safeguarding health, but also to stimulate the activities of labor groups precisely along the lines you indicate in your letter.

We have on our staff a safety engineer with years of experience not only in inspection work, but in developing organized industrial safety and health promotion. It seems to me that the best way of rendering service to you is to have our safety engineer, Mr. R. P. Blake, come to Manchester for a conference with you and your safety council. Unquestionably you can work out a plan for practical demonstrations of inspection technique and a sustained promotion program. If you agree with this suggestion I would be glad to have you advise me when would be a

convenient time for Mr. Blake to appear. I might say that around the first
of November Mr. Blake may be detailed to a job in the West which will
require two or three weeks.

V. A. ZIMMER

Manchester, Connecticut, October 23, 1936

Dear Mr. Zimmer:

Ref. your letter dated October 14, 1936.

We have discussed your letter by ourselves as labor group and as a
safety council with the management. It was decided that the most good
would be done, if Mr. R. P. Blake, whom you recommended, were to
meet the safety council, jointly with the management. The management
suggested as a possible date to have Mr. Blake come to Manchester, October 29, 1936. This is the only date that we could get before Mr. Blake
would make his proposed trip to the West. If this can be arranged, will
you please notify me, that I may make the necessary contact, to insure a
full attendance at the meeting. The management suggested as a possible
time for the meeting to open at 3.00 P.M. but if it is more convenient any
time that day will do, we will leave it to Mr. Blake to settle that. It is most
important that I be notified before hand, because the management have
three plants in which our group work, also the men work on shifts, so
you will see the necessity of my knowing the exact time so that the men
will be there and also that the management will not make any other ap-
pointments for that time.

We trust that this letter reaches you in time, before Mr. Blake makes
any other plans for October 29, 1936.

MILTON YEOMAN, Secretary

[Telegram]

WASHINGTON D C OCTOBER 27 1936

MILTON YEOMAN

MANCHESTER, CONNECTICUT

R P BLAKE SENIOR SAFETY ENGINEER WILL ARRIVE MANCHESTER
THURSDAY MORNING OCTOBER TWENTYNINTH STOP MEETING THREE
P M O K STOP UNLESS YOU ADVISE OTHERWISE BLAKE WILL CALL YOU
AT [YOUR] ADDRESS

V A ZIMMER

Manchester, Connecticut, November 2, 1936

Dear Mr. Zimmer:

We feel that we should thank you for the help you have been to us in our efforts to promote safety in the plants where we work.

Mr. Blake has been in Manchester and was taken on a tour through the plants through the courtesy of the management, the joint sponsors of this safety campaign. Mr. Blake was also present at a special meeting held of the safety council, where he gave us a safety talk.

We feel that it would please you to know that while in Manchester, Mr. Blake made a very favorable impression with the management of the company and with our committee. His visit has helped us more than we expected, and we feel that what he has shown us about safety will assist me greatly in the future.

MILTON YEOMAN, Secretary

States whose administrations were sympathetic to labor—such as New York, the home state of Secretary Perkins, President Roosevelt, and many other New Deal administrators—tended to heed the recommendations of the Division of Labor Standards, with resultant improvements in working conditions.

Brooklyn, New York, January 21, 1937

Dear Mrs. Roosevelt:

While holding meetings at Long Eddy, New York, my attention was called to conditions in the Acid Factory which is the only factory in that town. These conditions are worse than any I have seen in New York, and think if you will have Miss Perkins investigate this matter something will be accomplished for the unfortunate people living there.

I trust that you will keep the source of this information confidential as I really do not know who the owners of the property of the Acid Factory are, and I do not wish to get the minister of the church at whose home I stayed in any difficulty.

Thanking you for any action you can take in this matter.

A. McN.

Washington, D.C., February 1, 1937

Dear Reverend McN.:

I have been requested by Mrs. Roosevelt to acknowledge your letter of January 21, which was referred to the Department of Labor. I have reported to the Industrial Commissioner of New York the information contained in your letter without, however, making any use of your name.

I want to express the appreciation of both Mrs. Roosevelt and the Secretary of Labor.

V. A. ZIMMER

Washington, D.C., February 1, 1937

Mr. Elmer F. Andrews, Industrial Commissioner
80 Centre Street
New York, New York

Dear Mr. Andrews:

In an anonymous letter received by Mrs. Roosevelt the following statement is included: [He quotes A. McN.'s letter of January 21.]

Any action you deem appropriate in connection with this complaint would be greatly appreciated.

V. A. ZIMMER

New York, New York, March 4, 1937

My Dear Mr. Zimmer:

In reply to your letter of February 1st giving the text of a statement included in an anonymous letter regarding conditions at an acid factory at Long Eddy, New York, may I advise that we have had an investigation made of this establishment and for your information, I am enclosing a copy of the report of our Assistant Supervising Inspector, George H. Jones.

ELMER F. ANDREWS, Industrial Commissioner

Report of George H. Jones:

Made inspection of the acid plant of the Long Eddy Co. at Long Eddy, New York. The company is engaged in the manufacture of wood alcohol and acetate of lime, employing fourteen men. The work is done in two concrete buildings, a still-house and kiln building, both two stories in height. [He describes the plant.]

There are three openings on the second floor of the still house for purpose of ventilation; these openings are equipped with portable gratings which should be secured to ensure there always being in place. There is no lighting system for buildings: lanterns are used for purpose of illumination. Lights should be provided for both stairways. Suggestion made to owner that respirators be furnished the men when turning over the acetate placed on the floor to dry.

The following orders are to be issued:

1. IMMEDIATELY clean and keep in a clean and sanitary condition bowl of water closet (still house—first floor).

2. IMMEDIATELY maintain in a clean condition and free from water the space around the entrance to water closet compartment (first floor).

3. IMMEDIATELY thoroughly scrape and remove the caked material from the still house and kiln buildings.

4. Provide and maintain proper and adequate light in halls and stairs when necessary during all working hours (stairs—kiln building).

5. Provide and maintain proper and adequate light in halls and stairs when necessary during all working hours (stairs—kiln house).

7. *"Capital Is . . . Her Own Worst Enemy"*
Working Conditions during World War II

In 1941, the year the United States entered World War II, about 10 percent of the work force were still unemployed and those who had jobs faced severe problems in the workplace. Despite the growing strength of organized labor and especially of the CIO, layoffs were a constant threat to the workers in most industries.

The war, however, improved conditions for a great many workers. By the time it ended, wages had risen by 80 percent (prices, of course, had risen as well) and the composition of the work force, especially in the manufacturing sector, had changed dramatically.[1] As millions of young men entered the armed forces and the demand for labor increased, groups that had been underrepresented in the industrial labor force suddenly found opportunities beckoning. Southern farmers, both black and white, were lured north by jobs in defense plants in Detroit, Cleveland, Pittsburgh, Toledo, and other cities of the industrial heartland. Farther west, migrants from Texas, Arkansas, Oklahoma, and Kansas found work in California shipyards and aircraft plants.

Blacks were among the groups that most benefited from the expanding labor market and the scarcity of workers. Between 1940 and 1950 1.2 million blacks moved from the South to the North and West in search of

---

[1] David Brody, "The New Deal and World War II," in *The New Deal*, ed. John Braeman, Robert Bremner, and David Brody, vol. 1, *The National Level* (Columbus: Ohio State University Press, 1975).

better-paying jobs. Discrimination in the North spurred A. Philip Randolph, president of the Brotherhood of Sleeping Car Porters, to plan a massive march on Washington to pressure Franklin Roosevelt for redress. In June 1941, faced by the prospect of the march, the president issued Executive Order no. 8802, which established the Fair Employment Practices Commission.

As war-related production pulled the economy out of the Great Depression, women entered the work force in unprecedented numbers: during the course of the war more than 8.5 million women found jobs, an 80 percent growth in the female work force.[2] Women took jobs in the steel, auto, shipbuilding, and rubber industries, joining production lines that had welcomed few of them before. In 1940, 81,000 women held jobs as steelworkers and 30,000 women were employed in the auto industry; by 1944 those figures had leaped to 386,000 in steel and more than 200,000 in auto production. The chemical industry saw a similar growth in the number of female workers as 180,000 women gained employment there during the war, and the number of female aircraft workers rose 70 percent. In the Detroit area, defense plants that employed 36,000 women in the summer of 1942 were employing 156,000 a year later.[3]

The rapid growth of employment opportunities was accompanied by a recognition that the war-related speedup of production increased the hazards faced by industrial workers. Contemporary accounts noted that workers in iron and steel, shipbuilding, auto supply, concrete, slaughtering and meat packing, and fertilizer and leather production had extremely high injury and disease rates.[4] Similarly, in industries as diverse as aircraft, ammunition, chemicals, electrical products, machine and machine tools, plastics, and rubber, new workers were exposed to numerous skin irritants, poisons, dusts, acids, and X rays. The major concerns of industrial hygienists of the period were hazards whose effects were immediate and therefore a threat to war-related production. Their concern focused not only on absenteeism caused by injury and illness but on employees' resistance to working in dangerous conditions. Women employed in the ceramics department of a New Jersey factory "quit after

[2]Alice Kessler-Harris, *Out to Work: A History of Wage-Earning Women in the United States* (New York: Oxford University Press, 1982), p. 276.

[3]U.S. Department of Labor, Bureau of Labor Statistics, *Handbook of Labor Statistics, 1947,* Bulletin no. 916 (Washington, D.C.: Government Printing Office, 1948), pp. 17–20; U.S. Department of Labor, *Labor Information Bulletin,* February 1944, p. 4.

[4]U.S. Department of Labor, Women's Bureau, *Industrial Injuries to Women,* Bulletin no. 212 (Washington, D.C.: Government Printing Office, 1946), pp. 5–7.

working one or two days in the powder-filled air," and others threatened to "quit unless something is done about the heat."[5] While the long-term health effects of many toxins were well known, neither government nor industry showed great concern about the dangers to workers' health posed by such substances as benzene, toluene, asbestos, and silica.

The following two letters, written shortly before the United States entered the war, throw light on the hazards in store for wartime production workers. The welders who were exposed to the fumes described here were also being exposed to asbestos.

Baltimore, Maryland, June 10, 1940

Dear Madam Perkins:

At the Newport News Shipbuilding and Drydocks Company, Newport News, Virginia, there is a question concerning the health of the welders in this shipyard who are welding galvanized iron in the hold of the ship and in tanks in which no ventilation is provided to remove the acid fumes which are created by the electric arc method of welding on galvanized iron, which is poisonous to the lungs and produces a condition in which a man welding under those conditions develops boils all over his body.

These men gradually lose weight until finally they become unable to work. Members of my organization have reported this condition to me and requested that I take the matter up with your Department so that proper suction blowers would be provided to each welder so that the poisonous fumes would be drawn away from him and fresh air take its place.

Employees all become sick and numerous boils appear from the acid generated from this work, and the physician employed by the Newport News Shipbuilding Company will not let the men report that it is caused by the conditions. . . . If possible, when this investigation is made, I would like to be allowed the privilege of accompanying the inspectors to verify this condition.

Thanking you for past favors, I remain respectfully yours

NOAH M. JONES, Representative
International Brotherhood of Boilermakers,
Iron Shipbuilders, and Helpers of America

[5]U.S. Department of Labor, Women's Bureau, *Women Workers in Expanding Wartime Industries: New Jersey, 1942* (Washington, D.C.: Government Printing Office, 1943), pp. 28–33.

Kansas City, Kansas, April 15, 1941

Dear Mr. Zimmer:

Following are reports of our office furnished by officers of local unions, and you will note the comments of these men in their own language and written either by them or the Secretary to whom they related the experiences and the devious, improvised devices and means that they have tried to provide for themselves and use in order to protect their health against what they know to be injurious and in some instances, fatal. . . .

From L. A. Bailey, General Chairman of our District Number 66, Little Rock, came a lengthy report signed by the individual in part reading:

"It is a fact that the electric and acetylene welders and torch men are given no protection from the fumes. One of the brothers stated at this meeting that he was required to go inside of a boiler and remove front flue sheet braces with an acetylene cutting torch; when the job was completed, he had to check out and go home and lost three days from work."

J. L. Potteet, our Secretary at Pine Bluff, Arkansas, wrote:

"At times, especially under close quarters such as welding in the interior of a locomotive water tank they suffer from dizzy spells and stomach disorders. One welder had a bad spell of bleeding of the kidneys which he attributed directly to welding in close quarters."

From the officers of our local Lodge 403 at Hoistington, Kansas:

"My worst disorders are dizzy spells, vomiting and bleeding at the kidneys. Last year I was off work several weeks with my kidneys and dizziness. I was in the railway company hospital at St. Louis and the Doctors said it was kidney colic and auto-intoxication."

Our Secretary, John M. Price of Tacoma, Washington wrote:

"The case of E. C. F., a Welder, in Wichita Falls, who is a member of 576, employed by the M. & V. Tank Company there. They have always made him weld inside all the tanks against his protests; he has complained of his chest hurting him when he was welding, and has been in bed for about two months now and the doctor says he has tuberculosis."

Other letters and reports, where the welder has suffered similar attacks and disorders to those listed above, were received from [84 other workers].

WILLIAM E. WALTERS
International Secretary-Treasurer
International Brotherhood of Boilermakers,
Iron Shipbuilders, and Helpers of America

The urgent need for defense production following the United States' entry into the war increased the attention paid to the problem of workplace injuries. Accidents slowed production and aroused antagonism among scarce new workers.

Paterson, New Jersey, June 1, 1942

Mr. Paul V. McNutt[6]

Dear Sir:

I have read in the newspapers that you expected to order men to do defense work that they were fitted for or else order them into the army. I am sure you are trying to do the right thing but I am also sure that in some cases you do not know the reasons why some of these men take other employment instead of defense work.

The Wright Aeroplane Company here in Paterson has for years been notorious for its treatment of employees. An employee has been to them just another machine and not a human being. This is the reason why young men who are just as patriotic as you or I look for other employment even for less wages and longer hours. One of the reasons why young men leave the Wright shop is that the cutting oil used spatters over their faces and causes disfigurement. There are many cases where young men working at Wrights have been badly disfigured for life. They think this trouble could be overcome if the Company really tried to find a remedy. Another complaint has been that they had to work day after day in temperature either too hot or too cold. Especially in Winter the heat was unbearable. If a window was opened some caught colds. There certainly was no excuse for the Company to waste vast quantities of coal to overheat the buildings. I would respectfully suggest that as the government can now in war times tell a man what to work at would it not be well for the government to have an agency in the Wright company Shop whose duty it would be to look after the comfort of the employees to deal confidentially with the employees and entertain suggestions and complaints. In the interest of the workmen and I am certain it would also be in the interest of the Company. Mr. McNutt: Most of the men you have reference to are as patriotic as any living one would like to do defense work. Won't you make an appeal to their patriotism to do defense

---

[6]McNutt was at this time chairman of the War Manpower Commission; director of Defense, Health, and Welfare Services; and administrator of the Federal Security Agency.

work. Building Airplanes is the work most needed now. Also give them assurance that Uncle Sam will protect their health and comfort.

Very respectfully, I am compelled to sign anon.

Washington, D.C., June 5, 1942

Mr. John Roach, Deputy Commissioner
Department of Labor
Trenton, New Jersey

My dear Mr. Roach:

An anonymous communication addressed to Paul V. McNutt in care of the President has come to my desk.

While the nature of the communication precludes further action, I feel that you may be interested in his references to the cutting oils used in the Wright plant at Paterson. Evidently dermatitis and boils are attributed to the spattering of these cutting oils; and since both the quality and character of oils of this type are of interest to us all, I am passing on the — probably correct — information.

In the interest of a decent approach to serious subjects by such organizations as the United States Public Health Services, I am sending you under separate cover a disgusting little leaflet entitled "Benzol Gives Clara the Run-Around." The effect of this leaflet upon you will probably be identical with that experienced by me and, I feel sure, all those conversant with the serious hazard offered by benzol. You and I certainly have tragic memories that preclude amusement at this type of flippancy.

I. ERSKINE
Assistant Industrial Hygienist
Division of Labor Standards

The following two letters address the problems of workers who were unable to pass physical examinations.

Tulsa, Oklahoma, May 2, 1942

Mrs. Secretary:

I, the undersigned P. F. C., a painter with forty years active experience, am fifty eight years of age and fully able to do a hard day's work. I am a member of the American Federation of Labor, Brotherhood of Painters, Decorators and Paperhangers, Union Card 87145, issued to me at Terre Haute, Indiana, on July 18, 1911.

After having been examined, about February 1st, by the du Pont medical staff I was hired and put to work at Chouteau, Oklahoma, for one week during which I was given two more X-ray examinations and after which I was rejected by said board because of an alleged "spot" (tubercular) on my lung. Excepting "lead poisoning", for which I was treated and from which I was pronounced cured by Doctor McBride of Terre Haute about 25 years ago, I have never been disabled or inconvenienced by any lung trouble.

Immediately after losing my job with the du Pont's, I was given two thorough examinations by Doctor R. M. Shepard who bears a reputation as one of the best "lung specialists" in Oklahoma. Doctor Shepard pronounced my case as "doubtful." Which it must certainly be for I am not and have not been subject to any of the disabilities caused by tuberculosis.

Believing that there has been a cruel and unwarranted discrimination against me, I am volunteering the information that two men now taking treatment for syphilis and a man who has lost one hand are employed by the du Pont's at Chouteau. And I am addressing this letter to you with a plea for justice at your hands.

I, P. F. C. do make solemn oath that the statements herein contained are true in every detail.

P. F. C.

Long Beach, California, November 6, 1942

Dear Madam [Perkins]:

I am writing you to see if I can give you a little real evidence regarding the labor situation in Southern Calif. I will give you one true case: My Son in Law, F. R., who was in the U.S. Navy 5 years as a gunner on The Battleship, Nevada was injured by falling on the deck and bruising his spine when on maneuvers near Pearl Harbor a short time before war broke out. This injury turned into Arthritis and he was surveyed out and is receiving a small pension. He is partly crippled but able to walk around and has full use of his hands and arms but has a stiff back. Last week The Northrup Aircraft Co asked their employees to send in anyone they could find to work. Mr. H., an employee interviewed Mr. F., The Personnel Man and gave him the complete history of Mr. R. Mr. R. reports at the plant last Saturday, Oct. 31 and Mr. F. called in the Plant Supt. who also interviewed Mr. R. and told him that they wanted a man to sit at a bench and assemble Machine guns. The Supt. said that he was pleased to have him as he was thoroughly familiar with that equipment, having had 5 years of light gun training so they sent him to the Dr. who promptly turned him down as he was working primarily for an insurance Co. (Maybe German) and thought he would not be a good risk. This is one case. I can sight dozens who have tried the Douglas Plant. They are too old, too fat, Varicose Veins, a bad tooth. People that are able and want to work and many are working at harder jobs. These people want to work and win the war. They are able to work but denied that right by some insurance racket. These people are being turned down by Douglas by the hundreds after having stayed in line from 12 to 16 hrs trying to get a job!! Are we going to win this war or let some German minded Insurance Co lose the war by turning down hundreds of good workers for some minor and many times not any physical defect. Many are turned down without any examination. If you will investigate you will find that several hundred extra women were rushed out to Douglas to make a show for our President on his recent visit here. The workers of Southern Calif. are 100% behind Mr. Roosevelt and we don't believe he wants a show but wants the goods produced. The Oil Companies are also slack. They have recently started working a 40 hr week instead of 36. They should all be working 48 hrs at least per week during this crisis. I am not just giving my own opinion. I am a Field Gauger for the Texas Co and talk to hundreds of men and I am giving the general opinion. Our sons and relatives are rotting in the South Pacific and we believe that anyone who is able and willing to work have the right to do so regardless of the profits of some Insurance Co. I have great faith in you and in our President and I sincerely hope you can and will do something about it.

S. A. D.

Wartime workers, aware that the government now had a direct interest in their productivity and therefore in their health and safety, became more assertive in their efforts to improve workplace conditions.

Paterson, New Jersey, October 24, 1942

Dear Mr. President:

As spokesman for a group of workers employed at the war plant of "Electronic Mechanics Inc.," Clifton, New Jersey, manufactures of mycalex products for the Army and navy, I wish to inform you of conditions there:

1. Unsanitary
   We work with our hands under water and the place is not kept clean. Many of the women are getting ill and a so-called itch.
2. Unsystematic
   Machines (all government machines) are not kept in repair or taken care of properly.
3. Heat
   Heating facilities are very poor dressing rooms have no heat at all, which is very unhealthy.
4. Open to public
   Outsiders from nearby non-war plants are allowed in and out daily to patronize plant cafeteria without identifications.
5. Underpaid workers
   Workers are all underpaid, some of us can not live and cover transportation expenses on what we make. We are all women who need jobs badly and want to cooperate by not going from one job to another.
6. Insufficient guards
   It is a large plant, only six guards in all. 2 on each shift. They have to work 7 days a week and receive less salary per wk. than an 18 yr. old girl working on a drill press. The night guards have to walk 8 miles per night on rounds, and are paid less than the day shift.

I know you are all very busy in these critical times, but I also know that you believe in fairness for your fellow workers, so if you can possibly arrange to send a government representative to said plant, to investigate and clarify statements made, perhaps conditions could be improved. It is all government money invested, operating the plant, that's why we appeal to you.

Thanking you in advance.

WORKERS OF ELECTRONIC MECHANICS INC.

The war aroused the consciences of many workers and triggered anger at employers who valued profits above the effort to win the war.

San Francisco, California [April 3, 1943]

Dear Mr. Roosevelt:

I am sending you another local union paper. Please read it carefully where I mark it, its of great importance to you why labor is fighting for the right of free people and human welfare, as every stands for peace and are willing to go far for patient and tolerance, at the same looking out, and defending whats dear to our hearts. If someone comes and rob us of these principals we have to fight them, same as they are fighting it all over the world as the brutal forces are trying to enslave the whole earth. Arent we giving up our sons husbands willingly to die so that future generations may live in peace and continue on its upward progression? So do we have to guard the principals at home, less some one may take away these rights and we have to make room for progress of newer invention which newer changes all around are necessary and there is no room for greed. If labor fights, its because greedy people make them fight, not because it wants to.

Mr. Roosevelt people have faith and trust you, so do not make the mistake of turning the wrong way because you do not understand the complication. We all think you are wonderful President, and along with the people's and labor's help you have gone far. That work can be destroyed in one minute if you are not careful. If you were born of poor class like we were and gone through the same struggles you would understand what I mean.

I would have much more to say but today is Sunday and I have lots of work to do around the house as I work all week, and this has to be done.

With best of wishes and love to you and your wife and dear ones.

R. C.

Chicago, April 9, 1943

Dear President:

The reason I am working in a defense plant is to do all possible in my power to help the United nations and my country the United States to a quicker victory. The efforts of everyone connected in anyway with the war industries should feel it his or her duty to stand behind our men in the armed forces regardless of the sacrifice.

This is no time for self interests to seek gains and this applies to Capital as well as labor—naturally a reasonable balance must exist between the two for the economic welfare of the nation.

Still there is no reason for any forced demands by either Capital or labor. Both are guilty of treasonable acts and Capital is in many cases her own worst enemy and probably the fault for the lag in production, rather than labor.

Capital insists on promoting petty trickery on the part of her employees. She persists in refusing to make any effort to make working conditions meaning, tools, materials and conveniences on the part of production, any better.

There are many plants that handicap the war effort on purpose. This is
done for percentage profit gain on contracts.

There is not so grave a problem for a shortage of help as there is for
improvement in the tools and machinery we are being forced to use.

In plants where there is piece work. Unfair prices are put on the job
and the company stalls the man doing the job by imposing many hardships on him. It is hard if not almost impossible to make out or do a
good days work on this account and production is blamed on the worker
for the lag.

We can't win the war with individualism.

C. G.

The following three letters register the shock that many workers felt
when they entered an industrial plant for the first time. Working with
unfamiliar and dangerous machines, with little instruction about safety
measures, new workers were in danger themselves and were seen as a
danger to others.

Des Moines, Iowa, April 15, 1943

To Whom It May Concern:

Just a line in regard to a small problem which I would like to have
straightened out. I worked for the New Monarch Machine Co. for one
day which was 8 hrs. And I quit cause I was afraid of getting my hand
caught in the presser. That's the first time I ever done this kind of work
and they sure worked us steady. There were 3 of us new on that machine
and the others were afraid too. This isn't slavery Abraham Lincoln done
away with that this burns me up even if this doesn't [do] any good but it
isn't right. And I went down to get my money and they said I had .34
coming out of 4.00 four dollars the other money went to the doctors examination which I do not believe. This is the first time I've heard of a
case like this. They don't even have a good first aid just a little kit and
that's not what I'd call it. Well I'm sorry this came up but it makes me
sore. I didn't take the .34.

C. N.

Des Moines, Iowa, April 15, 1943

Dear Sir:

I have a problem of labor: I would like very much to have you help me out. I work for the Monarch Machine & Stamping Co. 1 day that is 8 hrs. I quit because I was afraid of my machine as they put three new people who never saw a press in their lives. They gave us a 5 minute rest period which isn't long enough to go to the rest room and back. Then we work fast and steady until we went home. Just a ½ hour out for lunch: I really didn't know which one was going to take my fingers off the man putting up steel plates or the press. I made $3.20 that night. I had 3 cents taken out for Social Security and 30 cents out for gloves that would leave me a check of $2.87. At least that is the way I had it figured out. When I went to get my check they told me I didn't have any thing coming. They told me because I had quit I had to pay for my own examination. They say they have a First Aid. It is nothing but a dirty box above the wash bowl. The top and bandage were all dirty and they didn't have any thing to wash out the cuts on your hands. I ask them what we would do if we ever got hurt and they said they would take care of us and pay our Dr. bill. I said just like you pay for the examination and my wages? Sir I really think I should have some thing for that days work. Its not the idea that I don't like to work hard. I do but I don't want to be treated like the people in Germany are. We are suppose to be a free country. But to work for places and People like that it doesn't seem that way. I am sorry to have to write you a letter like this but I want what's coming to me and so do other people. We are all trying to do what we can for our country but if we loose our hands then we are no good to our selves or our country. Hoping to hear from you soon.

M. L. L.

Wheeling, West Virginia, December 30, 1944

Mr. and Mrs. President Roosevelt:

Am writing to both of you as what I have to say is very important to the world of tomorrow. I know you are all very busy but you are the only one I can turn to as a mother.

I have a daughter 23, very well educated, but when this war took her husband she thought she could do something for him and her country and she went into a defense plant. He has been overseas 2 years 4 months. One day I was called to the hospital; my daughter lost two

fingers—index and middle finger. She just got over the second operation
of these fingers and her health is broken. But she isn't the only girl; there
were 5 girls in one week that worked at the Wheeling Corrugating in
Wheeling that lost fingers. They make their help work without guards
and tongs and bad presses. The girls are some day going to be mothers
and do house work. How can they do this without fingers? I taught my
daughter how to take care of a home before going out into the world and
because some people want to make money these girls have to lose some
part of their body. Yes, they have Government inspectors in but the
Wheeling Steel can buy them over and have them on their side. They
make these girls work in damp places, even stand in water. What do you
think our future mothers are going to be like? I am not speaking for my
daughter alone but for the other girls.

The C.I.O. tries to do every thing they can but the Wheeling Steel runs
Wheeling and round about town. I do think they should give these girls
artificial fingers as being a mother means dresses to make and button up,
and nearly everything means you need your fingers in the home to make
good mothers and to rear good citizens. So Mr. and Mrs. Roosevelt that
is why I am writing this letter to you as I have faith in you and know you
both will understand. But after these girls are hurt they try to put them
back on presses; they can't get jobs elsewhere. What can they do without
fingers? So if you will give this a little of your attention I will be so
thankful.

MRS. U. S.

Even experienced workers, when faced with speedups and dangerous
machinery, feared for their personal safety.

Rockton, Illinois, July 7, 1944

Dear Sirs:

I am writing you in regards to safety laws for drill presses. I have been
employed at a Beloit, Wis. factory for 1½ years up till the 18th of May
when my foreman refused to set a job up so it was safe for me to run. I
called in the safety man who also refused to do anything because the foreman said the job was safe. The foreman became mad because I called in
the safety man therefore he turned in for me to be transferred onto another job. He didn't tell the truth in the main office and that is where my
trouble is. He turned in there that it was due to nervousness and poor
eyes that I should not be allowed to have a machine. This is all lies. I have

worked under very dangerous conditions with this foreman. The jobs on the drill presses are only half set up and he is gone from the department so much of the time we lose a lot of time waiting for him because he won't let the setup man have the drill presses. The foreman took it upon himself to set them up and he fails to do it so the jobs are safe to run. He don't know any too much about this work when it comes to tapping and grinding drills.

Now, I have had jigs to fly completely off the table of the machine on to the floor also had them jerked out of my hands on tap and drilling both. This happens real often. On all jobs we have to hold the jigs down with our hands. They are guarded on some jobs from whirling and some jobs have no guards whatsoever, just held by the hands. I work on the night shift also one other girl. We both have the same trouble.

Now I have been waiting since the 18th of May for them to give me another job but up to date have not been called back to work. I need the work the worst way. You see they haven't fired me just tell me I will have to wait till some bench job is open.

Now, I would like you to please send me the laws for the drill presses as the C.I.O. union says if I can get laws to show how these presses are to be guarded, and the foreman is not doing it according to law they can do something for me. All they can do now is wait till I get back in there to work, then fight for a machine job for me on seniority rights as I have that over all the other girls in the department I was in.

I don't know whether your Bulletin No. 430, "Safety Code for power Presses and Foot and Hand Presses," is the law on this that I want, or not. The presses I run are power and hand.

I will greatly appreciate this if you send me these laws and whatever the expense is let me know and I will gladly pay it. Thank you.

Mrs. O. H. McC.

P.S. Please send whatever laws you have on safety for drill presses besides Bulletin 430.

Federal contracts were of such importance to industry that workers soon saw them as possible tools to use in their efforts to improve working conditions.

Fort Worth, Texas, December 16, 1943

My dear Mrs. Perkins:

I am writing this *personal* letter to your office for the purpose of calling your attention to a condition prevalent here in Fort Worth Texas in the meat packing industry in the plants of Swift and Co. and Armour and Co. operating under Federal License Number 3-F and 2F respectfully.

The conditions which I shall describe briefly are this—inadequate heating facilities—which results in absenteeism which indirectly hinders the war effort, for whether you know it or not the winds down here in this great plains region blow constantly.

In the Swift plant (which is 42 yrs old) the very same heating system which was in style when Sinclair Lewis [Upton Sinclair] wrote "The Jungle" is still being used.

Metal barrels are placed on the wet brick floors and chunks of wood are placed in them and are set on fire—this results in smoke filling the large rooms where—cattle—calves sheep and swine are being slaughtered and where approximately one hundred and fifty or two hundred men are employed—The temperature often is as low as 36 degrees F. and with these extremely high winds in the winter time it is much more unpleasant and disagreeable to work here than in the plants of the same company located farther north—I have taken the matter up with the local company officials but due to the fact all improvements must be approved from their home office in Chicago—nothing is ever done about it.

Why should they—Their offices are steam heated and air conditioned, and if [they] should be required to modernize their plant that would cost *money* and they would lose their company rating as efficient supervisory officers; so you see the problem is not so simple of solution as it might seem. In the summer time the heat is almost as unbearable as any place I have ever been often 110°F.

Now I am a meat inspector for the War Food Administration and I have had years of experience in meat packing plants all over the country—but these intolerable conditions certainly are wrecking the health of hundreds of patriotic working people including myself.

Yes I know they have a nurse and a company doctor—he comes down to the plant at 7 A.M. and leaves at 9 A.M. just long enough to look after the emergency cases—the nurse does stay all day.

Now these conditions have resulted in my weight dropping in three years from 210 to 157 lbs.

I've got some of the lost weight back now—I think if a few good government contracts were withheld until they corrected these unhealthful conditions in their plants—The officials would take due notice and govern themselves accordingly by having them fixed—you know it isn't a coal shortage down here, for we have millions of feet of natural gas going to waste in this state every day.

So far as I know a state factory inspector is non-existent.

In the Armour plant where hogs are killed—large gas flares are used to singe the hair off of hogs in the dressing process the odor and fumes are simply terrible as the fumes are not carried out of the rooms by means of vents, and to stay in these rooms working like mad from seven in the morning until six at night just about saps every ounce of energy out of the most healthy ones.

On top of this an air line of compressed air and steam is used to blow the loose hairs off hogs which have been scalded and scraped—the noise resembles a steam engine letting off steam—now imagine yourself being shut up in a room for ten hours a day listening to such an outlandish noise.

Now I have raised so much H-ll that this nuisance has been partly eliminated when I am in charge of the inspection on the killing floor but when other inspectors take my place they usually are not quite so active in making themselves heard on these subjects which I have tried to describe to you.

I thank you for this opportunity to bring these matters to your attention. I had to get up at 4 in the morning to write this, as you know I am on my way to work by 5:45 A.M.

We are getting this job done down here in southwest in spite of many difficulties but in peace or in war I still believe in free speech for it helps in overcoming so many unsatisfactory conditions.

                                                            D. R. W.

P.S. I do not care for this communication to be regarded as official in character I prefer it to be confidential and personal.

The following exchange of letters between an elderly worker and representatives of the U.S. Department of Labor suggests that the elderly were still subjected to discrimination, even during the wartime labor shortage and despite the Labor Department's continuing concern about the problem.

                              Philadelphia, Pennsylvania, February 5, 1945

Labor Department
Gentlemen:

There are items appearing in the Daily papers about the labor shortage in the different shops where defense work has been done.

To this I would say, it seems to me that there are too many unemployed men walking around the streets everywhere and are looking for
work and can not get it! Why, what is the matter?

Gentlemen, there are two damnable curses which ought to be removed
at once, for they are standing between the workers and the work. These
are:

1. The old age, and

2. The physical examination. They do not employ older men in the
most of the shops and they have to pass very strict physical examination
and older men can not pass it any more, but they are still good enough to
do some work. This curse is brought upon the working men by the different insurance companies for their own good. I am a first class machinist with long experience, but can not get a job because I have passed the
65th mile stone in my life, although I am strong and husky to do some
good work in machine shop.

The second curse is: as an older person I can not pass the physical examination anymore, but am willing to do some work for my country.
The physical examination curse is brought upon the poor working men
by the different insurance companies for their own good and it ought to
be removed entirely by the government and then there would be thousands of workers available to do some work for the government. But the
trouble is even in the government shops are practiced the same damnable
curse, they have the age limit there at 55 years and have to pass physical
examination, what for? The weaker one wants to make his living just the
same as the strong one!

If the physical ex. would be removed, at least for the duration, there
would be fair chance for many a men to get a work and make a good living, at least for the duration.

                                                                                    J. S.

                                                           Washington, D.C., February 14, 1945

Dear Mr. S.:

In your letter of February 5, addressed to the Secretary of Labor, you
have presented very pointedly a problem which has been constantly increasing for 20 years, or at least up to the advent of war conditions three
years ago.

As you indicated in your letter, the employment problem of the older
worker is closely linked to that of the physically sub-standard worker.

Relatively few persons over 45 can pass a strict physical examination, such as has been required by many managements in the past. However, shortage of manpower—and particularly of skilled workers—has prompted many managements to either greatly modify their physical standard requirements or abandon the pre-employment physical examinations entirely.

I am interested particularly in your reference to insurance companies as being responsible for hiring restrictions in respect to age and physical fitness. While there is plenty of evidence that many insurance carriers indulged in this practice some years ago, nevertheless within the last two years both the stock and the mutual insurance companies through their associations have issued a strong pronouncement to the effect that they do not encourage or advocate the rejection of workers from employment due to age or physical conditions. It may be, of course, that a particular insurance company does not adhere to this present policy and for this reason I would be glad to have you supply this Department with the names of plants where you have applied for work and have been told that you must undergo a physical examination due to the advice of an insurance company, or that you cannot be hired because of age for the same reason.

I would also be interested in knowing just what Federal or Government plant or shop has rejected your application for employment as a skilled machinist because of your age. It is our information that the 55 year old limit formerly existing in respect to Federal employment has been abandoned under war conditions.

I suggest that you call at the office of the local U.S. Employment Service and discuss your problem with one of the officials in charge. Certainly there are many employers in your area who do not require pre-employment physical examinations and who have no age hiring limit. Some time ago one of our field staff reported that a man 85 years old was regularly employed as a tool maker in a war plant and doing a very satisfactory job.

At your convenience I would be glad to have the information I have suggested above.

V. A. ZIMMER

Epilogue

The victory over Japan in 1945 unleashed many of the tensions that had built up between management and labor under the strains of the Depression and World War II. The death of President Roosevelt and the resignation of Secretary Frances Perkins in the same year marked the end of the New Deal for labor and of the effort to assimilate labor into the governing coalition. Labor militancy reached an all-time high in 1946 as unions sought to protect the gains in membership and influence they had achieved during the New Deal and war years. In the two years following the end of the war, more workers were involved in more strikes than in any comparable period in American history. Business leaders reacted strongly to this challenge to their dominance of labor–management relations, and conservative Republican senators and congressmen, spurred by a growing fear of communism at home and abroad, launched a series of antilabor initiatives. The Taft-Hartley Act of 1947 is perhaps the most famous of the legislative attempts to limit labor's power to strike.[1]

The attacks on labor were aimed not only at limiting the unions' power but also at undermining the government's ability to act on labor's behalf. The budget of the Department of Labor was severely cut in the postwar years as conservatives attacked the department with arguments that are now all too familiar: that government had become so large and bureaucratized that it threatened the freedom of all Americans; that regulation of labor should be left to the states. Sounding these themes, Re-

---

[1]David Montgomery, *Workers' Control in America: Studies in the History of Work, Technology, and Labor Struggle* (London: Cambridge University Press, 1979), p. 166.

publicans in the Congress sought to dismantle the Division of Labor Standards and disperse its programs to less enthusiastic administrators in other agencies. In a direct attack on the New Deal, Frank B. Keefe of Wisconsin urged his fellow representatives "to cut down, to get rid of . . . the Division of Labor Standards."[2] Congressman George B. Schwabe of Oklahoma was even more ideological in his analysis of the need to cut back on the size and authority of the Department of Labor. "We have come to the weaning time," he began. "That is always a difficult time, in politics as well as elsewhere. . . . I for one shall vote to wean as many [bureaucrats] as possible to keep our government American and from becoming communistic, and we all know that it has been tending that way a long time ago."[3]

While Keefe, Schwabe, and others carried forth the ideological attack on the New Deal and Perkins' Labor Department, other congressmen developed the programmatic mechanisms for destroying the morale and program of the Division of Labor Standards. Ralph E. Church of Rhode Island linked his attack on the division to the need for smaller government. "When Miss Perkins was Secretary of Labor she established the Division of Labor Standards. It was supposed to serve as a clearinghouse in the field of industrial safety and sanitation. But, like so many other divisions throughout the Federal Government, it gradually expanded its functions, and entered into the fields of labor education and labor legislation." Here he was echoing the head of the National Association of Manufacturers, who singled out the government's involvement in labor education as reprehensible and indicative of its pro-union stance. There was "a duplication of the work of this division with the Bureau of Labor Statistics," Church continued, and it was his opinion that "no useful purpose is served by having a group of Federal employees gratuitously work by helping states in the administration of their safety and sanitation laws. That is a matter that can be left to the States, to insurance companies and private organizations," he said, echoing the views of industry noted in a 1945 Congressional Appropriations Committee report.[4]

The concrete proposal that emerged from this conservative onslaught

---

[2]*Congressional Record*, 60th Cong., 1st sess., vol. 93, pt. 2 (1947), p. 2466. For an expanded discussion of the plight of the Division of Labor Standards after World War II, see Gerald Markowitz and David Rosner, "More than Economism: The Politics of Workers' Safety and Health, 1932–1947," *Milbank Quarterly* 64 (Fall 1986): 331–54.

[3]*Congressional Record*, 60th Cong., 1st sess., vol. 93, pt. 2 (1947), p. 2546.

[4]Ibid., p. 2479. The NAM leader's remarks are reported in *New York Times*, 25 March 1947, p. 22.

was that Congress use its power of the purse to purge "left-wing" New Deal agencies. "We promised the people a reduction in Government expenditures and a reduction in the number of people on the Federal payroll. . . ," Church went on. "It is part of our program to put this government on a sound financial basis and to take this Government out of the hands of petty bureaucrats and return it to the people."[5]

Within the limited context of New Deal liberalism, some administrators sometimes pushed the boundaries of their own role so that they redefined and expanded the limits of legitimate government activities on behalf of labor. They often interpreted labor's goals as more than mere economic self-interest. While they accepted limitations to direct federal intervention before World War II, after Pearl Harbor they broadened the government's involvement in labor issues by providing expertise, technical knowledge, social legitimacy, and even empathy for workers' plight. It was for this aid to labor that the New Deal, with all of its programmatic limitations, was attacked. In 1949 the Division of Labor Standards, the premier creation of the secretary of labor herself, was taken out of the secretary's office, its program dismantled, and its name changed to the Bureau of Labor Standards.

It was the symbiotic relationship with the labor movement that gave the Division of Labor Standards its power and also led to the conservative opposition to it. During World War II the division had to walk a very fine line between the demands of labor for a safe and healthful workplace and the interests of management and government in maximizing production and controlling the labor force. On the one hand, the division worked effectively with business to alleviate some hazards while defusing labor unrest. On the other hand, the division raised the specter of a public consciousness of a set of issues which could, in changed social and economic circumstances, threaten the hegemony of management over the conditions of work.

The division served as a catalyst for change. But the letters in this volume indicate that workers themselves provided the impetus for government action during the harsh years of the Depression. Labor militancy is often measured by the number and length of strikes and sitdowns. These events are valid reflections of the attitudes and concerns of organized workers. The words of the unorganized often tell a similar story of suffering, struggle, and hope.

---

[5]*Congressional Record*, 60th Cong., 1st sess., vol. 93, pt. 2 (1947), p. 2479.

Index

225

Library of Congress Cataloging-in-Publication Data

Slaves of the Depression.

Includes index.
1. Labor and laboring classes—United States—1914–   —Sources.
2. United States—Economic conditions—1918–1945—Sources.
3. Depressions—1929—United States—Sources. I. Markowitz, Gerald E.
II. Rosner, David, 1947–
HD8072.S6164   1987   331.25′0973   87–6671
ISBN 0-8014-1956-5 (alk. paper)
ISBN 0-8014-9464-8 (pbk.)